Gender, Development and Environmental Governance

Routledge Research in Gender and Society

1 **Economics of the Family and Family Policies**
Edited by Inga Persson and Christina Jonung

2 **Women's Work and Wages**
Edited by Inga Persson and Christina Jonung

3 **Rethinking Households**
An Atomistic Perspective on European Living Arrangements
Michel Verdon

4 **Gender, Welfare State and the Market**
Thomas P. Boje and Arnlaug Leira

5 **Gender, Economy and Culture in the European Union**
Simon Duncan and Birgit Pfau Effinger

6 **Body, Femininity and Nationalism**
Girls in the German Youth Movement 1900-1934
Marion E. P. de Ras

7 **Women and the Labour-Market**
Self-employment as a Route to Economic Independence
Vani Borooah and Mark Hart

8 **Victoria's Daughters**
The Schooling of Girls in Britain and Ireland 1850-1914
Jane McDermid and Paula Coonerty

9 **Homosexuality, Law and Resistance**
Derek McGhee

10 **Sex Differences in Labor Markets**
David Neumark

11 **Women, Activism and Social Change**
Edited by Maja Mikula

12 **The Gender of Democracy**
Citizenship and Gendered Subjectivity
Maro Pantelidou Maloutas

13 **Female Homosexuality in the Middle East**
Histories and Representations
Samar Habib

14 **Global Empowerment of Women**
Responses to Globalization and Politicized Religions
Edited by Carolyn M. Elliott

15 **Child Abuse, Gender and Society**
Jackie Turton

16 **Gendering Global Transformations**
Gender, Culture, Race, and Identity
Edited by Chima J Korieh and Philomina Ihejirika-Okeke

17 **Gender, Race and National Identity**
Nations of Flesh and Blood
Jackie Hogan

18 **Intimate Citizenships**
Gender, Sexualities, Politics
Elżbieta H. Oleksy

19 A Philosophical Investigation of Rape
The Making and Unmaking of the Feminine Self
Louise du Toit

20 Migrant Men
Critical Studies of Masculinities and the Migration Experience
Edited by Mike Donaldson, Raymond Hibbins, Richard Howson and Bob Pease

21 Theorizing Sexual Violence
Edited by Renée J. Heberle and Victoria Grace

22 Inclusive Masculinity
The Changing Nature of Masculinities
Eric Anderson

23 Understanding Non-Monogamies
Edited by Meg Barker and Darren Langdridge

24 Transgender Identities
Towards a Social Analysis of Gender Diversity
Edited by Sally Hines and Tam Sanger

25 The Cultural Politics of Female Sexuality in South Africa
Henriette Gunkel

26 Migration, Domestic Work and Affect
A Decolonial Approach on Value and the Feminization of Labor
Encarnación Gutiérrez-Rodríguez

27 Overcoming Objectification
A Carnal Ethics
Ann J. Cahill

28 Intimate Partner Violence in LGBTQ Lives
Edited by Janice L. Ristock

29 Contesting the Politics of Genocidal Rape
Affirming the Dignity of the Vulnerable Body
Debra B. Bergoffen

30 Transnational Migration, Media and Identity of Asian Women
Diasporic Daughters
Youna Kim

31 Feminist Solidarity at the Crossroads
Intersectional Women's Studies for Transracial Alliance
Edited by Kim Marie Vaz and Gary L. Lemons

32 Victims, Gender and Jouissance
Victoria Grace

33 Gender, Development and Environmental Governance
Theorizing Connections
Seema Arora-Jonsson

Gender, Development and Environmental Governance

Theorizing Connections

Seema Arora-Jonsson

Routledge
Taylor & Francis Group
NEW YORK LONDON

First published 2013
by Routledge
711 Third Avenue, New York, NY 10017

Simultaneously published in the UK
by Routledge
2 Park Square, Milton Park, Abingdon, Oxon OX14 4RN

Routledge is an imprint of the Taylor & Francis Group, an informa business

Library of Congress Cataloging-in-Publication Data

Arora-Jonsson, Seema.
Gender, development, and environmental management / Seema Arora-Jonsson.
p. cm. — (Routledge research in gender and society ; 33)
Includes bibliographical references and index.
1. Natural resources—Management. 2. Women in development. 3. Environmental policy. I. Title.
HC85.A76 2012
333.7—dc23
2012002378

ISBN13: 978-0-415-89037-3 (hbk)
ISBN13: 978-0-415-62961-4 (pbk)
ISBN13: 978-0-203-10680-8 (ebk)

Typeset in Sabon
by IBT Global.

For
N, S and S, S, M

Contents

Figures

Acknowledgments

This book has a lengthy past. It began before I knew it was to be a book, when I somewhat unwillingly, moved to live in Odisha in 1993. Little did I know then that it would change the way I think—about the environment and especially forests, about how they are inextricably entwined in rural life and about men and women who struggle against all odds for a democratic society. I would like to thank all the women and men, in Nayagarh district in Odisha, who took me along on this adventure, especially the women in the *mahila samitis*, who opened up new ways of seeing the world for me. When I began my Ph.D. research in 1998, there were several people who were indispensable as discussion partners and who helped me navigate the twists and turns of the gendered politics of the Nayagarh forests. I would like to thank Sarthak Pal, Manoj Pattanaik, Barna Bhai Panda, Jogi babu, Alaka Nanda for your help and advice and Bapa, Manoj Rathi and the many other BOJBP members for your kind hospitality in Kesharpur.

When in Sweden in 1996, I realized the need for a more 'global' approach to environmental issues around us. It is to my former colleagues Daphne Tuvesson and Anders Tivell that I owe thanks for exciting discussions and work together, in particular to Daphne for inspiration and support through the years. The 'dammiga damer' in Drevdagen, whom I don't name here—thank you for your support, for sharing your lives and dreams with me and for what I realize now are lifelong friendships.

As for the writing of this book, it wouldn't have been written if it wasn't for Louise Fortmann's and Rohan d'Souza's gentle but persistent questioning about when my book was coming out. Thank you Rohan and Louise for your support, Rohan, for pushing me to it whenever I wandered by your dingy and always very interesting corridor at JNU and to both of you for reading and commenting on some of the text. Over the years, many others have discussed, advised and commented on various versions of what lies in between these pages. I would like to thank Bina Agarwal, Arun Agrawal, Gunilla Bjérén, Berith Brandth, Andrea Cornwall, Carol Colfer, Kjell Havnevik, Gunilla Härnsten, Katja Jassey, Mary John, Janice Jiggins, Naila Kabeer, Nivedita Menon, Maureen Reed, Lars Rudebeck, Malin Rönnblom, Nandini Sundar, Alison Wylie, the seminar group at the Centre for Gender Research at Uppsala University, the Bay Area Feminist Philosophers Association and the CPEPER/ESPM group at UC Berkeley.

More recently, I would like to thank Erik Westholm and Thomas Håkansson for having read almost the entire manuscript and for their encouraging engagement with the questions it raised, and especially Erik for interesting discussions on the present and the future of our field. For reading various chapters of the present text and for indispensable help in thinking them through, I am grateful to my colleagues, Elinor Carlbrand, Kjell Hansen, Hans-Peter Hansen, Klara Jacobson, Kaisa Raitio and Cecilia Waldenström at SLU and to Biswamoy Pati at Delhi University.

Many thanks to my parents, Neena and Suren Arora who were forced to read various drafts, for their love and encouragement and to my brother Shankar Arora, whose commentary on the text was much more entertaining than the text, but that I shall keep for private reading. To Sunayana, Daljit, Kavita, Zorro, Prithvi and Nano and the Jonsson clan, thanks for being such a great family. Last but not least, I am indebted to Stefan Jonsson, for his unfailing support, for his reading and critical commentary on the many different versions of the manuscript, to Sebastian and Maya for making life so much more exciting and fun and of course for your tips on what makes for a good book. I'm not sure if I've managed to get down quite all that cloak and dagger action as yet! Maybe next time.

I owe thanks to Vetenskapsrådet, The Swedish Research Council for supporting the initial research (1998–2005) and to the Swedish Research Council Formas for financing further fieldwork in Sweden and the writing of this book (2007–2012). Thanks also to my editor Max Novick for believing in the book and for answering my many questions. Much of this work builds on my previous Ph.D. dissertation, *Unsettling the Order: Gendered subjects and grassroots activism in two forest communities, Doctoral thesis no. 2005:70*; Faculty of Natural Resources and Agricultural Sciences, Swedish University of Agricultural Sciences, Uppsala. 2005. I also wish to make grateful acknowledgment to the original publishers for permission to reprint as chapter seven, "Discordant Connections: Discourses on Gender and Grassroots Activism in Two Forest Communities in India and Sweden" in *Signs: Journal of Women in Culture and Society* 2009, Vol. 35, No. 1, University of Chicago Press. Certain paragraphs and thoughts from the following articles have been used in various parts of the book: "Research sounds so big . . ." Collaborative inquiry with women in Drevdagen' in Louise Fortmann *(ed.) Participatory Research in Conservation: Doing Science Together,* pp. 130–145. Blackwell-Wiley, 2008, and "Shifting images of the community: gender and the local management of forests", in Ildiko Astalos och Bettina Bock (eds.), *Gender Regimes, citizen participation and rural restructuring,* Elsevier, Oxford/Amsterdam/San Diego 2008.

1 Introduction

Three Places and a Jigsaw World

FIRST PLACE: A SHADY CORNER OF A VILLAGE IN NAYAGARH DISTRICT IN ODISHA, INDIA. FEBRUARY 1999

It was towards the end of February, but Odisha was already getting warm.[1] Summer was approaching. At least 30 women from a women's group had gathered to talk to me. However, answering their questions about why I wanted to write about them was not all that simple. Manju[2] asked me if I was married and how many children I had. I was reprimanded for not wearing bangles or *sindoor*[3] that showed that I was married (I was getting used to that now). Some women sang a song about how women and men together looked after the forests and the welfare of the village. I was then told that it was my turn to sing. They were not taking no for an answer. (The message was: If you want our information, you had better entertain us first). I managed to croak out a song, after which they began to tell me about themselves (probably to pre-empt any more singing on my part). I got to hear about their group, about all the work they did in the village, their negotiations with violent husbands and nasty mothers-in-law, struggles with rich landowners and their work for everyday village life. They spoke positively about the forest organizations in their villages, but also about their non-involvement in formal decision-making and about the problems of not being able to speak about and relate their work to the forests at forestry forums.

SEVERAL MONTHS LATER, ANOTHER PLACE: A FEW THOUSAND MILES NORTH—A COTTAGE BY THE LAKE IN DREVDAGEN, AN OUT OF THE WAY VILLAGE IN SWEDEN, JUNE 1999

It was an evening after midsummer but it was still cold outside. Thirteen women sat around an old fashioned fireplace in the middle of the one room cottage. The hordes of mosquitoes outside were kept out firmly by the closed door. The discussion centered on why we had decided to meet. Kerstin stoked the fire vigorously,

After the *gubb*[4] conference on local forest management last weekend . . . when they 'forgot' to invite us . . . it is about time we form our own network. We could take up things that women are interested in so that we all know that we have support from each other . . .

Cecilia: I am interested in the social issues. For a living countryside, we must look to the village as a whole . . . if we are ever going to be able to get anywhere with the forests.

Kerstin: I called around before this and spoke to some people about forming a women's network. I spoke to Sune Johansson at the *Hushållningsällskap.*[5] He gave me some tips. And then he said . . . aha, have you come so far . . . you have someone from SLU in your group.

I squirmed in my place, glad to be of help, but not quite sure how I would live up to it,

"How do you think I could be of help? I could document all that you do and talk about and maybe we could use that to think about what we are doing. And I could find out what other women's networks have been doing and what has been written on them and . . ."

THE THIRD PLACE: FORESTS TREES AND PEOPLE PROGRAM OFFICE, SWEDISH UNIVERSITY OF AGRICULTURAL SCIENCES (SLU) IN UPPSALA, NOVEMBER 1997

We were in a room constructed out of temporary partitions and overfull bookshelves that tilted precariously with FAO manuals on how to go about development. Piles of papers and books covered every inch of the room as I tried in vain to find a place to sit. Diane and I listened to Axel's account of meetings that he had been to. He had met men from a village and its municipality in mid-western Sweden who were trying to find ways to revive their forest community by working locally with the forests.

Axel: There are things happening here, people struggling for rights to the forests . . . issues that we have been working with in the countries in the global South for years . . . that nobody is looking at. We could learn so much from each other . . .

Diane: We can't just keep talking and devising solutions for the South and not see that we have similar problems here.

Axel: We need to look at ourselves and start from where we are.

My presence in these three places and the interactions with the people involved encapsulate how the research, on which this book is based, began.

The visits to Nayagarh and Drevdagen showed me that women in these villages preferred to work in alternative ways when it came to local development and environmental governance. In both places, I heard the women saying important things about needing to link environmental governance to other aspects of village life to be able to succeed in their struggles. Why was that proving to be so difficult? After my visit to India, another constant thought in my mind was 'what did the women get out of my research?' Was this going to be a book that would address another stack of books and a world of people far from their lives? Or could I do it in a way that might be relevant for the women that I spoke to?' I came to the conviction that future research had to be useful for the people immediately concerned. And that these issues needed to be seen in a 'global' perspective. There are processes taking shape in the 'developed' North, not dissimilar to those in the South. Studying them in relation to each other and unraveling the connections between them provide insights about environmental governance, gender and development that are hard to discern otherwise.

This book is about the entanglements of gender, environmental governance and development activities on the ground. It seeks to disentangle these strands to understand them and having done so, to be able to see them in their connections to one another. It is about working in and with, what J. K. Gibson-Graham (drawing on the eco-philosopher Freya Matthews) call a jigsaw world, where practice is shaped by and shapes everything else. This is an up-close, piecing it together, participatory approach to understanding (or performing) the world rather than a big-picture, spectator approach that captures and reduces everything via universal laws (Gibson-Graham 2011, 4). At the heart of the book are 'up-close' stories from two peripheral places (in relation to state and other decision-making structures in their countries): Nayagarh, in the countryside of the state of Odisha in India and the other the village of Drevdagen, in the sparsely populated area of western Sweden. I examine the minutiae of daily life, the negotiations of gender and power relations and how these shape environmental governance and development action. I then step back to view them as part of a larger puzzle that makes up our world and trace the tenuous connections between them.

The political meaning of their geographical location as marginal played an important part in gender relations and in the villagers' work with local development and environmental governance. This politics of marginalization was contested even as it was elaborated. It was, as Anna Lowenhaupt Tsing writes of her work in Indonesia, a marginalization developed in language, in dialogue with state policies and regional politics rather than in their isolation in relation to what is perceived as mainstream society. Gender was not parallel to this marginalization. Marginalization itself was gendered (c.f. Tsing 1993) and played an important part in environment and development politics.

The villagers in Nayagarh and Drevdagen regarded themselves as forest communities. Forests are both material resources but also symbolic, imbued with culturally constructed meanings and values. The forests were and remain intrinsic to the way of life in these communities and have played a major role in the sustenance and cultures in these places. Contestations over natural resources in Nayagarh and Drevdagen were central to questions of local governance and development. Natural resources are important for rural lives but they are also a source of significant wealth for governments and for the meaning that they hold for different people. The communities sought to 'redefine' their relationships with the environment and to authorities while claiming greater rights over the forests. Women in the villages in both these places chose to organize themselves in their own groups to work for themselves and their communities. This decision became contentious.

By working with the women in these two places and following the trajectories of their organizing, I foreground everyday practices of gender and power while questions of local forest governance form an important background. The women's organizing turned the focus to struggles over meanings and the contestations over what constituted rural development and local environmental governance. These struggles made clear that what environmental governance and development meant could no longer be taken for granted. The processes brought to attention how dominant meanings are sought to be established. Environmental imaginations were key to crafting gender relations and gender was integral to environmental governance and rural development. In thus arguing, I put environmental sensibilities at the heart of gender negotiations, while at the same time making a case for gender as integral to our analyses in order to be able to meet environmental and developmental challenges.

GENDER, ENVIRONMENTAL GOVERNANCE AND DEVELOPMENT

In speaking of gender, development and environmental governance as three pieces of a jigsaw, I do not mean that these are discrete and separate pieces. They are charged by each other—that is, while practices of development and environmental governance are gendered, environmental governance in local communities can be synonymous with development. These categories are superimposed on each other in particular ways in different, material contexts.

There are three important ways in which I conceptualize gender in these two rural contexts—(1) as a description of society based on sexual attributes, (2) as a category of analysis and also (3) how it becomes an issue or problem that needs to be dealt with in development and environmental governance. The first use of gender, as a description of society, is what we find all around us. When we allocate to the sexes different attributes, characteristics and roles, we are doing gender. It becomes apparent in the text as people in both Nayagarh and Drevdagen (especially in Chapters 4, 5 and 6) describe men and women on the basis of their sex with certain taken for granted attributes, for example, men as pragmatic or women as impulsive. These characteristics have valence because, regardless of actual practice, they were often used as the justification for and basis of action. Gender is thus part of the world we live in but it also a way of understanding the world. It is in this second meaning, of studying and understanding the world that I use gender as a category of analysis. This implies studying the organization of power in initiatives for local environmental governance and development (see chapter two for a futher discussion on how I use gender as an analytical category). Appeals to sexual difference were used to consolidate power relationships, but these were also crosscut by other categories of social difference such as age, class, caste or occupation. Gender was, and always is, entangled with and never separate from other forms of social difference. Gender relations were also central within the women's collectives as the women related to each other, organized themselves and built up an intersubjective space between them, creating a 'mood' for change. Third and lastly, I study how gender becomes an 'issue' in environmental governance and development, as a problem that needs to be solved. This is typified by the absence of women from organizations for local governance and by the professed need by mainstream organizations and development practitioners to ensure their presence. It also recurs in reiterations about needing to train and develop women and in exhortations to women in rural areas to involve themselves in income generation and community activities. I turn first to the issue of environmental governance and then to development to examine how gender is intrinsic to these processes.

Environmental governance is increasingly concerned with formal and informal decision-making, rule making mechanisms and actors and networks at various scales in relation to environmental resources. Environmental threats and the failure of previous centralized regimes to deliver effective development has led national governments and international organizations to regard political decentralization and a devolution of responsibilities over the environment as the path to sustainable development (Shakleton, Campbell, Wollenberg and Edmunds 2002). At the center of theoretical and policy discussions about political decentralization is a shift from ideas on 'government' by the state to 'governance' by a variety of different actors in the pursuit of collective interests (c.f. Peters and Pierre 1998).[6]

There are different emphases in the ways that scholars have theorized environmental governance, especially in relation to the actors involved in the processes of devolution. The literature from Sweden, for example centers predominantly on initiatives characterized by partnerships between public-private interests or in some cases with established civil society groups. Many such initiatives especially in the last decade reveal neoliberal influences, where environmental problems are sought to be solved by market approaches (see Bäckstrand, Khan, Kronsell and Lövbrand 2010). Another emphasis associated with the term governance, more noticeable in the literature in India, focuses on rural communities' struggles for viable alternatives to existing arrangements and their relations to the state (e.g. Agrawal, Chhatre and Hardin 2008; Edmunds and Wollenberg 2003). These concern the politics of decision-making and community action while a few have also studied the gendered nature of local environmental governance (e.g. Agarwal 2010).

To varying extents, approaches are dictated by context. Neoliberal currents and community action are present in both India and Sweden although community action is largely inconspicuous in the literature on forest governance in Sweden, and discussions of gender and power are singularly absent. In the present book, I analyze the micropolitics of everyday relations on the ground in cases both from India and Sweden to understand these wider trends associated with the idea of governance in particular spaces. In doing so I pay special attention to the subjectivities produced at the intersection of efforts towards environmental governance and development of marginal places.

At the time of the fieldwork in Naygarh and Drevdagen (in periods between 1992–2005), much of the discourse—in theory and practice—was framed around the term community-based natural resource management (CBRNM) or simply local management. Since then, recognizing community claims as beyond that of 'managing' the environment, the discourse has been in terms of 'governance.'[7] This is a term I use in the book to refer to processes of decision-making, accountability and for rights and relations to the environment that exceed that of 'management.'

My attention is on how environmental governance and development are realized through gender and power relations in everyday practice and decision-making processes that give rise to new relationships and subjectivities at collective and individual levels. Issues of management and governance, if anything, have gained more salience in the last few years with climate concerns dominating international agendas and with environmental debates once again focusing on forestry. In quotes from people in Nayagarh and Drevdagen I sometimes continue to use the term 'local management,' to suggest a more limited meaning but also when it was a term that participants used themselves, a language that was in use then. Their meanings though, become clear from the dialogues and stories.

Since the term governance has overtones of private interests, I often resort to the use of the term 'local' governance to emphasize the focus on community claims. Local governance or management implied a new kind of politics in the two settings, a politics where everyone could be involved. This made it imperative to study what is 'local' and who is 'local' in environmental governance and development activities. As women were sought to be included in the public space of 'local' governance by mainstream organizations, I examine if attempts at inclusion may not in fact undermine efforts towards equitable participation and sustainable environmental governance (Chapter 6)? If we are looking for potentially more democratic and effective environmental governance and development, we need to take account of the alternative spaces in which social groups such as those of women choose to work and what they might want out of their political participation and hopes for the development of their environments.

Development is primarily associated with economic progress and with a 'will to improve' (Li 2007) the lives of people, especially in rural areas. Ideas about development are linked in specific ways to conceptualizations of rural space (Chapter 2). Rural areas are seen as being left behind in the inexorable thrust of development and economic growth. Cities are centers of capital accumulation, entrepreneurship and cultural development. Rural women are often regarded as doubly backward, as rural inhabitants restricted to their homes and villages as in India; or in Sweden, as aberrations if they choose to stay on in the countryside instead of seizing opportunities in cities that promise greater equality in gender relations. While rural areas are and have been materially central to global flows in the natural resources and eco-system services they provide, they have been pushed further into the periphery from the centers of capital. These can be understood as the disintegrative effects of development as described by Cindi Katz—the uneven motion of capital finding producing and reproducing places and people in . . . relation to peculiar strategies of accumulation (Katz 2004, ix). But, as I go on to argue in this book, development is also what people do, as they consciously mobilize resources and networks, form new associations or revive old ones, seek new markets for entrepreneurship and construct a rural community. Dominant definitions of development associated with material improvement contended with varied understandings of what development meant to different people in Nayagarh and Drevdagen.

The 'conversation' about development, as Fredrick Cooper and Randall Packard (drawing on McClosky's metaphor of the 'conversation' in the social sciences) point out, "is an extraordinarily extensive one, taking place all over the world" (1997, 6). It also has distinct connotations for countries in the global South or North. In places located in such different parts of the world such as Nayagarh and Drevdagen, where differences in wealth and gender indices are so glaring, global space is often transformed into a time sequence. The West becomes the inhabitant of modernity that is in several respects interchangeable with development and westernization (Pieterse 1991). These conversations produce particular gendered subject positions such as gender equal and modern women or illiterate and victimized poor women, that contend with experiences rooted in specific material environments and relationships (Chapter 5). I analyze how these tensions are productive of change and the unexpected ways in which such tensions provided and closed off spaces for women to take action in the two very different contexts in Sweden and India (Chapter 7).

The challenge is to understand the implications of micropolitics and activism within communities for the definitions of local environmental governance and development and for people's visions for their futures.

By paying attention to day-to-day dynamics and changing subjectivities, I highlight localized norms and practices in the public arena of the village as yet another place where gender and power is established in its specific ways but is also contingent on meanings constituted in and connected with the wider society.

THEORIZING CONNECTIONS

There are different connections that I consider in the book. The first and obvious is the need to connect and converse across theories on environmental governance, development and gender as I outline above. Overlaying these are the connections between two distant places in the North and the South. These are sites and struggles with people wanting agency over their environments in conditions and cultures that are vastly different but in a wider context of changing environmental governance where environmental issues are increasingly being treated as 'global.' Cross cultural comparative studies often aim at abstracting emerging patterns in order to discuss what is universal and what is specific. This is not a formal conventional case comparison but what I have chosen to call a 'relational analysis.' Rather than abstracting patterns, I examine the specifics, but also the discourses that shape the specifics, the complex circulation of ideas in a world with many links. I use the cases to ask questions that are not obvious at first glance, both in the empirical settings and of the somewhat separate theoretical frameworks generally associated with studies in two such different settings in the North and the South. One aspect has been to 'reverse the gaze' on how questions of development and gender are usually asked, an approach that I describe further in this chapter. The relational analysis revealed the connections between Nayagarh and Drevdagen in an increasingly globalized world. Local governance and democracy were constructed in a context of struggles for their environment in both places in specific ways, but also within overlapping discursive contexts. These cases are not merely two instances of discrete cultures placed in a comparative status but as I discuss above, experience the contingent history of complex power relations in their own countries and in a larger world order. I analyze how categories such as 'being modern' are translocal in their cognitive capacity yet contested and changing and charged by their contexts, 'without an inherent rationality or coherence that they do not have' (Mitchell 2002).

Parallel to this are connections of scale. Rural space played an important part in the conceptualizations of the two places as small, marginal places far from centers of official power. While rural space was distinct, its uneasy relationship to the 'urban' and to government authorities outside the villages was present in villagers' conceptualizations of their places. As Zygmunt Bauman puts it eloquently, "Not all city life is modern; but all modern life is city life. For life to turn modern means to become more like life in the city" (1995, 126). And as the struggles for local governance and development in the two places got increasingly bureaucratized, one could discern disciplinary relations that were not merely localized in relations between the modernizing state and its citizens but went down to the depths of society (c.f. Foucault 1979, 27).

Several feminist geographers argue for a rescaling in the gender and environment literature to acknowledge the multiple ecologies that include habitat, home, household and the body as much as the city, the region, the nation and the globe. In other words, gender matters at all these levels but importantly, as they note, these multiple ecologies are entangled in complex arrangements that can only be understood through their multisited and multiscalar character (Hawkins and Ojeda 2011). This was clear in both Nayagarh and Drevdagen. The outside world was just as tangible in environmental and development discourses as in women's use of their bodies. But the women also changed the terms of discourse in the actions they took and laid bare the gendered nature of environmental governance and development as they sought new openings (Chapter 7).

It is important to be sensitive to specificity but at the same time to be able to grasp large objects of inquiry such as processes and ideas about environmental governance, development and gender that circulate in an increasingly globalized world. I believe, like Nancy Fraser that,

> "We also need approaches that promote our ability to think relationally and contextually, including frameworks that can connect various elements of the social totality, casting those elements not merely as 'different' from one another but as mutually interconnected. . . . We need, finally, theoretical frameworks that permit us to project utopian hopes, envision emancipatory alternatives, and infuse all of our work with a normative critique of domination and injustice" (1995, 159).

By mapping links between what may seem as discrete discursive contexts, I hope to further thinking on the construction of domination in the two places but also possibilities for emancipation. The politics of knowledge production is central to this endeavor.

THE POLITICS OF KNOWLEDGE PRODUCTION: TWO SITES OF STRUGGLE AND A UNIVERSITY

A current that goes through the book is an attention to the approach and the methodologies we adopt to study questions of environmental governance and how they produce distinctive answers to our questions. The research was situated in three different physical contexts. The ethnographic studies in Nayagarh district in Odisha in southeast India began as far back as 1993 and in the village of Drevdagen in the sparsely populated region of mid-western Sweden somewhat later in 1998. However, the bulk of the work in both places took place between 1998 and 2008, with extensive participatory research with the women in Drevdagen. The third place that I mention here is the university of which, I too, was a part (see Chapter 4). Universities are meant not to have a politics and yet in their role as formal producers of knowledge, research and education, they are enmeshed in relationships of gender and power as I discuss further in the following chapters. The production of scientific knowledge is never independent of the wider context and it felt important for me to situate the research. Recent discussions on environmental issues and more specifically on climate science have further called into public attention, contests about the boundaries of science and society (Berkhout 2010) and the partiality of science in face of uncertainty. The more facts become uncertain, the more important is the dialogue on values in dispute (Funtowicz and Ravetz 1993).

It is important for research to understand what people value and why they value it (Jasanoff 2007). I wanted to position my research with the women in the villages in India and in Sweden, to understand what they themselves might want from efforts for local governance, for the community and on what terms they wanted to participate. I realized fairly early in both places that unless I consciously made the effort, it was mainly men who volunteered to speak about the forests and village development, especially since almost all village forest committee and association members were men. I chose to view community efforts through the vantage point of the women's groups (see Chapter 2). This vantage point afforded me a 'double vision' (Gadol 1976), alerting me to the double meanings of words where previously their significance was taken for granted. It helped me understand the 'space off' (described in Chapter 2) of local governance and development, the underlying meanings and relationships of gender and power that determine outcomes.

Taking a vantage point from the women's groups rather than starting from the mainstream organizations, brought to light aspects of environmental governance that would otherwise stay hidden. Rather than trying to explain certain social phenomena, in this case local governance of the environment and of development initiatives or women's organizing per se, it became possible to think about the ways in which social relations were constitutive of these phenomena (c.f. Smith 1987). Long-term participatory research with the women in Drevdagen (a collaborative inquiry) forced me to situate the research and disrupt the division between theory and practice. It led me to an active theorizing or alternatively a more 'thoughtful practice' (Cuomo 1998), where theory is thoughtful practice. A similar collaborative inquiry was impossible to carry out in India because of financial and time constraints, since I was based at a university in Sweden. Because I went about my research in an unconventional way in Sweden and not in India, where my focus was on attending meetings, interviews and participant observation in the villages, it made me vigilant to methodology and 'process' both in research and developmental work. The transdisciplinary approach in Drevdagen and the joint process of knowledge-production also provided deep insights into the case in Sweden that I do not have in Nayagarh, despite a long-term involvement in Nayagarh.

In this volume, the material generated from these two processes is analyzed in relation to each other, sometimes in discussions with the women in Drevdagen. An initial report on Nayagarh was commented on by the women's coordinator in Nayagarh who wrote to me while I was in Sweden. When describing events in Drevdagen, I switch between 'we' and 'I' and do this for a purpose. It is to distinguish between the shared experience of the collaborative inquiry and the individual analysis presented in this book as I look back on 'us.' I was a part of the inquiry and changed by it, however in most places I use 'they' or the 'women in the inquiry' because the focus was nonetheless on the lives of the women. The analysis of the two cases parallel to each other is central to the design of the research. In the following section I briefly present the methods by which I carried it out.

THE RELATIONAL ANALYSIS

One aspect has been to *freeze activities and freeze time* when analyzing the material in their specific contexts. This means that I take as important that which was said and done at the particular time to explain the present. The focus is on the action that was taken and the words that were used at that particular moment as exemplars and acts that solidify meanings and indicate underlying assumptions or the structures of meaning rather than being properties of specific people. For example, I examine the existing situation and scrutinize relationships of power at that moment rather than merely accepting tradition as an argument to explain certain behavior, an explanation that harks back to the past, ignoring the power relationships that actually produce that behavior in the present. My relationship to the two places was different and I account for these differences by locating myself in the text. By being reflexive about my work I have strived to be objective about my own subjectivity or I have tried to adopt a *critical subjectivity* (Reason 1994).

I have used the cases to ask questions of each other, analyzing the ways in which meanings were established in each of the two contexts about the categories that were used rather than taking them as given (e.g. forests, equality, development). This entailed looking at the societal context and to study the discourses (e.g. state policies on gender, development and governance debates) that men and women call upon to explain their experiences and talk about themselves and others. I consciously *reverse the gaze* on questions such as development and gender equality, i.e. instead of assuming that development and equality are aspects that Sweden has reached in comparison with India, I examine instead the ways in which the concepts are constructed in each place. By exploring how these understandings gave meaning to and challenged wider discourses in society, I take the discussion beyond the micro-politics of the villages to identify and comprehend a wider discursive context that was constitutive of and constituted by the women's efforts. The book has implications for how local governance and gender equality are conceptualized in theory and in practice and importantly for the framing of policies that seek to bring about gender equitable and sustainable environmental management.

OVERVIEW OF THE BOOK

Disrupting the theory and practice divide I integrate theory, history, ethnography and methodological conceptualizations in the different chapters to unravel the entanglements of gender, environment and development and make them easier to grasp. In Chapter 2, "Crafting New Relations and Theorizing Connections: Gender, Development and the Environment," I begin with a theoretical and methodological discussion on the three constraining discourses that characterize this field: that equitable environmental citizenship involves managing resources through open and public deliberation, that greater individual equality presupposes greater space for collective agency and that the correct way to go about scientific inquiry is to maintain a neutral distance from the field and start with the right questions. I analyze and elaborate on the conceptual and methodological tools used in the book—power, resistance and agency, debates on space, theorizing on development and being modern, translocality and discourse and subjectivity. I end the chapter by outlining the participatory approach that allowed me to situate my research, to acquire a double vision and go beyond conventional understandings of environmental governance.

Chapter 3, "Policy Discourses and Material Places: Forests, Gender and the (Re)making of the Peripheries," is a reading 'against the grain' of the history of policy discourses on forest governance in India and Sweden over the years. Drawing on the work of scholars, in 'double vision,' I see difference where earlier only sameness prevailed (Gadol 1975)—in questioning and connecting gender to land ownership, forests, questions of deforestation, women's involvement in local democracy and increasingly to the emphasis on climate change. In Chapter 4, "Environmental Politics on the Ground," the focus is on development and environmental action in Nayagarh and Drevdagen. I give an account of forest activism in the two places and end by drawing on the connections between the two—on how ideas on marginality were a constraint but also provided opportunity, the importance of the social agenda for the political and for governance of the forests and the inherent interdependence of the political with women's labor.

In Chapter 5, "A Politics of the Possible: Gendered Subjectivities in Collective Organizing," I discuss how the women's collectives came about through a telling of their stories. The attention is on how gendered subjectivities come into being through the women's interactions with their material environments. The women drew upon prevailing discourses and conformed to conventional images about themselves but also created new possibilities of being in a process mutually constituted as they transformed the environments and politics around them. In brokering 'modernity' and 'tradition,' they built up their collectives, met across their differences and formed their subjectivities in action and talk, carving out an alternative space for themselves in the villages. This politics was resisted by the formal organizations in the villages and considerable energy put into maintaining the existing networks of relations. This becomes apparent when turning the analytical lens in Chapter 6 to the "Micro-politics of Rural Development and Environmental Governance." Here, I untangle how the 'local' is constructed in discourses on development and environmental governance in everyday interactions and how women's inclusion in decision-making forums does not automatically challenge gender inequalities. I also examine my role as well as that of my colleagues in these processes. By analyzing 'local governance' in Nayagarh and Drevdagen as 'problematic in the everyday' (Smith 1987), I unravel the assumptions and organizing principles underlying work with rural development and the environment that are otherwise taken for granted. These played an important part in gender relations in the villages but also reflect normative assumptions about development and environmental governance.

In Chapter 7, "Discordant Connections: Discourses on Gender and Grassroots Activism," I take an analytical step back from the specific to explore the space for women's agency in their particular contexts by analyzing the connections between them. The chapter throws light on two important insights: first, that in Sweden where gender equality has been actively pursued as the bedrock of modern societal organizing, the space to organize as women in relation to environmental issues was hedged around with ambiguities. Second, development discourses about equality and empowerment of oppressed third world women bear not only on how gender equality is conceptualized and practiced in the South but also shape the space for gender equality in the North. Analyzing the two cases in relation to each other, reveals the travel of ideas and conversations across distances. The chapter analyzes how discourses may be appropriated and can have a liberating effect at one moment while entailing domination in another. Understanding how this takes place opens an opportunity for interruption in an order and in a space that appears to have become narrower under the umbrella of development, welfare, and growth. It brings into question the category of development both in a Southern but especially so in a Northern context where the North and especially Sweden is taken as referent for questions of development and gender equality.

In Chapter 8, "Developmental Action and Environmental Governance: Flexible Spaces for Political Action," I discuss what happens when organizations whose power is challenged by ideas about rights in decision-making are in fact expected to assume charge of delivering democracy. Local governance as it was framed was limiting for the women in the two places but it also provided openings that they used to imagine different futures for their communities. The analysis in the chapter emphasizes the need for new ways to understand decision-making and the important role of space in adjudicating power in development and environmental governance. It draws attention to the need to theorize on multiple spaces and the connections between them in order to reframe agendas that are unjust. Finally in Chapter 9, "Up Close in a Jigsaw World: Guideposts from the Present," I conclude by pulling together the main strands of the book, discuss how I overcame the three constraints I outline in Chapter 2 and end with a discussion of participatory research and for possibilities for the future.

The contributions that this book seeks to make lie in problematizing environmental and development relations in a changing environmental and political situation wherein ideas about governance and the rhetoric on participation and partnerships is fairly established. Secondly, it is to analyze how assumptions about development and gender equality or empowerment take shape in reference to collective and individual agency. This approach brings into question development not only in the South, but also in the North. Lastly but importantly, I outline a methodology that may provide an opportunity to link the academic world to that of the research subjects in order to come to meaningful questions of relevance to both.

2 Crafting New Relations and Theorizing Connections

Gender, Development and Environmental Governance

Decision-making on environmental governance today occurs at different scales—from the rarefied settings of international and national bureaucracies and scientific experts to grassroots communities concerned with making a life in the environments. The questions often asked of environmental governance are: What will it take to save the environment in face of crisis such as climate change and the push to economic growth at various scales—in international fora, national settings and local communities? Who is going to control environmental management? Why are certain social groups such as women absent in formal governance and how can we create equitable forms of governance at different levels?

What if we were to ask these questions differently—How do global connections manifest themselves as men and women take environmental action? Where and how is environmental governance taking place at present? Is the marginalization of certain social groups a result of local gender and power relations or are they produced through far flung webs of exchange that need to be unraveled? This investigation begins in the present chapter with a conversation between a number of partly overlapping but also discrete bodies of literature on environmental governance, gender, development and scientific inquiry. The focus is not on the spaces afforded by the state such as decentralization and new forms of governance, but on the spaces carved out by local inhabitants and the spaces where formal governance and local processes meet. How might we study and theorize the messy realities of such meeting places and governance arrangements, not only at the local level but in a global and transnational perspective? What are the constraints that we need to overcome to move towards better choices about environmental governance and development?

To answer these questions, I discuss the theoretical, analytical and methodological means by which I negotiated the three constraining discourses that I encountered in the fields of environmental governance, gender and development. To deal with the first, that equitable environmental citizenship involves managing resources through open and public deliberation, I shift focus and foreground the background of processes of environmental governance and development. In other words, I turn the spotlight on how we might begin to *theorize* on the social and political contexts and inequalities that surround environmental governance to truly understand the mechanisms by which decision-making takes place. This entails an investigation into the multiple public and private spaces in environmental governance. By complicating the picture in this way, the point is to delve into specific and local details but to always hold on to their connections to wider systems outside of local contexts in order to discern patterns that sustain processes in different places. This brings me to the core of the discussion on the second constraining discourse, that greater individual equality presupposes greater space for collective agency or that women's political action results in greater personal independence. I discuss how we might need to think *analytically* about development and environmental issues in two very different places in the world, without adopting criteria or framework that will always be culturally specific. I use postmodern and postcolonial analysis, not merely to deconstruct dominating discourses but also to find moral and political positions by which to view the world. How may this be done practically without drowning in specifics or resorting to overgeneralizations? I explain this in the methodological discussion through which I confront the third constraining discourse, that the correct way to go about scientific inquiry is to maintain a neutral distance from the field and start with the right questions. I draw on participatory and feminist approaches that enable an analysis that remains close to the ground and yet able to speak to issues of wider theoretical concern. Importantly, this approach forces attention to knowledge production that happens not only in the field out there but in our universities in here.

EQUITABLE ENVIRONMENTAL CITIZENSHIP INVOLVES MANAGING RESOURCES THROUGH OPEN AND PUBLIC DELIBERATION?

The formation of groups and committees as well as associations at the local level has been regarded as evidence of an environmental citizenship that denotes both rights and responsibilities in relation to the environment. It has become an axiom that any research dealing with access and management of natural resources needs to start by looking at the institutions put in place for their governance. Policy and academic discourses are replete with references to the need for new organizational forms for environmental governance and development, keeping in mind issues of social equality. Neo-liberal policies have hastened this process. Both in literature and in policy, sustainable resource management and community development have been assumed to be accomplished by cooperative action between different social groups and institutions. Attempts to engage a diversity of actors in debates in environmental politics has been dubbed the 'deliberative turn.' At the local level, such a process has been considered possible by designing better institutional forms for resource management. The institutional approach was in part prompted by the rejection of the community (with its overtones of an organic whole) as a conceptual tool for understanding differing interests in resource management (Agrawal and Gibson 1999). It was believed that through a focus on institutions it would be possible to study the divergent interests of multiple actors within communities, the interactions and politics through which these interests emerge, and the outcomes of such political processes (ibid.). The attention has been on the ways it is possible to make these institutions efficient (Varughese and Ostrom 2001) and accountable to the structures above but also the people below (Agrawal and Ribot 2000). In general it has been agreed upon that smaller and more homogenous structures tend to function better (Baland and Platteau 1996: 343–345; Bardhan 1993) while others regard heterogeneities within these organizations as a challenge that may be overcome by good institutional design (Varughese and Ostrom 2001) or in some instances that heterogeneity might even help in successful management (Baland and Platteau 1996).

Although so far more rhetoric than practice, the deliberative approach to environmental management rests on the underlying assumption that broad participation in collective decision-making will bring about more legitimate and effective policy outcomes, promising new modes of environmental governance with increased attention to procedural qualities such as participation, dialogue, transparency and accountability (Bäckstrand et al. 2010, 4). The relative absence and invisibility of women is evident in institutions for environmental governance, both at the global level as for example in negotiations on climate change (e.g. Villagrasa 2002) and in organizations for environmental management at the local level (Agarwal 2010; Arora-Jonsson 2005; Sarin and Ray 1998). Environmental citizenship is at present evidently male-dominated. Research in India shows how new organizations and committees for environmental management could even erode women's former customary rights and access by replacing older customs and causing a breakdown in traditional rules of reciprocity and mutual aid with regard to the forests (Agarwal 1997). In Sweden, studies on rural development have shown women to be positioned negatively in terms of access to formal institutions for accessing credit and subsidies for their work in rural communities (Herlitz 1989). In certain areas, including the western forest counties where the village of Drevdagen is located, women got lower salaries but also tended to be more educated than the men (Forsberg 1997, 47). Thus, rather than the gender neutral institutions as they tend to get presented, local organizations and government bodies appear to be gendered entities in which women have had less room to maneuver than men.

There have been calls especially in India for the presence of a critical mass of women in organizations for environmental governance (e.g.

Agarwal 1997). But, the assumption that competing interests can be negotiated within institutions is also problematic. As Malin Rönnblom (2002) points out, although Sweden has come far in including a larger number of women in local level municipal institutions in Sweden, to be able to be a part of such organizations, and be present, does not necessarily mean that women can influence them. Solutions to such problems are usually couched in trying to increase women's competencies in order for them to take place in these settings. But, what if we were to turn the question around and ask, where are the women and what are environments in which they act?

Considerable feminist research has been devoted to understanding the work that women do in their environments and the value ascribed to it. "Struggles over resources are shaped not only by material forces and political power but also by the ideologies and understanding of what is meant by the environment" (Bhavnani, Foran and Kurian 2003, 16). What counts as work and whose definitions of the forest are taken as legitimate are crucial in understanding processes of power and gendered exclusion. Early feminists in the field of environmental studies, mostly in the south, have been influential in making visible the work of women in local development and environmental management (e.g. Harcourt 1994). The research that followed gave rise to debates between various strands of feminism in development studies.[1] The Women, Environment and Development approach that held sway in the 1980s to the early 1990s drew much of its inspiration from eco-feminism (e.g. Shiva 1989) that contended parallels between environmental degradation and the oppression of women by a male dominated instrumentalist science. Eco-feminism has been important in environmental studies for treating the non-human world as an active subject, not as a resource to be mapped or only a cultural construction, a perspective that has become increasingly more important in social theory. Some strands of eco-feminism however came to be criticized by proponents of what came to be called the Gender and Development approach for its tendency to essentialize the figure of the woman as 'carer of the environment' (Leach 2007). Eco-feminists also tended to neglect complexities and differences among and between women and men in their relationships to natural resources and disregard the gendered division of labor, property and power that determine men and women's relationships to the environment (e.g. Jackson 1993; Agarwal 1997). Within theories of development, post-colonial feminists like Chandra Talpade Mohanty have criticized the tendency of early western feminism to depict third world women as hapless victims subject to men's oppression. These ignored women's agency in the environments in which they are active and tended to subscribe to the assumption that greater development would bring equality (2003), a point to which I return in this book as well.

In Sweden, literature on women and their relation to environmental governance and development is scarce. Here again, what counts as work in the environment is important in understanding gender relations. In present day Sweden this is especially important considering the importance of work as a marker of gender equality (Hobson 2000). Researchers on farming show how women's work on the Swedish farm (Flygare 1999) as well as in farmer associations (Javefors Grauers and Eskilsson 2003) is downplayed and seen as a complement to the 'real' work of farming. Forest history from northern Dalarna shows the forests being worked mainly by women before the 1800s (Montelius 1977b, 37). However more recent studies in the northern forest communities have shown how both men and women tend to view men's activities in the forests as 'work' while other activities, in the forests by the women, are not regarded as work by both men and women (Kaldal 2000; Hansen 2000). In the next chapter, by reading history against the grain, I show how the masculinization of the forests in Sweden came about in a gradual process of defining property rights, work and trade in forest products and also contributed to carving out the forests as a male domain. Women's activities were thus erased from the stories of how forest communities live and survive. Reading against the grain draws attention to the real work that women do, as well as their histories and their differences in relation to environmental governance and rural development.

The social contexts of citizenship in which decision-making on resources takes place, have tended to be ignored in the vast literature on institutions for resource management cited earlier. Individual actors often get taken as coterminous with the formal organizations in which they are active, disregarding the informal ways in which resources are accessed and their use negotiated (Jackson 1998; Cleaver 1998). Frances Cleaver, for example, points to the need to understand that the interactions of daily life are as important in shaping outcomes and governing resource management and development as are public negotiations (2001). Studies in rural Sweden and other western European countries from the 1980s onwards point to the significance of 'networks' and informal, action-oriented groups parallel to established associations and political parties as women's preferred forms of working. They also emphasize the incompatibility of such forms of organizing *vis-à-vis* government bureaucracies and established politics (e.g. Rönnblom 1996; Forsberg 2001).

In contrast, analyzing the women's movement in India at the beginning of the 1990s, Nandita Gandhi and Nandita Shah write that women in India have by and large preferred to create space for themselves within existing organizations in order to make such organizations more flexible, accessible and sympathetic to women's voices, alongside autonomous groupings (1992, 295). Some of these preferences are reflected in the different forms in which the women chose to organize in Nayagarh and Drevdagen. Clearly, each instance is contextual. But the question that becomes interesting in the two different places in the book is what the forms adopted by the women tell us about the context in which they act. Is women's invisibility in public arenas such as government organizations or environmental committees the piece of the puzzle that is missing in sustainable environmental governance? How important is the 'public' nature of women's own work and organizing?

Feminists illustrate how citizenship is imbued with gender-specific assumptions and constructions of the public *versus* the private sphere. The popular belief that the private and public are two separate spheres with discrete boundaries is a legacy of early liberalism. In the words of John Stuart Mill, the division was between that "part of a person's life that which concerns only himself and that which concerns others" (1971, 98). The former was the realm of the private, where the state would not enter while the latter was meant to be open to all citizens equally and to state intervention. The public sphere has since then been increasingly theorized as the ground for democratic deliberation (Outhwaite 1996). The public/private division has been questioned by feminist scholarship for much of the 20th century, pointing to the injustices of the liberal perspective. Citizenship became associated with those active in the public sphere of the market and the state that was dominated by men while all that was deemed incompatible with citizenship was relegated to the private, female sphere of the home. The feminist slogan, the personal is political and the research that has followed in its wake turned the light on the inequalities that were left untouched within the private sphere (e.g. Pateman 1988).

Reviewing feminist scholarship on citizenship, Ruth Lister writes that the private sphere is characterized by the term 'ethic of care' where values such as care and connectedness are central and responsibilities stem from specific relationships in concrete circumstances. The public sphere on the other hand was seen to be driven by an 'ethic of justice' that emphasizes universal standards and abstract dictates of fairness and impartial rights (1997, 101–110). Several feminists including Lister argue for the importance of synthesizing these ethics. She argues for the need "to create a more powerful plural and relational ethic, which promotes the citizenship of women in their diversity in both private and public spheres" (ibid. 106), and at the same time to revalue the devalued side of this dichotomy (Fraser and Gordon 1994 cited in Lister 1997, 109) that consistently makes invisible the work that women do.

Lister's argument for a focus on citizenship as a process and not just an outcome is apposite for the women's organizing in Nayagarh and Drevdagen as the women's groups struggled to gain new rights and give substance to existing ones. The arena of community politics in relation to the governance of natural resources and rural development activities provides an ideal arena for studying participation of men and women and claims to political legitimacy and citizenship. Women's activism in Drevdagen and Nayagarh illustrates the inadequacy of the public-private split that comes more from theory rather than the messy practices of everyday environmental management and community development. Community activities and the labor that is put into them took place in an arena that straddled the public and the private. Lister writes that women's activism is breaking down boundaries between the public and the private. Critiquing the narrow definition of the formal political system, she argues for opening up formal politics to women in their diversity and for improving the links between formal and informal modes of politics so as to promote women's *equal* citizenship (Lister 1997, Chapter 6). Clearly such an approach demands an analysis of relationships of power in particular places, an analysis that is regrettably sidestepped by many theorists of deliberative environmental politics. In the following sections I turn to how this might be done.

Power, Resistance and Agency in Environmental Politics

Women's absence in committees and associations, the formal spaces for environmental and developmental decision-making, is often explained as a result of women's lack of power in relation to, and subjugation by, men in those committees. These formal spaces are seen as centers of power and decision-making. The assumption is that acceptance in these spaces would ascribe power to those who enter. Yet, the power that men and women can exercise has as much to do with what happens outside these spaces as inside. Michel Foucault's conception that ". . . power is not an institution, and not a structure; neither is it a certain strength we are endowed with; it is the name that one attributes to a complex strategical situation in a particular society" (1990, 93) is more useful to understand the events as they unfolded in the villages.

Power was not a property of the men or of specific spaces (c.f. Massey 1994) but was mobilized in relationships between people, although some of those relationships were difficult to dislodge. Those who exercised authority resisted change to the *status quo* and worked just as hard to maintain their advantages as those who opposed them. As Foucault writes, "Power is tolerable only on condition that it mask a substantial part of itself" (1990, 86), that it is not perceived as political. What is political is thus "not defined by the *locus* of its operation but by its nature as a *process*" (Hay 2002, 3), that is, by acknowledging the relations of power at work. The conceptualization of power as relational has enabled feminists to move from an oppositional discourse where power is something that men possess and women do not, to looking at the greater complexity of women's experiences in their relationships with men and women.

Foucault also writes that, "Where there is power, there is resistance and yet or rather consequently, this resistance is never in a position of exteriority in relation to power" (1990, 95). Power thus may be seen not as a resource to be possessed but rather as pervasively filtering through everyday life through language and practices. Criticizing Foucault's work for the neglect of the view of the subject and for neglecting the 'specificity of the sexed body' (Grosz 1990) even in his theses on sexuality, feminists such as Lois McNay (2000) and Davina Cooper (1995) have built upon his work for an understanding of agency on the part of subjects that may also exercise power. Power can thus be seen as both oppressive but also productive and generative (Cooper 1995; McNay 2000). This is particularly useful in analyzing instances where women in Nayagarh and Drevdagen did exercise power *generatively* and the processes that took shape around them, inside and outside of formal institutions.

This does not imply that all organizing by women in the different villages necessarily led to a generation of power by them. The terms 'resistance' and 'dislocation' have in some respects become maxims in that they are used to describe any situation where individual practices do not conform to dominant norms and impute to them a kind of inherently subversive status. If one was to accept however that individual practices never reflect overarching norms in a straightforward fashion, then the widely deployed notion of resistance loses analytical purchase (McNay 2000, 4). A more precise and varied account of agency is needed to explain the differing motivations and ways in which groups struggle over, appropriate and transform cultural meanings and resources. In this sense, agency may be seen McNay argues, as attempts to manage the often discontinuous, overlapping or conflicting relations of power and as autonomous action in the face of often overwhelming cultural sanctions and structural inequalities (2000, 10).

Maud Eduards' proposition that the seemingly gender-neutral concept of agency has an obvious male bias is interesting in this regard. She writes, "Agency is limited here to the capacity to initiate, guide and control developments—'to executive power' . . . The collective actions of women are also measured against this yardstick" (1992, 96) and are seen to fall short. "By defining the need for women to act together as women, oppression comes, in principle under attack, since sexual power relations are built on the notion of human, gender-neutral, agency" (ibid.). The women's organizing in Naygarh and Drevdagen was an assertion of and exercise of agency. In taking action together the women challenged the boundaries that were placed between themselves and where politics may be done (c.f. Eduards 2002, 78). They created a political space that challenged ideas about what local citizenship could be.

But the 'action' that constitutes the exercise of agency varies from context to context, as it may from male to female. It is often assumed that the formation of women's groups leads to a collective solidarity and women's empowerment across a broad front (e.g. see Everingham 2002). However, as Eduards points out, "The more women act, the more divided they seem" (1992, 95). Women's unity and cohesion cannot be assumed, just as all men's unity cannot be assumed especially when they may be divided by crosscutting interests such as age, race, place, caste or political conviction. Such unity has to be constructed. Moreover, where such unity does exist, it is fragile and conditional as much empirical work suggests (e.g. Reed 2000). In taking public action together in Nayagarh, women were acutely aware of the boundaries of age, caste and class. In collective organizing erasing of boundaries is not a given. Neither did all women in Nayagarh or Drevdagen choose to be part of the collectivity. This has meant trying to understand the women's actions beyond those reasons offered by their social location. I take up these questions by recognizing women's organizing and the building of a collectivity as a conscious effort (or struggle) for solidarity that was not self-evident even in the fairly homogenous and small village of Drevdagen.

'Spaces' of Democratic Deliberation

Lister's conceptualization of citizenship is an ideal basis for theorizing on the events as they unfolded in Nayagarh and Drevdagen. But it also gives rise to two theoretical complications (that arise from practice) that need to be unraveled. The first concerns the question of how women's activism is viewed, that is, when are women understood as being active and in what spaces? The other concerns the assumption of the relationship between informal political action and individual freedom that I take up in the following section. A range of literature on women's community activism has documented women protesting against toxic waste, against logging practices or organizing community activities in public spaces (e.g. Rocheleau, Thomas-Slayter and Wangari 1996). The tendency within feminist research, especially that on women's environmental action, to a "preoccupation with public acts" (Reed 2000, 366) in public spaces needs to be troubled. But to understand this better, I begin with clarifying the difference between what we call the public sphere and public space. Simon Springer's definition is useful in this context.

Referring to Habermas (1989), Simon Springer writes that the public sphere can be defined as the abstract domain of social life, ideally separate from the coercion of state power, where public opinion is formed. Analogous to civil society in its original Habermasian sense, the idea of public sphere is effectively silent on space. Springer argues that public space must be taken literally as a material space and that because belonging to any public requires at least minimum participation, individuals must physically come together and occupy a common space (Howell 1993, cited in Springer 2010). He builds his argument on two propositions. The first is the importance of visibility to political action—that *people need to be seen* for a democratic politics to take place (Springer 2010, 537 *my emphasis*). To answer the first question that I posed in the beginning of this section, women are seen to be active when they are visible. I show why this point of view is problematic.

The focus on visibility is also the reason that theorists tend to focus almost exclusively on public acts and fail to notice the not so obvious relations of environmental governance that take place in *spaces* that are not necessarily public or visible. For example, in an analysis of collective action on forestry issues, Bina Agarwal distinguishes women's involvement in resource management as having a propensity towards agitational actions or what we might call a time bound public action. She contrasts these to long-term, cooperative organizations that are often dominated by the men (2003, 3), suggesting that women's rich social networks in the villages might offer potential for them to 'learn to cooperate with one another' while building cooperative organizations and solidarity for more sustainable forest management, from which they are otherwise excluded (Agarwal 2010, 378). The cases presented in this book suggest that there is more to brief periods of agitational action than meets the eye. The work that women do in the environment, in public spaces (as well as private), tends to remain invisible, until those moments in time when the women choose to act as a collective in specific ways that contradict conventional organizing principles in public spaces.[2] Women's networks and actions related to their villages tend to take up multiple issues, and often do not take on the recognizable, more permanent forms that are seen as viable cooperative organizations associated with development work. Their deliberation on environmental and developmental decision-making may take place outside of official public spaces with a range of people but without the legitimacy accorded to the visible, male dominated organizations by actors within and outside their communities.[3]

Springer's second explanation for the differentiation of public space from sphere draws on the work of Lefebvre and McCann (1999). He emphasizes the significance of bodily representations or lived experiences to bring public spaces into being.[4] Through collective action, women bodily occupy spaces, doing politics, creating a tension not only in that space but in relation to the official space of formal politics. My argument here, like that of Springer is that "all groups, whether subaltern or dominant cannot constitute themselves unless they produce a material space" (2011, 539). That public space is important for identity formation is well recognized (e.g. Massey 1994; Roseneil 1995). Where I differ, is that space does not have to be public and that the personal or in-between spaces that women bring into being are indeed political as well as fertile grounds for identity formation. What may these spaces be in material terms? As the women straddle the public and the private, take action in these in-between spaces, they often do so from within what Fraser calls 'subaltern counter-publics' (1993), strategically separate spaces. Women in Nayagarh and Drevdagen created alternative spaces in ways that may or may not be agitational or 'theatrical'[5] but their actions invoked political repercussions all the same. This prompts thinking on the limitations of 'official spaces' that characterize processes of deliberation and the need to imagine new ways to conceptualize spaces of environmental governance. These are discussed further in Chapter 8.

Public space as formulated in its current liberal formulation is premised on that you leave your subjectivities behind (Iveson 2010, 217). The women who came into male dominated organizations in the villages were expected to do so as neutral individuals, unconcerned with particular issues or their identity as women. In that sense, their need to participate might have been fulfilled but to fulfill their strategic interests, they needed to draw on their subjective experiences of difference. Scholars have grappled with this paradox and many feminists challenge the dichotomous pairing of difference *versus* equality by noting that equality is incommensurate with difference only if equality means 'sameness' (e.g. Lister 1994, 97–98).[6] But what might this mean for gender and environmental governance in diverse settings? Inclusion in organizations for environmental management or deliberative politics does not necessarily ensure a democratic politics. How do women and men engage as citizens rather than be managed as subjects? The analysis in the book presents insights on alternative forms in environmental governance (Chapter 8). It makes a case for the need to analyze the multiple spaces and ways in which decision-making on environmental and development issues takes place. Understanding and acknowledging them as political is key to understanding the production of citizenship.

For women in the two places, local citizenship, environmental or otherwise also meant being involved in what they termed development activities but were not always recognized as such.[7] Ideas about development with its correlate of being modern played an important role in defining citizenship in environmental governance and local development. It is to these that I turn as I examine the second constraining discourse.

POLITICAL ACTION AND INVIDUAL RIGHTS RESULT IN GREATER SPACE FOR WOMEN'S AGENCY?

The apparently commonsensical assumption that I confront in this section is that political action by women results in greater personal independence for them. The other side of the coin is the idea that development and individual equality and rights lead to greater space for agency for women.

When speaking about the large numbers of women imprisoned by the colonial authorities in the struggle for independence in Odisha in the 1940s, Annapurna Maharana, a Gandhian worker, told me laughingly,[8]

> "Once they were baptized (i.e. been to jail) for their participation in the movements on an equal footing with the men, they could never be the same."

She cited a verse from Mirabai,[9] *ab to baat phail padi* (now the word has spread), meaning that even though women went back to the confines of their home, the experience of making a difference in their own right, had made them different women. The question this poses, also, is what happens when women active in a collective go back home as individuals? Does collective political action lead to greater personal freedom and agency? Lister proposes that "informal political action can enhance self-esteem, which in turn can strengthen women's position in the family thereby making it easier for them to assert their economic or physical independence (which in turn effect each other)" (1997, 114). The converse, the assumption that greater individual freedom and level of development leads to greater gender equality in collective deliberation or public spaces, is ubiquitous in policy making and programs for development. While erasing the boundaries of the public and private, informal political action in Nayagarh and Drevdagen did enhance the women's self esteem but did it necessarily 'strengthen their position in the family'? Similarly, are greater individual rights and economic stability not conducive to collective political action? Herein lies the heart of the argument about the two cases that I analyze in Chapter 7.

Another longstanding dichotomy within feminist theorizing, that of strategic *versus* practical gender interests, has held sway in development studies. Advanced by Maxine Molyneux (1985), it has been expanded on by other researchers. Strategic interests are those derived from an analysis of women's subordination and the formulation of strategic objectives to overcome them. Practical gender interests, on the other hand, arise from the concrete conditions of women's lives and are usually a response to an immediate perceived need and they do not generally entail a strategic goal such as women's emancipation or gender equality (Molyneux 1985, 232–233). Though useful to understand some aspects of discrimination, this division of women's lives in practical and strategic interests can be counterproductive in understanding the effects of their activism. One could assume that women's articulation of solidarity is a response to their subordination and attempt to overcome strategic disadvantages. However, it is impossible to separate the two (Arora-Jonsson 2005, 54, 306). As I illustrate further in the book, the articulation of needs and making claims, has in itself challenged structural disadvantage. On the other hand, strategic considerations such as a conscious involvement of women in organizations for resource governance and articulation of the problem such as discrimination of women, could well become a tool to rubberstamp existing inequalities (Chapter 6). Also, the issues that women choose to take up when they mobilize are rarely only about discrimination or strategically gendered. They are tied to their aspirations for other things—such as a living countryside, equitable management of resources *vis-à-vis* state authorities or upper caste men and women, a desire to preserve their husbands' employment and contextually crosscut by other motivations and relationships of power. Although motivated by practical needs and interests, these can have far reaching consequences for what are regarded as strategic interests.

The two cases suggest that the politics of the public and the private, despite being dependent one on the other, have partly different sets of logics or organizing principles at work in the different spaces (and spheres) that continue to work to maintain this divide. These are explained only by examining the wider relations in which the peoples and the places were embedded including discourses on equality and development that connect particular places and national contexts. What work do gender equality and development or the related concept of being modern do in organizing the social sharing of global values? It is to this wider context that I now turn in the next section. I first examine the contexts/relationships that produce assumptions about gender equality and development and second, I propose tools for their analysis.

The Context and Condition . . . of Development

When men and women in Drevdagen and Nayagarh, told me about their work with development activities, in its most concrete form, I took development to mean the changes that they wished to see in their villages. But development was also something that was sought to be done for them from outside, for example by state agencies, regional policies and by various development agents. The 'development context' of Nayagarh is unmistakable—foreign development agencies and NGOs active in the field, funds that could be applied for from government as well as foreign donors and numerous schemes started by the government often aimed specifically at women, such as the Development of Women and Children in Rural Areas as well as the existence of the women's development program as part of the forestry network activities.

Drevdagen is not a 'development context' as it is normally understood, located as it is in a country in the North with a relatively high standard of welfare. Even writing about them relationally evoked skepticism. Yet, similar assumptions colored ideas about development in these places in the North and South. Development is about being ahead, pulling the present behind and building futures in relation to particular pasts (c.f. Tsing 2003). Postcolonial theorists have shown how economic development has come to stand in for all kind of development—social, cultural and political (Loomba, Kaul, Bunzl, Burton and Esty 2007). According to Ien Ang, the nature of global capitalist modernity is such that at the international level the option for the non-white, non Western 'other' is either to 'Westernize' or be ostracized from the 'world community' or 'family of nations' (2001, 402). 'Development' has been positioned as the way to reach this state of Westernization, with assumptions of a linear progression into modernity that has been synonymous with what Ang terms as the white/Western hegemony.

Development is also a term used in relation to the sparsely populated rural regions of Sweden. Gunnel Forsberg, a geographer in Sweden, criticizes the terminology of 'rural development,'

> "Is it really underdevelopment that is the problem in the countryside?" she asks, "And if it is so, underdeveloped in relation to what? In the term is an assumed criticism of the countryside from the point of view of the city and the urban as the norm. The countryside is compared to this and is considered different" (1996, 36).

As I cite Bauman earlier, to be modern is to be urban. Katz writes,

> "all over the world 'development' driven by global economic restructuring produces similar contradictions between resources available and possibilities engendered, leaving people scrambling to make themselves viable in the face of the relentless, uneven development that is the hallmark of capitalism (see Smith 1984 in Katz 2004, 240).

While keeping in mind processes of economic restructuring that marginalize certain areas, it is the ideological currents that drive and are intertwined with economic processes that are the focus of my analyses of environmental politics and local development. On the one hand, development causes dislocations and can exacerbate inequalities. On the other, social groups who challenge dominant definitions of development are able to derive legitimacy from a discourse of development itself. Women in Nayagarh and Drevdagen who spoke of development often gave new meanings to dominant discourses about development and environmental governance. For Light Carruyo,

> "Development as a field of research and practice provides a language to talk about the relationships between nations and economies, but continues to struggle with understanding the complicated relationships between people. Understanding these relationships, as well as people's hopes, dreams, visions and the meanings that they give to the process of improving their quality of living, is at the centre of understanding development" (2003, 200).

Development, as Amita Baviskar writes, "is also ostensibly about increasing human welfare, empowerment and the exercise of democratic freedoms, and about establishing sustainable and just ways of using the physical and biological environment. This idealization, coupled with the experience of exploitation creates the possibility of a politics of resistance that combines conflict with collaboration, criticizing" projects of development and change "while engaging in dialogue and negotiating" (2001, 354–355) with state agencies and others driving that change. The "marvelous ambiguity of the word development," leads Cooper and Packard to note,

> "What at one level appears like a discourse of control is at another a discourse of entitlement, a way of capturing the imagination of a cross-national public around demands for decency and equity" (1997, 4).

In Nayagarh and Drevdagen, 'doing development' was clearly linked to ideas about gender and often regulated through similar institutional means. Postcolonial feminists show how notions of gender are interweaved with those of development. Convictions about women as vulnerable victims that would be saved by development (Mohanty 2003) were eagerly adopted by development agencies in their early work. This attention overlapped in the 1990s with a valorization of women and their agency. Women were sought to be enrolled in projects of development, this time as saviors of their environments. In India, the fate of women became linked to mainstream development agendas and not only due to feminist efforts. "Suddenly women are everywhere. Development experts cite 'gender bias as the cause of poverty in the Third World'; population planners declare their commitment to the empowerment of Indian women; economists speak of the feminization of the Indian labor force" (Tharu and Niranjana 2001, 494).

Debates on gender mesh directly with and actively reconstituted conceptions of national identity and notions of development (c.f. John 1999) not only in India but also in Sweden. 'Women' have been an important factor in Sweden in debates about rural depopulation. In popular perception but also policy and some academic literature, women's flight from rural areas has been attributed to a lack of gender equality (e.g. Dahlström 1996) and the minimal choices available for modern, educated women in backward areas.[10] The assumption is that gender equality and empowerment logically follow development and modernity, and *vice versa*. In such invocations of gender and development, ". . . 'women' seems to stand in for the subject (agent, addressee, field of inquiry) of feminism itself" (Tharu and Niranjana 2001, 495). There is a sense, therefore, in which the new visibility is an index of women's increased importance. But clearly, as Susie Tharu and Tejaswini Niranjana point out, this apparent success is also problematic. Power differences are made technical and gender bureaucratized while new dependencies arise as ideas about freedom, love and work in 'modern' ways take hold in everyday imaginaries. This becomes evident in the connections between development and gender that I unravel in Chapter 7.

. . . Of Being Modern

Men and women in both places drew upon various meanings of development, modernity or 'tradition' to define themselves as communities capable of managing their environments. Ideas about modernity were related to environmental and development activities (e.g. the modern woman, a new democratic environmental management, progress) in conscious awareness of connections with distant peoples. Being developed is about being modern though what that might mean is not the same everywhere or at all times. This assertion is not just a way to "qualify a universal or a metanarrative by scrupulous attention to local conditions" (Loomba, Kaul, Bunzl, Burton and Esty 2007, 19) and not only to understand the "multiplicity of simultaneous modernisms" (Predd and Watts 1992, xiv). Rather it is to understand the ideal of modernity as a "node of connection." For this I draw on the work of Stacy Leigh Pigg who explores people's beliefs about healing and modern medicine in Nepal. Pigg maintains that modernity,

> "becomes cosmopolitan not because "western" ideas spread through the world, homogenizing it, but because heterogeneous meanings and social concerns can be organized through it. . . . the idea of modernity has become a modality for engagement within and between social locations" (1996, 192).

This was clear in relationships of gender, development and environmental governance in both Drevdagen and Nayagarh. Aspirations for development were linked to images of democracy and ideas about gender to modern, independent and empowered women, able to take part in new ways in managing forests. Modernity was a lens through which people viewed others but also a mindfulness of how others might view them, as developed or as needing to develop. It is imperative to speak of these communities in relation to each other as interwoven in debates that characterize the present. At the same time, the nation remained an enduring ideal in debates about development in both places. Modernity although shifting and challenged, was regarded as a positive quality. How then to justify all that was not modern and progressive? What role does *tradition* play in this matrix? Pigg argues that "the dichotomy of tradition and modernity makes sense only within the narrative of modernization" (ibid. 163). It is not only the forms and practice of these engagements that need to be understood but also the connections that they draw upon in the course of struggle. I examine the dynamics of environmental and development action in the two places and the categories and connections that they drew upon through three tools of analysis throughout the book: by viewing the community as translocal, by using gender as an analytical category and lastly by tracking discourses and analyzing the formation of subjectivities among the women active in these two places.

Tools of Analysis

Translocality

In the course of studying the two different contexts in relation to each other, it became apparent that a locality or place in itself is translocal or transnational space. This premise makes it possible to comprehend how power is mobilized and status quo sought to be maintained or challenged in specific contexts by reference to development, gender equality and environmental governance in far-away places. The villages of Drevdagen and Nayagarh were "constituted in and through relations to wider systems, not simply impinged upon by them" (Pigg 1996, 165), for example in ideas about empowered or independent women, the right way to govern resources such as the forests or to organize for community development. The challenge is to unravel the connections between "processes of localization and processes of interconnection and acknowledging the impossibility of delimiting 'a' culture in the face of overwhelming evidence of the cross-currents in which these views are positioned" (ibid.). In Nayagarh, development practitioners, foreign donors and discourses on modernization, local democracy and on empowering poor rural women generated "a sense of difference while at the same time holding out the promise of inclusion in a global cosmopolitan culture" (ibid.). But in a rural community in Sweden as well, tropes of being modern, developed or traditional played as much a role in structuring everyday life in environmental governance and rural development. This needs careful attention to discourses mobilized and the formation of subjectivities.

Keeping in mind the translocality of specific places, it is possible to analyze how *development* connects distant places just as much as it divides. There is an obvious linear economic divide between Sweden and India at the national level, one an industrialized country considered to be developed, the other still developing. An awareness of this economic divide was tangible in both places just as discourses on development provided a language for the people to mobilize towards their different ends. Uneven development between nations but also between urban and peripheral areas within nations when analyzed in relation to each other prompts rethinking difference through connections.

Gender as an Analytical Category

To use gender as an analytical category is to study the organization of power relations between and among men and women. In its most common usage, gender refers to social differences ascribed to the male or female body, the knowledge that establishes meanings about sexual difference (c.f. Scott 1988). Gender differences can also be found among groups of men or among women linked to ideas about sexuality (Connell 2003). Using Teresa de Lauretis' allegory of 'technologies of gender,'

> "we might then say, (like sexuality) gender is not a property of bodies or something originally existent in human beings, but the set of effects produced in bodies, behaviors, and social relations, in Michel Foucault's words, by the deployment of a complex political technology" (1989b, 3).

As I write in chapter one, the allocation of distinctive attributes on the basis of sex/sexuality is a doing of gender. Gender differences between the sexes may thus be understood not as the natural order of things, but historically, culturally and socially created. Sexual difference plays an important role in organizing social relationships and differences in power. Gender and sex are forms of knowledge that are articulated by language, and their meanings have changed over time and across cultures (Scott 1999, 71). It is the articulation of sexual difference that becomes interesting to study and how relationships of power may be consolidated by appeals to sexual difference (ibid., 78) and how that might interact with other categories of social difference.

Feminist philosophers have emphasized how knowledge production is a political activity. Binary categories governing western reason (such as mind over body, culture over nature, self over other, reason over passion) are correlated to the binary of male and female and marked by a hierarchy that privileges the masculine. These apparently neutral divisions are implicitly sexualized and maintain unequal power relations between the sexes (see Grosz 1993, 195). What are considered to be male characteristics such as reason and mind are privileged over those associated with the feminine such as the body or passion that are viewed as negative especially in the public sphere.

And yet the body is important. Unequal power relations are as much about the physical body as the privileging of masculine characteristics. Moira Gatens puts it lucidly, "there is no neutral body, . . . the subject always is a sexed subject." There are at least two kinds of bodies; the male body and the female body (1991, 145). For example, the very same behaviors (whether considered masculine or feminine) had different personal and social significance in the villages when acted out by the men on the one hand and the women on the other. As Gatens writes further, if one accepts the notion of the sexually specific subject, that is male or female subject, then one must dismiss, or at least as I see it, seriously qualify the notion that patriarchy only can be characterized as a system of social organization that valorizes the masculine gender over the feminine gender (ibid.). This reasoning also applies to other differences like color and age that are vested in the body.

Elizabeth Grosz points out that even for those who acknowledge the corporeality of knowledge production and view the body as inscribed by social norms (from Nietzsche to Foucault) or those who emphasize the lived body (such as Merleau Ponty), ironically tend towards not a tangible or concrete corporeality but one that is "philosophical" in their reduction of the 'body' to a single masculine model. She argues instead that,

> "The inscribed surface is not neutral and may require different typographical procedures and result in very different kinds of meanings, depending on the kind of (sexed) materiality to be inscribed" (1993, 202–203).

In studying development and environmental governance it becomes evident how gender in relation to categories such as age, caste and family lineage was central in the making of meanings in the two case study sites. All knowledge claims are local (see next section) but some are more powerful than others, appearing to be universal or commonsensical, in 'how things are or who needs to do what.' This was clear in villages in Naygarh and in Drevdagen. Working with development activities in the villages in Nayagarh and Drevdagen was at the same time, a doing of gender. In both places what may be considered as instances of equal relations between individual men and women existed within larger orders of inequality between the sexes, and especially within forest management, where being male was privileged and women were disadvantaged. Yet, it is difficult to speak of an overarching or universal patriarchy that subjugates women to men. Gender relations are established in both multiple and complex ways and take different forms in different institutional contexts. "Different societies differ . . . on the specific social interpretation that they give to biological difference . . . Some societies allow large areas of overlap in the lives of men and women while others are organized in ways which maintain a rigid segregation" (Kabeer 1999, 5). In some respects Drevdagen and Nayagarh fall into these two different categories in the interpretation they give to biological difference: one where overlap is regarded as desirable and the other where the ideal is a segregation between what women do and what men do. In neither case can one way of being be considered more gender equal than the other without taking account of the contexts. Ideal images of social practices need not correspond to how life is lived in the everyday. Conflicting practices thrive at the same time and in the same place. Gender relations are dynamic and continually in motion.

There was, nevertheless, a regularity in gender relationships as they recurred in recognizable forms within both places. Norms were challenged by both women and men but a great deal of effort was also spent in trying to reproduce them by both women and men, accounting for what some feminist research has called the 'sluggishness' of gender relations (Eduards 2002). One difference between men and women as groups is, as Naila Kabeer writes, that men have a collective interest as men in organizations of social life which give them a privileged status; they do not only have a strategic gender interest in resisting attempts at transformation, but also have the greatest capacity to resist such transformation (1999, 28).

Now that greater knowledge has made it increasingly difficult to sustain the idea that there is something 'natural' about the organization of gender division of roles and responsibilities in any particular community, resistance to change has tended to take on the rationale of tradition or the 'sanctity of culture,' evident in the arguments used in relation to the events in the villages. This, according to Naila Kabeer, moves us away from disputes over 'facts' to disputes over 'values,' over not how things are but should be. But as she points out, culture is constantly changing (1999, 7) and in many ways this becomes apparent in both case studies as women and men in both places question dominant images of Indian or Swedish culture.

By studying gender relations in each particular context one is able to see how power and gender relations express themselves in particular ways in environmental governance and local development. Finally, it is worth noting that situated criticism does not preclude general claims to justice or appeals to general norms. But it requires that these, too, be regarded as situated, i.e. genealogized, framed by contextualizing narrative and rendered historically and culturally specific (Fraser 1995, 64), not only within local contexts but also in their national and transnational connections.

Discourse and Subjectivity

Definitions of discourse span a whole range of meanings. At its most basic level, discourse is definable as language in use. However, discourse is also more than language. Discourse may be seen as the set of social practices that make meaning and have material effects. In other words, one way of using discourse, as defined by Foucault is to understand it less as the actual utterances/texts that are produced but as the rules and structures which produce particular utterances and texts (see Mills 1997, 7). "This necessarily draws attention to the power *of* discourse to delimit topics of analysis and to the power to *make* discourse" (Bacchi 1999, 41), in the cases in the book for example, in the power to delineate what local environmental governance and development includes or excludes. The power of discourse, may be seen in discursive practices that provide subject positions, as subjects are produced through power-knowledge relations (Foucault 1990). By analyzing these utterances and texts, proponents of discourse analysis have sought to shed light on the rules and practices that are taken for granted, *i.e.* to make visible processes by which meanings are established and taken as obvious. It is important to move from more obvious interpretations to look at subtler and more insidious discriminatory and discursive practices (Mills 2002, 208) in order to be able to interrupt them.

Discourses are, however, not fixed but are the site of constant contestation of meaning (Mills 1997, 16). Subjects are able to engage in novel actions and to modify social conditions, in other words they have the power to make discourse, and they possess self-awareness. Following Julian Henriques, Wendy Hollway, Cathy Unwin, Venn Couze and Valerie Walkerdine, I employ the concept of subjectivity to refer to individuality and self-awareness—the condition of *being a subject*—but understand in this usage that subjects are dynamic and multiple, always positioned in relation to particular discourses and practices and produced by these—the condition of *being subject* (1998, 3, *my emphasis*). The analysis of the women's organizing in the two places illustrates with great clarity how they as subjects were both culturally constructed (c.f. Foucault/Butler) *and* capable of critique (c.f. Habermas/ Benhabib).[11] The attention in the book is on the formation of women's subjectivities as they related to each other and to others in the village and beyond and 'situated their selves' while at the same time creating an intersubjective and shared context. In the words of Seyla Benhabib, it is the relations we form and the associations we inhabit that define the kind of individuals we will become (1992, 71). This intersubjectivity, though fraught, contributed to building up the women's collectivity as well to our changing subjectivities over time.

Ideas about development and environmental governance and the villagers' relationships with each other as well as with outsiders encouraged new subject positions. These, in turn, related directly to the ways in which environmental governance was conceived and local development took shape. Several different currents existed concurrently, some more so than others in the two different contexts. A 'new' environmental consciousness with local people as carers was central while women as guardians of community cohesion formed part of local subjectivities. Ideas about freedom were interwoven with the myth of individual autonomy and modern women. Elizabeth Povinelli shows in her essay on language, how the legacy of worshipping freedom-as-individual-autonomy is further intensified by neoliberalism (2007). Strains of this can be seen in the two case studies, for example in expectations on people to organize according to certain principles, in structures reminiscent of the market and the contestations that this aroused in the villages. Ideas about neutrality, equality of all individuals and the small-scale female entrepreneur subsisted uneasily with discourses on community well-being, women's empowerment and arguments about collective marginalization by central authorities.

Men and women in Nayagarh and Drevdagen drew on diverse discourses and experienced subjectivities in complex forms as they mobilized in collectives. Processes that entail resistance and dominance, the search for alternative spaces and the significance of gender and sexuality need to be studied, "not as distractions from the "real problems"" (Loomba, Kaul, Bunzl, Burton and Esty 2007, 14) of environmental governance but as integral to our coming to terms with a new epoch in policy making and environmental prerogatives in local, national and transnational arenas. Environmental governance and local development were envisaged in both forest communities in their specific ways, but also within overlapping discursive contexts. Women's desire for freedom was linked closely to aspirations about development and gender equality. They drew upon fragments of discourses to define themselves in different periods as they formed individual and collective subjectivities (Chapter 5). Gender inequalities in environmental governance were concrete material practices that the women sought to challenge.

I use the material produced during the course of my research (information from notes, transcriptions from recordings, journal entries, etc.) both as descriptive of the particular contexts, in some sense as a 'realist tale,' and also as discourse. While a realist tale is an attempt to provide an account of 'what happened' I also analyze the descriptions as text to foreground what is the background in the realist descriptions. Employing theorizations of power, discourse analysis and an understanding of subjectivities as aids to understanding the ways in which meanings were produced in the two contexts, I adopt an approach that requires "learning to see the effects of power in contrast to seeing the expected realities" (Treleaven 1998, 71). Studying the connections between the two sites throws light on the contradictory workings of environmental processes in different parts of the world as well as on the structures of power organizing environmental governance transnationally.

I now turn to the methodological approach and practices that made this eclectic theorization possible bringing me to the third constraining discourse within this field.

THE NEED FOR NEUTRAL DISTANCE AND THE RIGHT QUESTION?

I entered the field of environmental governance that was already hyperrepresented—in theoretical orientation by studies on institutions and organizations for environmental management and in practice, by organizations represented almost only by men. The question was, how then to study institutions for environmental governance and development, without reinscribing existing power relations? The decision was to study them differently. I started research, not from these organizations, but from women's activities outside of them, a multi-site ethnographic approach where formal organizations represented just one perspective on environmental governance and development. Juxtaposing women's collective actions with forest organizations opened up a discursive field that went beyond calling for the inclusion of women into existing organizations, as victims of patriarchy or as silent heroes toiling in the environment. In the next section I explain this approach that involved taking a stand from the women's groups to analyze environmental governance and development. It undermined established assumptions about research neutrality that call for reflecting different views relatively and equally. Following this section, I discuss how the choice of negotiating the research question together with the women was a will to overcome 'epistemic injustice' (Fricker 2007) by acknowledging that environmental knowledge is produced in many settings outside of the academy despite academic power to determine the right questions to study and what environmental knowledge is. It meant extending the field not only to 'over there' but to here, the university where my colleagues and myself were part of defining what counted as knowledge on environmental governance.

A Different Vantage Point: Eschewing Neutrality and Distance

My initial contacts in the villages were with the men in the forest organizations. A conventional approach to research on local forest management initiatives involves starting with institutions and organizations that claim to work with environmental governance and development. That choice by itself sets the frame for the research. The contacts remain primarily with formal representatives, in most cases men with a privileged status in the villages, unless a special effort is made to speak to other people not within these bodies in an effort to gain everyone's opinion equally (in other words a neutral position). When studying environmental governance thus, from within public arenas for decision-making, as so many have done before me, you would see what you do not find, that is, the presence of women. My choice of undertaking research from the vantage point of the women in the villages, rather than the more obvious focus on the formal village institutions, initially prompted by women's absence from public forums, originated from wanting to go beyond obvious assumptions about the benefits women would derive from deliberative democracy to understanding what the women were doing and what might they want from such forums.

In studying environmental governance and local development from the women's actions and perspectives, I wanted to use "different criteria; perspectives and values than those dominant now. . . .and present not a more encompassing knowledge but rather a "less encompassing knowledge" (Grosz 1993, 208). Extensive feminist and social science scholarship over the years has made irrefutably clear that power relations are implicit in what is produced as knowledge, and that the making of science is a political activity (see Fonow and Cook 1991; Alcoff and Potter 1993; Denzin and Lincoln 2000).[12] This understanding stems from a constructionist paradigm that assumes a relativist ontology (that there are multiple realities), and a subjectivist epistemology (that the knower and respondent co-create understandings) (c.f. Denzin and Lincoln 2000, 21). But I also felt the need to go beyond a relativism or a "disavowal of politics insofar as all positions are rendered equivalent" (Grosz 1993, 194) and to understand the power relations that underpin and produce these realities.

A group of men speaking for their village or about environmental management as representatives are rarely questioned about the bias entailed by their claim to be speaking for their village (a bias both Nayagarh and Drevdagen showed). Even in participatory research, gender gets hidden in seemingly inclusive terms: 'the people,' 'the oppressed,' the 'campesinos' or simply 'the community.' All too often 'the community' is actually the male-community (Maguire, 1996, 29–30). Taking a stand or positioning oneself, as I did as part of the women's groups in the villages, is seen to undermine the need to reflect everyone's views equally. But, as the feminist philosopher, Donna Haraway writes,

> "We do not seek partiality for its own sake, but for the sake of the connections and unexpected openings situated knowledges make possible. The only way to find a larger vision is to be somewhere in particular. The science question in feminism is about objectivity as positioned rationality. Its images are not the products of escape and transcendence of limits . . . (*they are*) views from somewhere" (1991, 196).

In line with the reasoning on public and private spaces discussed earlier, the attention to the process of the women's organizing *vis-à- vis* initiatives of rural development and environmental governance highlighted what de Lauretis calls the 'space off' of the public in Nayagarh and Drevdagen. Borrowing terminology from cinema, de Lauretis explains 'space off' as the elsewhere of discourse here and now, the blind spots of its representations. She writes,

> "I think of it as the spaces in the margins of hegemonic discourses, social spaces carved in the interstices of institutions and in the chinks and cracks of the power-knowledge apparati. And it is there that the terms of a different construction of gender can be posed—terms that do have effect and take hold at the level of subjectivity and self-representation: in the micropolitical practices of daily life and daily resistances that afford both agency and sources of power . . ." (1989b, 25).

Though I did not know it then, these micropolitical practices would have been impossible for me to see without being a part of them, although this was not the motivation for my choice of methods. While my intention was to conceptualize the process and not the women, I had chosen to work with the women in order to do so. I was aware of the fact that by doing so I might be reinforcing the differences between them and the formal associations, differences that they may have negotiated in other ways. This was pertinent for Sweden where I undertook a collaborative inquiry over a period of two years with the women in the village. The intention with the inquiry and participatory research was to provide space for other views and insights to come forth. Not doing so would have meant accepting the existing order as 'natural' instead of understanding how it was constituted. In the following section, I elaborate on what prompted me to work in this way and why finding the right question together felt important.

Finding the Right Questions for 'Scientific Knowledge' on the Environment

> "In order to rapidly advance scientific understanding of environmental issues, it is necessary to promote properly focused research by

competent institutions," National Environment Policy (Government of India, 2006, 50).

"Universities and colleges and individual researchers have an important role in producing, managing and spreading knowledge to various actors, not least the local actors," White paper on environmental policy, Sweden. (Skrivelse 2001/02:173).[13]

Institutions and universities are regarded as producers of scientific knowledge that would lead to better environmental outcomes. However, a great deal of research in the past decades has emphasized how the production of knowledge is not restricted to conventional science. Nevertheless,

"people who do not have the right social markers (Epstein 1995, 411), which depending on the circumstances may include academic degrees, the 'right institutional home, majority ethnic or male gender, may be excluded from the category of credible knowers" (Fortmann 2008, 6–7).

In research people's interest are always mediated by academics in institutions that are themselves never value or culture free. The social sciences while claiming to do impartial research, construct the "conceptual practices of power" (Smith 1990 in Harding & Norberg) both for the worlds they study but also within the academy.

There have been debates within feminism acknowledging that although feminist theory is gaining recognition within academic circles, in order to do so, it has lost some of the activist roots that made it so vital (Lather, 1991, xviii). While conceding that gender theory has given us precise concepts to be able to analyze society more precisely, the 2005 governmental inquiry on gender equality in Sweden rued that what we have come to lack instead is its connection to the practical work for gender equality (SOU 2005, 66). Much like Marxist theory of which Campioni and Grosz write, although presented as dialectical partners, feminist theory and practice especially in the academy tend to be judged increasingly by theoretical criteria. "To speak of practice is only to be done in terms of what it means to . . . theory. It remains secondary, undirected" (1991, 383). Sandra Harding and Kathryn Norberg state,

"social research turns the chaotic and confusing experiences of everyday life into categories of people in society, categories that reflect prevailing political arrangements. The social sciences then assign causal relations to people and social relations in these categories. These causal accounts enable institutions to govern our everyday lives in ways that fulfill the interests and desires of these institutions and often not of the most vulnerable groups in our society" (2005, 2009).

It felt important for me that the women who chose to work with me felt that the research was relevant to them, that it created 'practical knowing, a knowing gained through practice, knowing *how to* do something and for something' (Reason 1994, 42). Participatory research, I hoped would give rise to categories from the social context during our process. Attention to the women's choice of subjects in Nayagarh, and more so the collaborative inquiry in Drevdagen, opened up the space for negotiating the research question for the inquiry that was of relevance to both, the women and myself rather than them answering questions that I deemed important.

I was inspired by Paolo Freire's *praxis*, which he describes as the connection between action and reflection. However, it was not an 'emancipatory project'[14] (1970) that I had in mind. I wanted to keep the framework of the inquiry open to the possibility of embracing its own concepts, to be of practical use, and to be accountable to the research subjects. According to Audrey Kobayashi,

> "A *critical* perspective transcends methodology to view qualitative methods as a basis for challenging dominant ways of understanding, and for exploring the contradictions that give rise to social inequities and patterns of marginalization. It demands an ethical positionality" (2001, 56).

Beyond a critical scholarship, my bias was towards an activist scholarship that engaged me in working towards change, not necessarily for the world at large, but for positive change for the women involved and for producing knowledge that the women would desire. This meant that emphasis in the research was not only on understanding or expanding theory (thinking on the subject of the environment and development), but also on linking the theorizing closely to practice. Referring to a dictionary of Marxist thought Patti Lather writes of praxis as 'philosophy becoming practical' (1991, 12). The inquiry was not designed explicitly to change unequal gender relationships. But by seeking to work as women to change their situations for the better, it did in fact become a *feminist praxis* (Stanley 1990). It was not a language of 'change' that the women themselves used but that of wanting to build on neglected or under-valued aspects of village life. My agenda at that point was to support their efforts by following and analyzing the process. As far as I was concerned, undertaking research as a collaborative inquiry was not merely a methodological question. It was an approach or a *förhållningssätt*,[15] an active way of being.[16]

The participative inquiry process created space for reflection as we made sense of our individual and joint experiences within the group and outside of it. In Nayagarh my research pushed me to pay close attention to the stories that the women chose to tell and to how they wanted to relate them. This way of knowing is a confirmation of everyday experiences as a legitimate source of knowledge, and of the importance of a concern with the local and the specific, while maintaining an awareness of wider relations and how similar issues are experienced in such different places. I wanted to be open to different dimensions of knowing—in action, cognitively and from feelings and emotions. I use the term experience elaborated by de Lauretis as,

> "... the general sense of a process by which, for all social beings, subjectivity is constructed. Through that process one places oneself or is placed in social reality and so perceives and comprehends as subjective (referring to, or even originating in oneself) those relations—material, economic and interpersonal—which are in fact social and, in a larger perspective, historical. For each person, therefore, subjectivity is an ongoing construction, not a fixed point of departure or arrival with which one interacts with the world. On the contrary it is the effect of that interaction that I call experience" (1984, 159).

The frame for the inquiry in Drevdagen emerged in discursive activities from within it. The women took up their agenda in a process of dialogue and meeting at what Haraway calls the 'points of affinity' (1991). As the women (we) related to each other, met, told stories and discussed our lives an assumed inter-subjectively understood and shared context was being jointly created. This was facilitated by shared experiences and a familiarity with the surrounding environment of the village as well as our recurring meetings. In our separate ways the women and as I both related to 'local forest management' and 'village development.' We also had different agendas: as an 'academic researcher' and as 'resident researchers' or 'civil scientists' (Fortmann 2008) in Sweden or as the women's groups in India. And although in one sense I inhabited the same critical plane as the women in the research, I was very unlike them in most respects: age, ethnicity, education, background, urban residence, language were among some of the differences.[17] Different parts of these identities intersected and were important at different times. In Drevdagen, I was much younger than most of the other participants. Coming from India, I was from another culture, obviously different and knew little about living in the *glesbygd* until I began to work in the village. In Nayagarh there was also an evident class difference (with its associated markers including that of education) which was not as relevant in Drevdagen. Compared to my male colleagues from the university who were working in the village and who had been active in development aid as professionals and consultants for several years, I was younger, a Ph.D. student, and had worked as a volunteer with NGOs in Odisha. My relationship to these two places was different and that would also account for some difference in seeing different facets of the organizing in these places. It is in the writing that my difference *vis-à-vis* the women became most apparent, but I will elaborate on that later in the book.

The shifts in the frameworks of the inquiry made a comparison with Nayagarh in terms of strict categories difficult and also alerted me to the importance of methodology. The focus of the research shifted from the *issue* to the *process*, to the importance of understanding the 'social arrangements' around the issue of local environmental management and village development, that is, as I cite Dorothy Smith earlier, to think about how "social relations were constitutive of these issues" (1987). Some of the most significant moments of the inquiry in Drevdagen are difficult to conceptualize. The energy that arose amongst the participants was felt and experienced as important. But how might moments and energy be analyzed? As one of the participants who spoke to me about our process said to me after she read one of my papers,

> "I don't know really how to describe our process . . . there was an upswing . . . among us and in the village then . . . it felt that we could do things . . ."

This has important lessons for studies of the environment and rural development. Environment and development politics lie at the heart of rural claims to citizenship. Addressing environmental change and rural development equitably will always fall short of its aspirations unless people at different scales and levels and especially those without the 'right social markers' are part of defining and negotiating the knowledge that prompts that change. But, importantly, as Louise Fortmann writes, inclusiveness will not in itself resolve the dilemma of contentious definitions or alone manifest scientific practice and knowledge production in new ways. Rather, it helps us avoid engaging in epistemic injustice and erasing important kinds of knowledge (2008, 4). Moreover, studying how environmental management or local development is defined not only in the 'field' out there but also in rooms and corridors of universities or development organizations complicates the picture of knowledge production. We are forced to situate and examine our own assumptions more carefully in producing scientific research, examining what is allowed to be said and what is not—for not to speak or "to speak is never neutral" (Irigaray 2002).

CONCLUSION

In this chapter I outlined the theoretical, analytical and methodological underpinnings of the writing and theorizing of the research material. But as Kurt Lewin writes, there is nothing as practical as a good theory, and this I put to test in the following chapters. My theorizing stays close to the empirical examples and the discussions on deliberative democracy while illustrating the multiple ways in which men and women negotiated environment and development questions in the course of their everyday lives. The analytical discussion finds substance in how singular narratives to explain resource struggles offer us little to understand a world crosscut by discourses on development and modernity. The methodological approach allows me to situate myself in the text and offers a way to go beyond conventional approaches to understand environmental governance and development in new ways. By exposing the limits of the present, this is an attempt to sketch out the contours of the currently impracticable in order to create better locations for imagining futures, justly.

3 Policy Discourses and Material Places
Forests, Gender and the (Re)making of the Peripheries

Forests, both in India and in Sweden have assumed center stage in discussions about the environment. The threat of climate change and the need to respond to it has galvanized policy debates on sustainable forest governance. Discussions on sequestering carbon through afforestation and conservation, and forests for biofuels, have become an important part of climate considerations. Policy makers, climate negotiators and private interests have entered the already acrimonious debates among environmentalists, conservationists, foresters and local movements. The experts, private companies, policy makers or foresters spearheading various alternatives at national and international scales are often far removed from the geographical sites of action. The current emphasis on experts is in sharp contrast to past decades that have been marked by a discourse on political decentralization and people's participation, regarded by many as a paradigm shift in environmental governance. Grassroots struggles around the use and access to natural resources especially in the global South had occasioned much of the shift to participation. Are the two processes—firstly, of decentralization and increased local participation in environmental management and secondly, the shift of discussions and negotiations in relation to climate change to the global level reconcilable? Where do local people fit into this scheme of things? And what does gender have to do with it?

To unravel some of the forest entanglements that answer these questions, I turn to the gendered history of the processes and conceptual framings of policy discourses in India and Sweden over the years that have shaped contemporary forest governance.[1] The points of reference are two distinct geographical spaces, Nayagarh district in Odisha, India and the village of Drevdagen in the county of Dalarna in Sweden. These sites are located in what are considered by urban majorities in their countries to be marginal areas, in 'out of the way places' (c.f. Tsing 1993). Like many other such areas that appear as statistics and words in documents found on official desks, these are the material and tangible sites of natural resources, especially forests. It is here that environmental and developmental activities take place, in the spaces that are assumed without being named in national and international discussions on the environment. However, for the people living in these areas the physical context (the geographical space) of Nayagarh and Drevdagen plays a special role in local commentaries on their lives, resource governance and village development. They call themselves forest communities, even when the forests do not directly provide the material basis for their lives, particularly in Sweden. Ownership, access to and the use of the forests has been pivotal in generating resources, power and influence in the family, the community and *vis-à-vis* the state in both places. And although the relationships to the forests might vary greatly in the communities studied in the book, they have forests at the heart of their cultural and social identities as well as material practices. Power and gender relations are intimately bound up in economic, social and cultural constructions of the forests and in struggles for control.

I discuss policy discourses that span the two ends of history—in India from the taking over of forests as state property by the colonial state in the 19th century to the newly instituted *Forest Rights Act* of 2006 with individual and private property as the cornerstone; in Sweden, moving from the institution of private property and appropriation of forests as state property in the late 1800s to the present when public participation is being discussed cautiously in the context of wider currents of neo-liberalism, an economic and political philosophy that advocates minimum state intervention in markets and people's relationships to the economy. In both places current climate solutions play an important part in forest debates. The parallel reading of history across the two geographical sites brings to the fore the connectivity and differences that are central to understanding contemporary life and processes of uneven development in the national contexts but also internationally. They highlight the importance of environmental discourses and their consequences in the present 'global' age but also in forestry of the 1800s and how old issues take shape in new ways in different places.

Certain discourses, that is, shared representations about what the environmental problems are and how resources ought to be managed, held sway in each national context at a particular time. These discourses were shaped by narratives that *defined the environmental problem of the time* and on which I focus in this chapter: (1) deforestation, (2) the importance of the environment (especially the forests) in nation building (leading in turn to the need for a delineation of property rights and a symbolic masculinization of the forests, more apparent in Sweden), (3) the need for local democracy and equal participation for men and women in environmental management, more vociferous in India, (coinciding paradoxically with the increasing importance of experts and resource bureaucracies and market actors) and lastly, (4) the urgent need to deal with climate change as a dominating presence in environmental discourse. These discourses play an important part in structuring environmental governance, citizenship and gender relations in the geographical spaces they touch. They reveal a process of marginalization, due not to the distance of the areas of Nayagarh and Drevdagen from national centers, but a marginalization brought about in an interactive process between policy, local material practices and government intervention. Marginality, with the center-periphery distinction, is not conceptualized as being parallel to gender. Rather, the tensions in which marginalities occasioned by geography or living in the periphery are gendered and a source of both constraint and creativity (Tsing 1993, 18) are at the heart of the analysis.

There are striking similarities in the two places in the progression of events and their motivations, though at times separated by several years. The discourses are not coincidental or merely a product of chance, but are in fact historically contingent and contextual. They bring to light, shared histories and struggles as well as particular aspects that contribute to the connections between them. The analysis illustrates how gender is embroiled in the politics of science and knowledge production at multiple scales in processes that resonate across space and time as a result of wider webs of connections.

DEFORESTATION

Narratives of deforestation recur insistently in forestry discourses, regardless of North or South, though the periods vary as do interventions. Striking in both Indian and Swedish forest history, regardless of the physical situation, is the purposes to which this discourse was put to use by the state. Narratives on deforestation gained ascendancy in later years, but its precursors can be seen in arguments against shifting cultivation in the 1800s, both in India and Sweden. These narratives formed the basis for the takeover of forests as state property as deforestation at the hands of the local populations was sought to be halted by rational and scientific forest methods.

India: Scientific Forestry, Revenue Extraction and Deforestation

The taking over of the forests as state property in India began during British rule. On an all-India basis the systematic public management of forests began in 1864, with the appointment of the first Inspector General of Forests. Simultaneously, a decision was taken to convert the forests into state property. This appropriation of forest land was justified partly by the destructive habits of food gatherers and shifting cultivators living off the forests, by the fear that “the forests are disappearing before the axe of the charcoal burner” (Oldham, superintendant of the Geological Survey of India in 1852, cited in Chaudhari 1982, 305) and the consequent need for modern, scientific forestry. Drawing on official documentation, Ravi Rajan in his book, *Modernizing Nature*, shows that by the early 19th century, arguments for conservation were bolstered by a well-developed field of inquiry that linked deforestation and water flows to climate variations. Forest bureaucrats were instrumental in developing a commitment to a strong, autocratic control over forests and forest enterprise much like their French and German counterparts (2006, 64–68, 92). It was argued that only the state could appreciate the importance of the indirect and long-term benefits of the forests. The commercial and strategic value of the forests lay at the heart of the colonial state's decisions (Guha and Gadgil 1989) while at least in its early stages it was also prompted by an urge for conservation based on scientific principles and the need for social control (Grove 1995). In *Green Imperialism*, Richard Grove describes the work of a coterie of educated and independent state scientists and environmental commentators, drawn from the ranks of medical and botanical branches. These enthusiastic proselytizers of a conservationist message provided the ideological basis for the pioneering of a forest-conservancy system in India on a hitherto unequalled geographical scale. This environmentalism was influenced by French anti-capitalist physiocrat reformers, Romantic scientists and others who also turned to the unitary thinking of Hindu philosophers (1995). Much of the scientific knowledge at this time was born out of these meetings in the colonies (Arnold 2006). The onset of private interests in the realm of forest management was viewed with great alarm. The thrust was therefore to exclude private operators from the forests (Rajan 2006).[2] Scientific forestry meant the institutionalizing of certain sorts of territorial claims on the basis of timber quality. Forest lands were demarcated into different categories with certain tracts of land for exclusive use of the forest department.[3]

The taking over of forest land by the colonial state was concurrent with efforts to exact more and precise revenues. This led to delineating the rights of the big landholders and princely states over agricultural land in the second half of the 1800s (Kumar 1982). In large parts of what is now Odisha, revenue settlements created a land market and heightened class and caste differentiation (Pati 1993). The demarcation of the forests and legal enactments by the colonial government gave differing rights to differing categories of people for different purposes within the same patch of forests. The rights to forest produce of certain categories of people, like agriculturalists, were recognized as superior to that of others, such as artisans. Thus, along with a hierarchy of land, there was a hierarchy of users and a negative hierarchy of rights (Sundar 2001, 334). "While forest dwellers were being sorted into types by tribe and caste, the forests themselves were arranged in categories by dominant genera and species. Such description and the laying down of taxonomic structures to represent biotic communities presaged colonial development projects in which human and natural resources were harnessed for imperial purposes" (Sivaramakrishnan 1995, 6).

Delving into a range of official and other sources in Odisha, Biswamoy Pati shows how increasing monetization opened up a market in land as well as the ranks of the landed society in coastal Odisha. There was an effort to induce forest dwellers to take up settled agriculture and to exact revenue on forest produce such as *lac, hides, kendu* and *tendu* leaves. This peasantization of tribal communities, claims Pati, also led to a process of Hinduization as they were tied closer to landowning classes. New taxes and the monetization of customary dues led to several rebellions and revolts by tribal communities and others who now had to pay revenue for customary rights that they had exercised for centuries[4]. Those that came up against the colonial judicial structures were blamed of crimes against property and several communities became labeled as 'criminal tribes' (1993).

The conversion of forest land to state property continued after India's independence in 1947 when the formerly private land belonging to the princely states, the *zamindars* and the *taluqadars* (big landholders), came under state control. This was also the case for Nayagarh which was formed out of the erstwhile princely states of Nayagarh, Daspalla and Khandpalla in central Odisha. Villagers claimed that feudal and customary rights were eroded, and the pressure on the forests continued to increase. In legal terms, forest inhabitants became 'encroachers' in their own homes, a term from the colonial lexicon that continued to be used by later bureaucracies. Stories about confrontations with male forest guards abound in accounts of the people in Nayagarh, especially those of tribal and *Dalit* women who spend time looking for minor produce in the forests. In the decades following independence, environmental degradation, once again, became a central part of the discourse on forest management. Roger Jefferey and Nandini Sundar maintain that the narrative of deforestation was used by the state in post-independence India to extend its authority in rural areas. Foresters began to define 'the forest problem' as deforestation or more precisely as the loss of large timber trees that are commercially viable and therefore able to earn revenue. The explanations for deforestation were complex and encompassed discussion of commercial interests as well as destruction by local communities. These were used as a description of an objective physical situation to justify intervention. Alternative constructions of the 'forest problem' such as the problem of lack of access by local populations to forest resources, and their resultant poverty and marginalization or even alternative constructions of the forest as requiring a diversity of forest products have been submerged by this definition (1999, 20–21).

Gendered Division of Property and Labor

There is little research on the effects that state policies have had on the gendered division of property and labor except for peripheral references that provide some indications. Pati cites British reports from the colonial period that make references to changes in tribal lifestyles in Odisha. Greater monetization of local economies and the land market exacerbated social differentiation and gender inequalities. As tribal communities adopted Hindu customs and dowry transactions became more common, a man's wealth came to be associated with the number of wives he had. Daughters became expensive as communities were drawn into mainstream dowry practices and parents were subject to the vagaries of an uncertain market. There are mentions of female infanticide as well as witch hunting (1993, 33–34). According to Agarwal, in the patrilineal system prevalent in most of India, historically women appear to have had few individual claims to land. Yet in matrilineal societies women inherited property and also enjoyed social independence and relative equality in marital relations. However, she points out that despite men's restricted access to property ownership in matrilineal systems, their rights of control over that property on the one hand, and their access to public bodies on the other (with links between those domains) often enabled them to consolidate substantial social prestige and political power. In addition, men's control of public decision-making gave them critical influence over the modification of legal and social rules especially as conditions began to change in significant ways, especially under British colonial rule. In short, ownership rights in landed property clearly conferred important benefits on women but their virtual exclusion from property management (in some groups) and from jural and overall public authority (in all groups) circumscribed the power they could derive from those rights (1994, 1466–1467).

The gap between ownership rights and managerial control have an important role to play in women's independence *versus* dependence on male relatives both in India and in Sweden as I will show. Unfortunately the dearth of research in this field in Odisha gives no indication as to how legal prescriptions have impacted on or perhaps been subverted in everyday practice and gender relations. But importantly, as Agarwal also points out, contestations over rights extend beyond households to encompass the complex institutions of community and state, to the arenas where decisions are made and unmade and need careful attention.

Early Forestry in Sweden: Countering the Place of Timber

On his travels in Särna in Dalarna, Carl von Linné, known as the father of modern taxonomy and ecology wrote disapprovingly of the slash and burn practices of the inhabitants of this mountain area,

> "Forest fires that raged at several times had destroyed the great forest that lies between Åsarna and 9/4 m from Särna . . . Of the fallen trees one saw that the fire had raged at several times. As a result, there now lay one great tree on top of another, fallen down . . . half rotten, leaving only a few odd trees standing sparsely here and there. The earth was gone, little was green, instead just one stone on the other, as if the whole land was . . . mounds of stone. We had never before seen such badly managed forests especially considering that it was so large."

He rued that trees were left to rot when they could have employed usefully as timber and went on to write,

> "The great forest although so destroyed does the public no good with its wonderful timber for logs, masts and shipping timbers. . . . and were it possible to transport them on the river Dalelfven to the sea at not too great an expense there would be timber for a long time to come" (von Linné 1734, 257–281).[5]

The historian Sigvard Montelius writes that the importance given to timber by the state from the mid 1800s onwards overshadowed the important role that the forests and cattle rearing played in the economy of the mountain areas of Dalarna (1977). The forests were central to this lifestyle. The *fäbodvallarna* were the grazing land with small cottages carved out of forests where the villagers could stay with their animals for the summer months. A fully developed *fäbodväsende*, a pasture grazing system, existed in northern Sweden by the end of the middle ages and complemented the small farms in the villages (Montelius 1977b). The cultivated land around the villages provided relatively little for the people (c.f. Montelius 1977b, 1973; Holmbäck 1920). This is confirmed by Linné who writes that he failed to understand how one was expected to cultivate the soil when it was just stone on stone (von Linné 1734, 281). Cattle-rearing, especially in the mountain areas, was the main source of livelihood.

Access to land in the forest was related to the land that a particular *socken* (parish) had in the *bygd*.[6] Åke Holmbäck writes that every farmer owned land down in the village, the *slogar*,[7] and also had a share in the *fäbodar*. He bases his work on archival material, which included law books, official documents such as correspondence between the various authorities and with the *sockenmän* (parish men), royal proclamations and meeting protocols. Holmbäck presumably implies male farmer since he writes *sockenmän* but it is difficult to know exactly. Legal documents or references, did not always correspond to the use and management of the forests or the customary rights of the landless. One such case is highlighted by Kurt Alinder (1945) in his reading of documents from a boundary dispute in 1725 in Särna-Idre. Forest land, on the other hand was owned jointly by the *socken* (Holmbäck, 1934, 243). Since access in the forests was dependent upon the size and area of the village, village boundaries were often shifted in order to improve access to the forests (Montelius 1977b, 23). It was not uncommon that the *fäbodar* shaped the *socken* boundaries and not only *vice versa*. As long as the villages were small and the forest land extensive, the grazing grounds were sufficient for everyone. But when villages expanded the grazing cattle from neighboring villages came closer (Holmbäck 1934, 242). In many a case, at the heart of what may seem like puzzling and unreasonable conflicts about village boundaries, were actually disputes over a *fäbodställe*, a *slåtteräng* or a *myrslog* (marshy area used for making hay) in the forests (Montelius 1977b, 23).

The *fäbodar* were important in organizing relationships of gender in the villages. As compared to southern Sweden, cattle-rearing in the north, especially since the middle-ages, was women's work and shepherds were mainly women. The *fäbodväsendet*, a bulwark of the economy, was a women's world, dominated by unmarried young girls. Living in the *fäbodar* in the forests in summer, they formed a close-knit female working culture based on constant association with the cattle. Men did not usually permanently stay on the *fäbodar* (ibid. 81). For a man this work in the forests with animals could imply a loss of manhood (ibid., 19).[8]

Villagers in Drevdagen speak of the village as a *fäbod* that was settled permanently in 1814 by people from Särna-Heden, south of the village. The new settlers moved there with a small number of cows, sheep and goats. In a book, one of the inhabitants, Hans Halvarsson, writes,

> "These were the settlers' savings and the basis of their livelihoods. The surplus milk provided butter and cheese for winter needs and the wool/fleece was carded and spun into wool/yarn" (1999, 7).

The 'ignorance' of the use of timber that Linné wrote about in the 18th century began to change from the 1800s. An increase in mining (*bergbruket*) and the accompanying demand for timber and charcoal meant that the forests became a sought after commodity, especially from the point of view of the crown. Timber for export to the English ship-building industry also contributed to the pressure. With the increasing importance of timber, work in the forests became the livelihood of many men who began to sell timber to the state and later to sawmill companies. Many of the *fäbod* cottages began to be used by them during that period. Since then, the forests have been linked to the importance of timber and to male loggers. The *fäbodar* in this part of Dalarna however continued for longer than in the agricultural areas of Dalarna further to the south.

The Gendered Construction of Property Rights

Much like in India, increasing state intervention in the forest areas coincided with en effort to formalize property rights. This took place in tandem with a change in the forests from being a female sphere to the construction of the forests as a masculine domain. Up to this point, individual ownership of land was recognized but there were also complicated forms of joint ownership and ownership regulated by marriage and inheritance (Alinder 1945). The liberal ideas of the 1800s played a part in the increasing move towards delineating forest land as private property (Montelius 1977a, 41). The benefits of dividing collective forest property into individual ownership became almost an axiom in the second half of the 18th century and the first half of the 1800s (Pettersson 1995, 130). Individual landownership thus came be seen as an important new category in the management of the forests, a move however that appears to have consolidated property rights mainly for men.

Over time, the rights of the formal owner of the property acquired greater significance, even if the land continued to be used or managed as common property. Historian, Maria Sjöberg, writes that in combination with land reforms, state regulations began to prioritize the individual at the cost of (among others) village organizations. The collective characteristics of property rights were slowly toned down (2002, 115). The intricate distribution of property in small strips of land in many parts of Dalarna in the 1800s is believed by many to be the result of the fact that women as well as men inherited property. Sjöberg argues that this view is misleading. Much of what has been taken to be the rights pertaining to individuals were rights actually held by men, although marriage was decisive in regulating property relations. She argues that, seen from a gender perspective, individual ownership in Sweden cannot be seen as established before the law of 1920 when women were declared *myndig* 'legally adult' and acquired the legal right to both possess and manage property (2001). There are qualifications to this as well. The new law applied to women in legal marriages that took place after 1920. In practice, women did not have the economic right to manage land until a new law in 1950 (Niskanen 2001). Women before this time therefore, had limited and unequal scope to exercise power since it was not possession as such but management that conferred power and agency (Sjöberg 2001).[9] Individual property rights thus went hand and hand with an increasing masculinisation of property law and state intervention in forest use and ownership. Despite the change in laws, by 2007 only 38 percent women as opposed to 62 percent men classified as forest owners (Statistics Sweden 2007) and only 29 percent owned agricultural land (Pettersson and Arora-Jonsson 2009). Research has shown that much of the forest land is jointly owned forests and it is usually managed by the men in the family (Lidestav 2003).

Through defining private property, the state extended its power over the natural world. The privatization of land by the state was justified by the fact that it would reduce the logging of the forests. Once again, this argument was used to pave the way for the takeover of large parts of the common forest land by the state. Boundaries were drawn between what came to be considered crown land and individual landowners' forest land. Towards the end of the 1800s the claims to land began to be formalized by the crown through the process of *avittring*, delimitation of crown land, and the forests were divided up during the *storskifte*, the great distribution of landholdings. When drawing boundaries between individually owned forests and the crown land, the authorities decreed that all farmers would keep as much forest as was needed for their use, and the remaining land would be taken over as crown forest. It is interesting that the crown appropriated forest land on the grounds that they could then supply the populace with timber for building (Holmbäck 1934, VI; Alinder 1945, 120).

In 1865 four crown forests (*kronoparker*) were created in Särna by the crown and a fifth was added in 1878. Minutes of a meeting held in Särna with the villagers on September 9, 1864 reveal how the crown justified its actions. A.E. Ros, the head of the *Skogstyrelse*[10] spoke to the villagers of the appalling state of the forests because of excessive logging to fulfill the demands of the saw mills. He justified the setting up of the crown forests by saying that the forests needed to be secured for the future and from the adverse effects of deforestation on the climate, an argument reminiscent from the Indian context. Such protection, they explained to the villagers, would be undertaken by the authorities based on scientific methods and would serve as an example to other forest owners (Alinder 1945, 120). The authorities also claimed that the takeover of the forests by the crown would put a stop to the destruction of the forests and to social problems like drunkenness and gambling that had resulted from the large inflow of money from illegal logging (Björk cited in Ericsson 1997, 16). These forests eventually came under the control of the *Kungl. Domänverket*, the *Royal Swedish Forest Service.*

As a result of the great redistribution of land holdings and delimitation of crown lands, another category of land, the *besparingsskog*, or the commons, was created in Dalarna (Ericsson 1997; Carlsson 2001). After the farm and village lands were determined and the borders to crown lands were decided and fixed, the next step was to allocate a portion of the land allotted to the farmers as a forest commons or *besparingsskog* (Carlsson 2001, 4). This initially occasioned considerable protest from the villagers (Montelius 1977a, 42). According to Kardell, the formation of the *besparingsskog* may be seen as an effort to declare incompetent private forest owners' management. The 'owners' of the commons were not granted the authority to sell or manage the forest commons on their own, and it was not until a law in 1938 that it was made clear that the *besparingsskog* were the private property of the owners (cited in Ericsson 1997, 7). Although they are very different contexts and times, there are striking echoes of such contestations over community rights taking place in India today as the ownership of private land and community rights are under the anvil with the passing of a new forest act.

The demand for wood for household needs, mining and making charcoal (*järnhantering*) was accelerated by the demand for timber from sawmills and forest companies, major actors that gained ascendancy in the latter half of the 1800s. As male farmers gained ownership rights that could be bought and sold, companies proceeded to buy out forest land from the men and began to log the forests in order to supply the sawmills with raw material. The state's tussle with private companies has clear parallels to the colonial state's antipathy to private interests in India in the 1800s. During the late 1800s and the first few decades of the 1900s, the sale of land by villagers to forest companies resulted in a political debate that came to be called the *Norrland Question.* The sale of the forests to the companies was criticized strongly by the state. The 1900s saw the enforcement of several laws, the so-called *Norrland Laws* (1906–1925), that prohibited companies from buying forests from small forest holders. The crux of the debate was between the efficiency of small-scale management by individual owners or communities *vis-à-vis* the benefits of large-scale management (Sörlin 1988), a debate that in a different way is pertinent to the case of Drevdagen today.

Historians have expressed surprise that the appropriation of the forests as *kronoparker* in Särna-Idre did not bring forth protest from the local inhabitants (Björck cited in Eriksson 1997, 17). Protests evidently occurred elsewhere in Dalarna, as described by Holmbäck for the area of Lima, Transtrand and Orsa (1934). One explanation may be that the forest land available in Särna-Idre was still vast, and largely inaccessible to the authorities, as compared to the other areas where pressure on land was increasing. Also, a change in formal ownership did not as yet change access and activities in the forest and social relations continued as they had been. Interviews with older men and women in Drevdagen revealed that they continued to use the forests and the *fäbod* economy continued in the early decades of the 1900s. However, as claims and obligations turned into rights and with changes in context and in forest relations, different attitudes took root. This can be seen in a landmark ruling in the area of Drevdagen discussed in the following chapter. There are men in and around Drevdagen today who have title deeds to pieces of forest land that were taken over by the state in the latter part of the 1800s, for which they claim that they were never compensated. Some relate stories of how their ancestors were cheated out of the land, as it fell under the management of the *Royal Swedish Forest Service* in the late 1800s. At least one person from a neighboring village has taken up this cause and is in the midst of a protracted legal battle with the state.

In hindsight, the production of this new territorial power of the state in both countries laid the grounds for the developments that followed—the making of the nation state in independent India and the welfare state in Sweden. Both nature and state were redefined as forests were framed through acts of centralization and territorialization.

FOREST COMMUNITIES AND THE MAKING OF THE NATION

Nation making in India, post 1947 as well as in Sweden in the post WWII years followed somewhat similar but also divergent trajectories. Common to both however was the important role of policy making in relation to its natural resources such as the forests. As suppliers of resources and raw materials, both the geographical spaces and peoples of Nayagarh and the areas around Drevdagen were drawn into the project of nation-building. The process was fraught, contested but often internalized. While the people in these areas were now citizens with rights in a new nation and welfare state, their marginality or peripheral status *vis-à-vis* the center was redefined.

National Interests and the Environment in India

'National interests' overrode other considerations. Nowhere is this shift better couched than in the Indian Forest Policy of 1952 that states, "The accident of a village being situated close to a forest does not prejudice the right of a country as a whole to receive benefits of a national asset" (Government Of India 1952, 29). Although the recognition of people's rights on forests as state property existed in post Independence policy in India, this changed over time. The displacement of communities from the forests for various developmental projects continued in independent India. The colonial state had laid the ground by appropriating forest property. The new state continued with a fairly autocratic forest management.

'Industrialize or perish,' the admonition of the influential engineer and statesman of the time, Sir M. Visveswaraya, became the motto of the times. Massive state investments in industrial infrastructure—power, minerals, metals, communications and forest based industry were provided to industry at highly subsidized rates and with virtually free access to crucial raw materials such as forests and water. Conventional management practices were however unable to keep step with escalating commercial demand. A new strategy of intensive forestry was called for—plantation forestry with monocultures such as eucalyptus, teak and rosewood followed by other varieties as new ways of processing wood became possible. Industry lobbied intensively for captive plantations for their purposes, though they did not always succeed (Gadgil and Guha 2004, 185–186, 192).

The continuing advance of commercial forestry fuelled conflicts not only between the state and commercial interests on the one hand and the rural poor on the other but also between settled cultivators and pastoralists as they clashed over diminishing resources. The most ready option for many was wage employment in commercial forestry operations through a so-called contractor system with low wages and no gains from commercial forestry (ibid. 229, 232). The inroads of conservation thinking and the making of national parks and sanctuaries further displaced thousands of people, confounding the simmering discontent between forest dwellers and forest authorities. The consequences were a scramble for resources and intense conflict that spread as people driven out from the countryside migrated to the cities.

The all male and mainly upper caste bureaucrat-politician nexus constructed an elaborate web of rules and regulations in order to maintain control over resource extraction and utilization.[11] Foresters saw a clear line between 'professionals' and non-professional users of forests in line with ideas of scientific forestry (Guha and Gadgil 2004).[12] Vandana Shiva argues that the masculine, violent and reductionist view that dominated scientific forest management sought to replace the worldviews of forests as living environments, of the feminine principle of *praktriti* or nature that encompassed the thinking of forest dwellers (1989). The Forest service in turn was constructed around dominant 19th-century representations of masculinity emphasizing independence, adventure and rationality (Hannam 2000b). Although researchers point to that not just extraction but conservation thinking prompted the work of many colonial foresters (e.g. Grove 1995), towards the turn of the 20th century, reductionism, in that the forests were reduced to their importance as producers of commodities such as timber from a reduced number of species and maximum extraction, appears to have become the overriding concern of the Indian Forest Service (Sivaramakrishnan 1995).

Nevertheless, as Jefferey and Sundar point out, it was impossible for the state to turn a blind eye to the rights of the villagers,

> ". . . the state and other actors have historically been forced to recognize the moral legitimacy of the claims of local people to have access to forests, often in response to movements of resistance. Even Forest Department Working Plans, geared towards maximization of revenue under the guise of 'scientific management' contained a symbolic nod towards accommodating local rights, in the form of a section on agricultural customs and wants" (1999, 18)

Several communist led tribal mobilizations in the first quarter of the 20th century contextualized the demands for land and forest rights.[13] These pressures forced welfare measures to be undertaken. Independent India attempted to set up mechanisms in the constitution that would democratize community institutions and allow local communities and tribal people to shape their own destinies. Nevertheless, the development paradigm that guided natural resource policy continued to govern management practices.

The Advent of Commercial Forestry in Sweden

Forest policy in Sweden in the years after World War II aimed to increase production of timber. This was the time of intense industrialization in Sweden as the rest of Europe lay ravaged by the war. Employment in the cities provided an option for many. To some extent, this created the space to negotiate the terms of work in the forests. The forest industry's need for raw material, and the trade unions' will to secure members' employment, created a common stake and became an important factor within forest politics (SUS 2001, 30). Working conditions in the forests and the home began to improve largely as a result of the work of the trade unions in the area. The *syndicalists*, a left-oriented trade union movement, had many supporters in this area. Villagers in Drevdagen referred to a famous court case between the 'blackfoot' strike-breakers from Mora who came to work for a forest company while men from Drevdagen and the surrounding areas were on strike. In his book, Halvarsson describes how the changes in the forests changed the lives of the young boys in the village. They found work in the lumberjack teams (*huggarlaget*) as soon as they were old enough and during the summers there was lucrative employment for them as *rallare* and *timmermän* (manual laborers working on civil engineering projects) or in floating timber down the rivers (1999).

In her account of forest workers in the 1900s, Ella Johansson vividly describes the images of masculinity that were created of the individualistic, hardworking lumberjacks and drivers (*körare*). This was coupled with notions of freedom that work in the forests provided. It is in this period that the forests as the domain of certain men, capable of taking care of the forests and associated with timber extraction, became the overriding image. What began to be seen as formal ownership in the forests was first and foremost ownership of the 'timber' in the forests. Work in the forest was associated with timber extraction and almost exclusively with men (2000, 57). Ideas of 'real forest work' were internalized by people in the rural areas as well (Kaldal 2000; Hansen 2000). Forest activities not associated with timber carried out by both women and men, did not necessarily find place in the formal definition of forest use. Furthermore, gendered construction of property rights during the first half of the 20th century played an important part in creating perceptions of family farming as a mainly male form of enterprise (Niskanen 2001) and by extension of forest ownership and work in the forests. This had important consequences for the position of future generations in terms of land ownership and management, in forestry and according to Iréne Flygare, also in farming (2001).

Commercial forestry helped to sustain small scale farming in this area by providing villagers with a stable basis for other activities. Technical developments and rationalization within forest management in the 1950s fractured this stability. This period witnessed the beginning of greater state regulation in prices and large-scale rationalization in agricultural politics whose effects were to be felt in this area through the coming years. Seasonal work in the forests was gradually replaced by fixed annual labor contracts. Timber floating was replaced by a network of roads that began to be used for transporting timber. Although images of foresters changed in form from the rough and ready lumberjack to the white-collar forester at his computer (Brandth and Haugen 2000) masculine images continued to maintain their dominance.

The Making of the *Glesbygd*: The City as the Measure

Gradually, industrialization absorbed much of the forest labor force. In my interviews with the villagers of Drevdagen, a narrative emerged of a clear cause and effect between state policy and the ensuing migration from the village, especially with the older generation. In the words of Halvarsson,

> "The 1960s had barely begun when a very tangible worry began to infect the village population. When we eventually could decipher the authorities' and the media's message, we unwillingly worked out that we lived in the wrong place in our country . . . Out in the field, closest to us this propaganda was spread by the labor market authorities, who also had the requisite means to pressure people. Their "information" got absorbed to such a degree that the villager who chose to stay on risked being marked as backward, if he insisted on staying on in this out of the way spot and not catch hold of a sure chance in the big town!" (1999, 10)

People were encouraged by state authorities to move to towns and were given moving grants, *flyttbidrag*, to set up homes in urban centers. As the wave of industrialization subsided, "there were no matching moving home grants," said Gerd, an elderly woman, who had returned to the village with her husband when work in the cities had dried up.

The depopulation of many peripheral areas became a policy concern in the 1960s, especially as it coincided with the making of the welfare state. In policy and in research, migration flows between various parts of the country gained attention in the Swedish discussion of regional balance. The emigration of young women as compared to men from the countryside became a part of the discussion in the 1980s and a cause of alarm—especially in the media and political debates. Political measures that sought to solve the *glesbygdsproblem* became part of the building of the welfare state with its ideals of solidarity and equality. Translated literally, the *glesbygd* means sparsely populated areas. The term is associated with the inland areas in the north, north-west and south-east Sweden. It refers to large contiguous areas with sparse populations, long distances to towns, employment and services. For the mainstream in urban areas it also came to be associated with the not so modern and backward periphery of the nation.

BECOMING CITIZENS IN MARGINAL PLACES

The making of the nation in India meant that the concerns of forest dwellers and communities carrying out small-scale cultivation found their way into policy documents and the constitution of the new nation. The fifth and the sixth schedule of the constitution provided for special mechanisms for *Dalit* and tribal communities that would democratize state institutions. Many were hopeful that the victory of the Congress party would inaugurate a new era. Several small farmers consolidated their gains after the confiscation of land from the princely estates and landlords in Nayagarh. Women and men in Naygarh could vote, were subject to the cajoling of local politicians during election time, and though diffuse at times, they knew that they had rights in the new nation. People were drawn into a maze of schemes and subsidies of which they could avail. Over the years, they have been the recipients of schemes promulgated both by the central and state governments. In the 1990s when I carried out most of my fieldwork, the DWACRA (Development of Women and Children in Rural Areas) was the ubiquitous scheme. More recently, the NREGA (National Rural Employment Guarantee) offers potential wages for 'works' in development projects for infrastructure and the like. However, the gulf between policies and their operationalization and the results of schemes and projects vary immensely.

A similar but much more intricate system of subsidies or *bidrag* characterized the area of Drevdagen in the years following the 1960s. The 1960s were characterized by a strong desire on the part of the Swedish state to provide equal welfare in all parts of the country. Individuals were tied directly to the various organs of national authorities through welfare policies such as social security, health insurance and housing policy. The sparsely populated regions, especially the northern counties, became identified as *stödregioner* (regions that needed support) through targeted regional policy. In the words of Bengt Johanisson, Lars Olof Persson and Ulf Wiberg, once the compensation concept had been launched, the *glesbygdsproblem* as we know it today began to get cemented (1989). Kjell Hansen (2000) provides an interesting example of the state's housing policy. While providing resources, the housing policy played a disciplining role in establishing a discourse on the right sort of standardized housing, whether it suited the terrain or not. The price one had to pay for access to such resources was marginalization. The right to describe what the rural problem was, and what measures were needed, was taken care of by the representatives of the state. The housing policy thus contributed to a new, centrally identified discourse on the rural areas. Cities were the touchstone of state measures. Images of the *glesbygd* in media and policy discourse were and continue to be laden with an understanding of areas marked by deficits in contrast to the cities.

Scholars point out that the solutions to the problems identified by the state did not make a significant difference or lead to improvement in the rural areas. During the time these efforts were undertaken, the pressure to align natural resource management and public services to the market was increased. The major part of the productive and future-oriented investments in the *glesbygd*, were concentrated de facto on the central towns. The negative effects of earlier projects, of clearing forest land and forest exploitation affected the *glesbygd* to a much greater extent than for example the efforts to establish hydro-power units, peat-cutting and exploitation of minerals, which can be assumed to have only local effects, giving limited employment (Frånberg 1994, 6; Johanisson, Persson and Wiberg 1989). Referring to state subsidies, Gun-Marie Frånberg writes that once having decided what was good for the rural areas, the state then provided the means to make the benefits come true. In doing so, the important interdependence between people that formed the basis for the informal economy was weakened (1994, 7). Such measures have been regarded as a cultural disarming of the countryside (Allardt 1975; Frånberg 1994) or what Hansen describes as the 'unintended consequences' of wanting to improve welfare in the country (1999, 41). Using Fraser's terms, this can be seen to fuel misrecognition in the course of trying to remedy distribution by stigmatizing the recipients and casting them as deviants and scroungers (2003, 64).

Gendered Effects of Welfare

For women in the rural areas these changes were double edged. The expansion of the public sector professionalized a range of activities such as childcare, some kinds of nursing and care of the elderly that hitherto had been carried out as unpaid labor in the home, traditionally by women. The public sector provided employment and hence economic independence in the larger struggle for gender equality. The disproportionate recruitment of women into public sector services was related to the fact that most men were already in the labor market. By the 1990s, Sweden had the highest female employment rate in the western world at 85 percent. The employment rate for men was 90 percent. Extensive female labor market participation was a precondition for the formation of the welfare model (Forsberg 1999, 81–83).

Progressive gender equality policies changed lives considerably. However, Sweden also has one of the most gender-segregated markets in the world with women in lower paying professions. Gunnel Forsberg's research in 1997 on the distribution of economic power and resources between women and men, showed that the most gender segregated labor markets were those in the western forest communities. On an average, there were 2.5 women employed in public services compared to every one man. Women had a much lower level of income compared to the men and many were employed only as part-time labor, despite the fact that their level of education was the same as that of the men. A large part of the social infrastructure, more specifically the services sectors, consisted of women workers, and in addition a large part of the social infrastructure was maintained by women through unpaid labor within their family and circle of relatives, reflecting the existing relationships of power between the sexes (1997, 43–45). Nevertheless, the public sector, she believes, plays an important role in deciding the level of freedom that the women have, and in gender relations.

At stake in both India and Sweden from the 1950s onwards was thus a concern for the welfare of the people by improving national wealth through the control of natural resources, deploying forms of what Foucault (1991) calls governmental rationality to manage process and relations, all in the name of improvement of and for the population. As becomes apparent from the two study sites of Nayagarh and Drevdagen, this politics of marginalization was contested even as it was elaborated and a reluctant acceptance of belonging to a nation or a welfare state from which they benefited was in constant tension with an intransigence occasioned by their marginality. It was a marginalization developed in language (the *glesbygd* or contrarily the *ban jatis* or forest castes as the communities in Odisha went on to call themselves), in dialogue with state policies and regional politics rather than in their isolation from what is perceived as mainstream society. Nayagarh and Drevdagen are nevertheless very different 'out of the way places.' Rather than only a geographical entity, the *glebsygd*, like Gayatri Chakravorty Spivak's phrase for the 'third world' may be regarded as a proper name for a generalized margin (1990). The areas of the *glesbygd* were born out of a contradictory marginality: made marginal partly by attempts to bring these areas into the ambit of the welfare state. In Nayagarh, marginality was constructed as a result of the inability of the state to reach these areas, especially in the case of the forests, despite the pervasive presence of various arms of government such as the forest department. Underlining these processes were the material resources that the people also called their homes. How schemes and projects are put into action (or not) and how ideas about marginality intersected with questions of gender, class or caste on the ground determined different trajectories as well as put 'limits to government' in both places as I go on to show in the following chapters.

LOCAL PARTICIPATION AND DEMOCRATIZING RESOURCE GOVERNANCE

The period of centralization eventually gave way to a different politics—nationally in the two places but also in international discourse. Beginning in the 1990s, political decentralization went hand in hand with a period of economic liberalization in India and a retrenchment of state services in Sweden. In India, the *Panchayati Raj Act* in the 1990s devolved political power to local village councils or the gram panchayats with mandatory representation for women. In Sweden, a transfer of political power down to the municipalities characterized the political process.

The discourse on participation and local governance coincided with neoliberal impulses globally. Private interests gained importance and government interventions in people's relationships to the market were officially eschewed. Regional policy in Sweden, envisaged as equal development and welfare in the whole country changed to an emphasis on competition between regions for development funds. In the new 'competition state' each region is encouraged to develop its own unique conditions and develop strategies for various parts of the territory (Westholm 2009) drawing on civil society and private actors. Competition and growth, not social welfare or support as in the past, became the new motto. Services in rural areas were cut down and privatized.[14]

The influence of neoliberal ideas in environmental and developmental policy making is evident in both places. Liberalization policies from the 1990s in India spelt the entry of transnational companies for infrastructure but also in extraction of resources, such as mining.[15] New policies often led to a change of livelihoods and employment, dispossession and not infrequently to the flaring up of violence between the villagers and representatives of the state such as the police and the forest department. The state's forestry apparatuses in Sweden were restructured to enhance private and corporate authority over economic, environmental and social action. Self-certification schemes gained in importance.[16]

An important strand of the push towards decentralization was a strident discourse on the decentralization of environmental governance. Policies evolved in the context of a growing consensus among international aid agencies and governments, both in the North and the South that endorsed local management or participation as the paradigm for the sustainable development of rural areas and forests. New ideas and language began to impose themselves on the public imagination. Development agencies (e.g. World Development Report 2000/2001), academics and practitioners (e.g. Ostrom 1990) and demands from local movements, especially in the South, for a greater recognition of local communities' needs and roles in governing forest resources, converged on an understanding for the need for people's participation in environmental governance.

Neoliberalism tends also to reinforce and celebrate strong private, individual and exclusive community rights (Heynen, McCarthy, Prudham and Robbins 2007, 18). This 'coincidence' in both Nayagarh and Drevdagen was not entirely fortuitous. "The community as a counter force to market led reform fails to come to terms with the extent to which community has become the neoliberal form *par excellence* of modern governmentality" (Watts 2007, 290) as men and especially women (see Larner 1998) are expected to take care of local development and care without any real delegation of power. The retrenchment of state services in the latter half of the 1990s affected women severely in rural areas in Sweden. Researchers have argued that rural areas with their lack of services on the one hand, and the care-taking that women are supposed to carry out on the other hand, have the potential to trap women in unequal relations (Friberg 2004). It may be assumed that women would be less inclined to move to places that do not have the services provided in other parts of the country and that restrict their freedom. The stories from Drevdagen present a more complex picture. Despite the absence of public services, the choice several women made to live in the countryside was motivated by a desire to exercise agency by working with development activities and in the creation of a living countryside. They sought a freedom that they believed they did not have in the cities and I elaborate on this in Chapter 5.

In contrast to processes of political decentralization and market solutions, ideas about people's participation were not merely an administrative exercise. Although enmeshed in wider webs of power and capital, they bore with them and kindled ideas about people's voice, gender equality and hopes for democracy that played out in unexpected ways in both Nayagarh and Drevdagen.

A New Moral Economy for India's Forests

Community participation in resource management became an accepted element of the discourse on forestry in India, so much so that it led Jefferey and Sundar to question whether this was indeed a new moral economy for India's forests.[17] However, they also point out that while various social forces in India and abroad have combined to create a new moral economy for subordinate groups in Indian forests, they have not been on the basis of the historical rights of people but rather granted only when villagers have demonstrated their entitlements through work in restoration, such as in projects such as Joint Forest Management (1999). Joint Forest Management aimed to inaugurate new partnerships in forest governance. It stimulated a great deal of debate about forest governance, its identity and purposes. Odisha was the first state to pass a resolution on the subject in 1988. There were various reasons given in my interviews as to the why Joint Forest Management was introduced, depending on who was asked. The official reason was that Joint Forest Management (JFM) was an attempt to encourage participation between local communities and the forest departments, in order to satisfy the villagers' fuel-wood needs as well as preserve standing forests. Degraded land was set aside for plantations to be managed jointly by the Forest Department and the villagers.[18] These attempts overlapped with the Social Forestry Program in Odisha, funded substantially by the Swedish government. Both JFM and social forestry came in for immense critique in Odisha, especially where local groups were already managing a great deal of forest land. The host of joint committees that were set up were dominated by forest officials. As one scathing report put it, the ethos was, "I manage, you participate," (Saxena 1996).

A much more dynamic local movement was growing in Odisha at the time. Local groups, with men in the lead (almost none from among the lowest castes), had taken over the protection and in some cases, the management of forests and were engaged in struggles with authorities for rights to the regenerated forest. Democratic environmental governance in the form of JFM has mainly been a flanking project while the vast number of grassroots networks in Odisha herald a new form of male democracy. The community forestry movement in Nayagarh is one such instance. There emerged considerable criticism of the male-dominated nature of these 'local' and 'community' efforts in various parts of the country (Agarwal 1997; Sarin and Ray 1998). Research revealed that in several places women were forming their own groups to bring forward their demands that encompassed much more than forest management (Arora-Jonsson 2005), also a focus of this book. The women's efforts coincided with discourses on women's empowerment and the need for inclusion promoted by development agencies, women's groups and academics and gave rise to unexpected results.

As these events gathered force, discontent due to the appropriation of land for joint forest management, local movements but also development failures and conservation projects that displaced several people, and campaigns by activists contributed to what has been hailed by its proponents as one of the single most dramatic events in recent forest history in India, the promulgation of the *Forest Rights Act*.

The Forest Rights Act

The passing of the *Scheduled Tribes and Other Traditional Forest Dwellers Act* known as the *Forest Rights Act* (FRA) in 2006 was the result of protracted discussions, lobbying, bureaucratic twists and a long-term campaign by activists. The act acknowledges the "historical injustice to the forest dwelling scheduled tribes and other traditional forest dwellers who are integral to the very survival and sustainability of the forest ecosystem" (Government of India 2006). It has provisions for forestland to be handed back to their traditional users—tribals—and others who have used it for three generations (75 years) or more. The lands cannot be taken away before their rights are ascertained and then bought by the state government. Individual right to the land is to be accorded in joint titles in the name of both the man and the woman except in the case of single women. The FRA recognizes community rights and other traditional rights to the forests such as minor forest produce, water bodies as well as the rights of access for pastoralists or nomadic communities. Here it is the *Gram Sabha* or the village council that has quasi-judicial powers and has to agree that all rights have been settled before the land can be transacted. Individuals as well as communities can make joint claims to land under this act. It is a landmark act that, at least, theoretically, offers forest inhabitants the potential security of forest rights.

Before it became the act, *The Forest Rights Bill* of 2005 was vehemently opposed by foresters, as well by a number of conservationists who argued that the act paved the way for the complete destruction of the forests by local communities (Secretariat 2009). The act left several proponents disappointed and angry over what they saw as a dilution of many of its rules in the final version. Nevertheless, the implementation of the FRA, appears to be like the status of many other laws, the major hurdle.[19] Many communities in Odisha appear to be largely unaware of the act or confused about its provisions and according to journalists, the forest department was doing little to dispel misconceptions. There are surprisingly few claims for community rights and many suspect that the state forest departments are doing their utmost to thwart these particular rights (Sahu 2010a). In the neighboring state of Andhra Pradesh, Sagari Ramdas writes that this is partly because some of the land that the villagers are now demanding had been claimed under the forest department as part of Joint Forest Management programs (2009). For the first time in history a local village body, the *Gram Sabha*, has the authority on deciding on legal rights. The act stipulates one-third representation of women in the *gram sabha* and once again brings to the fore questions of representative democracy in environmental governance. Transferring community rights to forest land would imply relinquishing control over vast swathes of forest land apart from adjudicating what is for the community and what is not. Unlike in the history of the *besparingsskogar,* the privately owned forest commons in Sweden where the state has continued for several years to maintain regulatory control (Holmgren, Lidestav, and Kempe 2004), there is no such provision in the *Forest Rights Act.*

The assumption that public property is collective whereas private property is individualized obscures a wide range of collective and private modes of property in both countries. Forests, especially in the north of Sweden are managed for production by state owned corporations. Sweden's success at privatizing forest property in the late 1800s to early 1900s was an earlier example of a process born out of a desire for profitability by changing people's relationship to the forests. Debates have taken a different turn in Sweden. While Sweden at present is moving marginally towards discussing public participation and deliberation in state owned forests, India's move to privatize forest land, although implemented very differently in different places, will lead to new environmental and social outcomes and reconfigured state control over nature.

Bringing Home Participation in Sweden

Although Swedish development aid supported social forestry as well as local forestry groups in the global South including in Odisha, moves towards people's participation were slower to be adopted within Swedish domestic policy. During the 1970s, the environmental movement gained ground in Sweden, known colloquially in the 1970s as the 'green wave.' By the decade of the 1990s, the dominant view of the forests in Sweden was that of the forests as a resource and raw material that kept the economy in place but also as valuable ecosystems. Since 1993, forest policy that for some time had one overriding goal of timber production, also accommodated environmental goals. Discussions center on the close to hostile relationships between environmentalists and proponents of commercial forestry but in the polarisation between environmental and forest production aims, social aspects concerning local community livelihoods are not considered relevant. Although there are references to the 'social values' of the forests, both in the literature and in policy documents (SUS 2001, 43; Skrivelse 2001/02: 173), these references are restricted to seeing the forests as spaces for recreation and for sport, arguing that these needs should be taken into account. Such social values are seen to be important especially with respect to forests close to towns (*tätortsnära skogar*) and also where tourist activities take place. The social value has to be with forests as places for recreation, not as social or economic basis for communities living in the areas. The relationships of the people living around urban forests tend to be taken as symptomatic of peoples' relations to forests in general. Certification standards, such as the Forestry Stewardship Council stipulate the need to address social issues. A major part of the Swedish forest industry has registered to apply these standards. These may be a potential mechanism and have been important for certain communities—but are not undisputed.

The focus on social or recreational values appears to fit with the argument that western environmentalists are moving towards a post materialist perspective in which forests are not central to economic production but rather to the enhancement of the quality of life while in contrast, the debate around the forests in countries such as India is firmly rooted in questions of production and use (see Guha and Martinez-Alier 1998). While urban preoccupations with the tiger and wildlife for example belie this simple division in India, my research in Sweden[20] points to people in the countryside who do actually rely on nature reserves or company forests for their livelihoods, such as for tourist enterprises or processing forest products, the latter mainly a female preserve. In confrontations between environmental aims and those of forest production, local men and women have chosen to position themselves variously in different situations. Community groups in the countryside have argued that rights to the environment are linked closely to local development and the survival of their communities in the countryside (Isaksson 1999). Voices outside of the production *versus* environmental debates have however been largely drowned out in the noise of production and environmental goals in policy making on the forests, and are rare within academia. Moreover, reaching greater gender equality in the different arenas of forestry in Sweden has been slow (Ds. 2004).

Ideas about people's participation made an inroad through a different policy discourse, that of environmental policy. The White Paper on environmental policy has called for 'innovative methods of local management with the participation of different groups' (Skrivelse 2001/02: 173, 85). It states that there is a need for a dialogue with citizens and to develop new forms of working for nature conservation that respond to the needs of local participation and to the need to anchor policies in local situations. With this aim in mind, a number of pilot projects have been initiated (ibid. 5–6). Some of these changes have been catalyzed by bureaucrats and practitioners who have moved from an international context in the South to work with environmental policy in Sweden, highlighting a changing knowledge base among forest and environmental experts. The Swedish state, especially in the 1990s, saw itself as a proponent of gender equality not only within the country but worked actively and lobbied for greater attention to questions of gender in international forums including environmental arenas such as the Food and Agriculture Organization (FAO), the International Tropical Timber Organization (ITTO) and the World Forestry Forum. The apparent lack of discussion on gender and local participation in domestic environmental policies and practice is ironic.

There have been some overtures at supporting public participation in the management of nature reserves in the country (Naturvårdsverket 2003). The White Paper links the environment to sustainable development and argues the case for cross-sectoral collaboration in order to meet new development needs. It states that it is important that gender equality is taken into consideration and that, women and men, the 'new Swedes' and 'the handicapped' are given opportunity to take part on equal terms in these processes. This is deemed important in view of the fact that women and men can have partly different views on nature—and the cultural environment and how we should preserve, use and develop the environment. The formulation is questionable in the light of the case in Drevdagen. What was it that made working for the forests different for the women and men? Was it merely a case of different views? In the multitude of local action groups working with local development in the countryside and in the context of a devolution of political responsibility, what local participation and development mean is not necessarily self-evident. Political decentralization and environmental governance are two very different processes and in the latter, there has been careful control of what participation may imply.

THE RISE OF EXPERTS IN 'GOOD GOVERNANCE'

While the initial period of scientific forestry may be seen as one of identity building all over the world, the present period is not short of an identity crisis. Discourses on people's participation and changes in definitions of objectives and partnerships have implied a fundamental rethink of forestry. Training and education grounded in natural sciences is hard put to deal with changing social and environmental concerns. "Forest administrations are increasingly conscious that their work is as much about managing people and social processes as it is about managing biophysical processes" (Sundar, Jefferey, and Thin 2001, 245). However, ethnographic work with foresters in India shows that although the actual work that the forest officer is expected to undertake may have changed beyond recognition, the recruitment and training methods have not. An authoritarian and hierarchical culture *vis-à-vis* local communities prevails (Hannam 2000a).

Changing objectives have nonetheless contributed to opening up the field of forestry to a host of experts other than foresters, especially in India. These range from development practitioners, economists, social scientists, consultants, activists, NGO workers, as well as academics engaged in debates about the future of forestry.[21] The difference they made to the state of the forests or to the lives of the people is moot and varies. International organizations have grown in importance in questions of the environment and development, though with uncertain legitimacy and contested results. While on the one hand, they have promoted the rhetoric of participation and ownership, foreign aid with its need for quantifiable targets and outputs has contributed to strengthening the authority of forest departments. As Sundar, Jefferey and Thin point out, "the formal forest bureaucracy has re-legitimized itself as providers of employment: in nurseries and plantation work and as responsible for ending encroachment and smuggling" (2001, 240).

More recently professional foresters are confronted with, to them the somewhat disagreeable scenario of, having to share the field with a series of experts interested in climate change but who may know little about forestry. It has also brought to the fore questions of 'global governance' or a shift to what a recent report on forestry calls, "the acceptance of the view that forest problems cannot be addressed purely by governmental and intergovernmental agreements" (Rayner, Buck, and Katila 2010, 14). Policy coordination with actors such as NGOs, business organizations, multinational organizations and other forms of private authority is considered inevitable. This shift is seen to be captured by the term 'governance' rather than government practiced by nation states. In another chapter, the report points out,

> "Part of the global governance discourse is the quest for *good* governance. There is a broad consensus about its essential elements: a rule of law, accountability and transparency, participation, and effectiveness and efficiency" (ibid. 62).

This aspiration for good governance is viewed by some as "a deliberative turn" in environmental politics (Bäckstrand et al. 2010). Interesting in this literature, largely on the North as compared to the literature on participation in the previous decades that focused on the South, is the change in nomenclature of participation. While previous versions of environmental participation, mainly in the South, assumed participation and deliberation with people working and living in the environments, the participants now tend to be one step removed from the environments themselves, and are to be found in the rarefied settings of offices and conference rooms of public and private bodies. The attention to climate change has furthered a push towards what Mike Hulme calls new kinds of knowledge production that call for "a managerialism on a planetary scale" (2010, 561). And once again, the current landscape of industries, governments and other bodies with a say in these issues is predominantly male (Buckingham 2010).

The advent of governance however, does not mean a withdrawal of the state. In the case of forestry in Sweden, Peter Schlyter and Ingrid Stjernquist write that for the Swedish government, faced with complexity, uncertain problems and conflicting interests, deliberation emerges as an economically and politically safe stop gap strategy. It occurs not only in the shadow of hierarchy, as often suggested, but at the mercy of what is deemed possible, expedient and effective by government and central authority (2010, 192–193). State actors in Sweden are in a favorable position to act as enablers and facilitators—steering these networks at a distance (Hysing 2009).

Incongruously, while for many years Swedish development aid (Sida) promoted local forest management in the South, including in Odisha, drawing on discourses on democracy and equality, often with references to themselves, participation of local communities in forest management in Sweden has been negligible and mainly in relation to private interests as Schlyter and Stjernquist point out (2010). The ubiquitous references to good governance in Sida's policy prescriptions do not have a corresponding resonance in domestic policy. According to Cooper and Packard,

> "the insistence on good government' reproduces much that was previously said about the 'good economy': a bland assertion that the West has defined objective standards for others to meet, a generalized set of categories (elections, multiple parties) that define those standards, irrespective of the actual debates that might be going on in specific

> contexts over how more people might acquire meaningful voices in their own lives" (1997, 23).

Ideas are thus mobilized in aid of contradictory impulses in environmental governance. It is important to analyze these contradictions and also when they are words and when they bring about political gains. Further, as Wendy Larner cautions, neither does all that we see as neoliberal effects come from a single rationale. Contemporary forms of environmental governance are complex (2007), not least in the local environments themselves as I examine in the chapters to come.

THE NEW CLIMATE ON ENVIRONMENTALISM AND DEVELOPMENT

As debates on climate change and the need for action have gained importance in policy-making, forests have once again come under national microscopes. At the 2010 World Forestry Congress in Seoul, the incoming president of the IUFRO (International Union of Forest Research Organizations), Niels Elers Koch, summed it up thus,

> "Never before in the history of mankind have so many people demanded so many different products, goods and services from the forests."

Scientists and policy makers outside the forestry sector are increasingly making their mark in discourses on forests and climate change. The 'rule of experts' takes precedence as global climate concerns based on complicated graphs and meteorological evidence override local concerns. Climate discussions and negotiations are far removed from lay people. On a more philosophical note, climate change "arguably displaces the very notion of community by displacing human beings, both as a species and as a source of norms, in favor of an impersonal, but naturalized, object of concern" (Jasanoff 2010). Also, for the first time perhaps, rifts in the scientific community on climate change, sensationalized by the media, charges of having doctored results in what has come to be called the 'climategate' episode as well as differences in response to climate change epitomized by the debates by the economist Nordhaus and Stern have brought into the popular realm, longstanding debates about the authority of science. This has implications for policy making on climate change and for the ethics of science (Berkhout 2010).

Such discord is amply demonstrated in forestry debates in Sweden. Commercial interests and the environment lobby are once again pitted against each other with the forest sector arguing for increased production and the environmentalists wanting to preserve old forests. Both sides have resorted to scientific arguments to press their cases. Some foresters have argued that the best way to reduce carbon in the atmosphere is to plant more trees as young trees tend to sequester more carbon than older growth trees. This would mean a commercial system with continuous logging and new plantations that would fulfill environmental objectives.[22] This argument has been scorned at by some environmentalists who find little evidence to support this thesis. They argue that logging practices are detrimental to efforts to sequester carbon and that the boreal forest ecosystem is extremely good at sequestering carbon.[23] They draw on research from Sweden and Canada to show that the old boreal forests of the far North are ideal for carbon sequestration.

Two main trends haunt the new forest debates—forests as carbon sinks and forests as repositories for future energy needs. Climate debates have also brought to the fore North-South political divides.[24] Nations in the South such as India have argued for sensitivity to the disparate historical trajectories including colonialism that have been the cause of an unequal world, the right to develop as well as the developed countries' acknowledgement of responsibility in polluting the atmosphere (Agarwal and Narain 1991). In the beleaguered climate negotiations, what most countries do appear to concur on at present is trade in carbon. An overriding preoccupation of governments in the North as well as the South has been with Reducing Emissions from Deforestation and Forest Degradation (REDD), later expanded to REDD+, a program that hopes to reduce the amount of carbon in the atmosphere by promoting plantations in the South as well as instituting a system of payments that would encourage people in the South not to cut standing forest.[25] REDD may be likened to the promotion of plantations and forestry in the South by development aid in the previous decades except now with a significant difference. There is now professed need to engage the private sector in market based mechanisms for REDD+ and a courting of capital investment that goes beyond conservation or fuelwood needs.

Environment policy in India has concentrated itself on justifying action on the bedrock of development. Development, in this thinking, implies national development and growth. There are overtures to wanting to market India's forests in the growing carbon trade. In a document released in August 2009, titled 'India's Forest and Tree Cover: Contribution as a Carbon Sink,' the then environment minister states,

> "Forestry is at the centre-stage of global climate change negotiations. . . . It is India's view that we need an agreement on a comprehensive framework for compensation and positive incentives for forestry as part of the ongoing climate change negotiations" (Ramesh 2009).

REDD+ initiatives with their focus on forest conservation, sustainable management and the enhancement of carbon stocks have aroused expectations but also a great deal of apprehension concerning its feasibility and potentially negative implications. Questions of being able to create an effective mechanism (Angelsen 2008) and whether governments are actually going to be able to put into practice effective policies and programs that reverse deforestation and degradation plague discussions on REDD+. There are apprehensions that the REDD+ to which a national approach and an architecture needing detailed carbon oriented forest management plans, reliable baseline data, quantitative monitoring, reporting and verification (MRV) of emissions reductions, and resources for brokering deals between buyers and sellers is integral, will reverse the gains made in the era of decentralized and participatory forest management (Phelps, Webb, and Agrawal 2010). There is also the worry that in a market system, more powerful players might grab the lion's share as the history with Clean Development Mechanism projects has shown (Skutsch and McKall 2010).[26] Despite these fears, development practitioners and others who believe that REDD+ is here to stay (keeping in mind the billions of dollars already invested) have tried to make a case for the importance of local management and women's participation in implementing REDD+.[27] What might such payment systems mean for women in village communities?

According to Subrat Kumar Sahu, a journalist who interviewed villagers in Odisha, the idea of forests as carbon sinks is viewed with increasing suspicion by communities already managing their forests, especially as they recognize that private interests are waiting to be let in (2010b). Sagari Ramdas describes an example from Andhra Pradesh where the government channeled afforestation funds through NREGA schemes and JFM committees, bypassing local governance bodies such as the *gram sabha* and the *panchayat* that are meant to approve such use of forest land. Women were also granted several individual titles under the FRA and paid NREG wages on private lands if they cooperated by planting cash crops on their land, making them vulnerable to irrigation problems, volatile markets, agricultural chemicals and a total change in their livelihoods. According to Ramdas, ominously like development interventions of the past, these measures tend to dispel women from their central role of growing food on these lands and try to settle farmers working on shifting cultivation. Citing another study she writes that in some districts women were 'encouraged' to grow biodiesel plants (*pongamia pinnata*). The degraded forests, which they would have regenerated with indigenous species, and agriculture lands that supported food crops such as *jowar* and other pulses, were replaced with mono-plantations of *pongamia*, as they were assured a regular income from the sale of seeds. After one payment from the World Band for neutralizing carbon emissions, a few years done the line, 80 percent of the trees perished, most families were forced to sell their cattle, were subject to an increased dependence on chemicals and ruined their land in the process. What also emerged was that the women were completely unaware of the reason they had received the money and had no idea about the ramifications of carbon trade and the relationship of their self-help group activities to climate change. Criticizing a report by Poffenberger et al. (2002) that glorifies women's self-help groups as the solution to developmental and environmental problems or carbon offsets as in this case, Ramdas points to how in an immensely patriarchal system, international payment systems and national hierarchies continue to experiment with poor women's lives (2009).[28]

The push to preserve standing forests in REDD+ might well intensify what Agarwal calls the gender inequality paradox—persisting shortages amidst plenty, that is, the lack of fuel-wood, an item of daily use for women amidst regenerating forests and growing biomass (2010, 323–359). Issues shown by research to be important for rural women such as cooking energy poverty, access to forest resources have not received the attention they deserve either from women's organizations or from the environmental movements more generally (ibid., 419). The issue of fuel-wood and cooking energy was a major issue in forest debates in the 1970s. It appears to be symptomatic of the times that the discussion on biofuels that has now made a comeback into climate debates has moved from domestic needs to a macro-scale that encompasses issues of carbon credits, afforestation schemes and international trade. Energy conservation discourses now overlap with forestry discourses, but on a large scale. Outlining the changing discourses on biofuels, Reginald Cline-Cole dubs the present period as the 'gentrification of the woodfuel discourse' or the reframing of the poor-man's energy crisis from woodfuel to biofuel. This change is discursive but also material as it is accompanied by "progressive supplanting of direct or solid -woodfuel by derived or 'recovered' liquid or gaseous fuels produced from woody biomass" (Cline-Cole 2007, 143). The discourses rely ultimately on the widespread belief that 'renewable energies are the energies of the future" a fusion of renewable energy and sustainable development concerns that fit comfortably both in the North and South. Technical knowledge is considered to be of paramount importance in this field. This fits with discourses of ecological modernization,[29] and technology transfers currently dominating policy discourses in the North. In countries in the South, as the example above from Andhra Pradesh demonstrates, it involves, "exploring neoliberal opportunities to market the wider adoption of renewable wood energy as both an acceptable policy option and attractive investment proposition" (Trossero 2002 cited in Cline-Cole 2007, 144).

CONCLUSION

The deliberate attention to very different geographical locations and historical times in this chapter puts in relief scientific forestry and its troubled trajectory, not only in the complex and socially differentiated society in Odisha but also in the relatively homogenous communities of northern Dalarna. Policies in the 1800s resulted in the separation of agriculture and forestry, though not quite as successfully in India, as in the area around Drevdagen. One could argue that Sweden fared relatively well, Europe being the home of scientific forestry. However, stories from Drevdagen reveal ruptures in this tale as do the hostile debates between conservationists and production forestry while local narratives wait to be told. Also in India, as environmental historians point out, science did not come ready made into the colonies but was formed in the encounter though put to use for imperial purposes.

The making of scientific forestry in both contexts was embedded in its gendered material practices and places as much as it was made in wider webs of power that may be seen as an attempt at centralizing knowledge on forests. In Sweden, the close association of the forests with the masculine was written into history in the 1800s. Young men with no property of their own served ideally as lumberjacks and loggers and came to symbolize work in the forest. Masculine representations that came into play continue to define forest activity and importantly the status that these activities acquired, not only locally but also in the larger political economy of the country. Property relations more generally were central to these concerns and to the restructuring they entailed in people's lives. In India the recent *Forest Rights Act*, although in a different period and place, brings up past questions about individual property rights and gender but in relation to a new context and scramble for natural resources. Indian forests, in contrast to Sweden, are to some measure also acknowledged as women's workplace, though the world of forestry and decision-making is dominated by men. Despite the entry of new actors, as far as control of natural resources is concerned, the state is a key institution in rural areas and will be likely to continue, albeit in new forms.

Nation making redefined marginality in both contexts. From being marginal geographically, marginality became political as these areas were drawn into the nation state and its people become citizens in an 'out of the way' place in a reconfigured central state. Citizenship meant acquiring new rights in a new nation but it was also about needing to conform to the interests of the nation—of being displaced with little compensation or dispossessed in India or as in Sweden, being told how to live: the houses they could have, the work they could do and as many in Drevdagen argue, an estrangement from their environment.

Discourses on participation collided with neoliberal models and impulses internationally from the decades of the 1990s. Development and growth shored up by legions of experts suggesting singular models, belie the complexity and knowledge making in particular environments. Contextual histories made up forestry science both in India and in Sweden, while, they also related to certain 'universal' ideas. This is all the more pertinent in the emerging 'global' discourses on the current environmental focus, the problem of climate change. Although framed as the new global environmental problem, it has served to bring to the fore North-South divides and questions of history as nation-states stake their rights to a common atmosphere and the right to 'develop.' Sheila Jasanoff highlights the contradiction as she writes, "The emissions framing ineffectually bucked the tide of scientific opinion; the development framing, by contrast, asserts a nation's sovereign political right to imagine the future of its citizens" (2010, 248).

But what kind of a future are we imagining and what does it mean on the ground. To come back to the questions posed in the beginning of the chapter—are the processes of decentralization and participation reconcilable with current global environmental and national policy making. Where are the decisions on the environment to be made and at what levels? What does this imply for opportunities for people and especially women who have been outside the purview of environmental decision-making? According to Jasanoff, "Living creatively with climate change will require re-linking larger scales of scientific representation with smaller scales of social meaning." She asks, how will this knowledge be reconciled? (ibid. 238), how is democracy to be ensured, particular interests to be recognized?

Science and knowledge production is integral to these endeavors. Counter narratives of forest histories from the ground in Sweden have been few. With few exceptions (e.g. Jensen 2002), struggles being waged by local people over forests have remained in the realm of popular literature and journalism (e.g. Ersson 1985; Isaksson 1999). The greatest challenges to conventional production forestry in Sweden have come from environmentalists and conservationists. Their recourse has also been science. In India, scientific forestry has been challenged on the basis of its unscientific nature, but also in its disregard for indigenous knowledge, by conservationists but largely through people's movements and as a result of projects of development.

It is in this context that the following case studies need to be examined. A large part of the fieldwork that forms the basis of this book was carried out in the mid 1990s to early 2000 when local participation had gained ground and become an important discourse to be reckoned with. The studies identify fragments of these expressions as small scales of social meaning link with larger scales of discursive formations and questions of power and gender are an inevitable part of the dialogue between them. How the inhabitants of these places dialogued with these changes, from acceptance to confrontation and how gender was entangled in these efforts forms the basis of the next chapters.

4 Environmental Politics on the Ground

The focus of this chapter is on the dynamics of development and environmental action at the sites of the activities, in Nayagarh and Drevdagen. In Part I on Nayagarh, I start with the beginnings of the forest protection movement in Kesharpur, the village that became known nationally and internationally for spearheading the community forestry movement in their own village and beyond. I describe the history of the movement, its philosophy, the men who were active in it, and the women who are significant by their absence in the history as told by the movement's proponents, and in the written accounts of its activities. Much of the account of the history of the movement has been taken from field work carried out in Kesharpur in 1993 (Arora-Jonsson 1995, 23–30).[1] It is an account where, at the time, I did not always question the term, 'people' when mainly men have recounted the history of the villagers' activities. I noticed in hindsight that the term 'people' is generally used instead of men and therefore, in the present text, I have put *male* or *female*, and *caste* in parentheses when I do know the specific identity or a question mark when I do not. I do this in order to try to give a more precise picture of two of the important principles by which power is organized in the community, although there are certainly others. This choice is not to minimize the importance of the revolutionary efforts of the men working with community forestry. It is a retrospective means to highlight that it is a history of the movement as presented primarily by the male leaders of the forest movement and also to highlight how categorizations such as 'people' are taken to be synonymous with the entire community when they actually mean 'men' from a particular social group.

Part II of the chapter is a parallel history of the village of Drevdagen as told by men and women that I interviewed between 1998 and 2002. The first phase of my inquiry in Drevdagen (1998–1999) consisted in speaking to the women and some of the men about their plans for the village, and the ongoing efforts for local management of the forests.[2] Some narratives recurred and formed dominant images of a Drevdagen identity, the familiar currents in the larger stream of stories about everyday life. There was a strong sense of being actively marginalized in the making of the modern state counterpoised by stories of rebelliousness and of defying authority.

These narratives are complicated by conflicting images that depended on differences in age among the tellers, on gendered differences and their length of stay in the village. There are differences in how especially women of different ages, spoke of their understanding of sex/gender roles and of the forests as the men's domain.

I go on to discuss the forest issue in the village and the history of the work devoted to it. The attention here is on the involvement of my colleagues and myself in village activities. These early events formed the basis for the diverging trajectories taken by our work in the village and our involvement in future village and forest activities. Drevdagen's efforts are situated in the context of debates between the proponents of environmental protection and those of forest production. In this arena local community members have tried to enter as actors. An attention to gender relations within the village complicates the picture. Frames used for understanding environmental issues are pressed upon to make room for questions of rural development that cannot be separated from questions of the environment and the forests.

PART I: THE FOREST COMMUNITIES OF NAYAGARH

Nayagarh district is in the state of Odisha on India's eastern coast facing the Bay of Bengal. Odisha has a greater proportion of its people living below the poverty line than any other major state in India. For most people, living off the land is a precarious occupation, since more than three-quarters of their holdings are so small as to be considered marginal and uneconomic (Human and Pattanaik 2000, 3). Differences in wealth are extreme. Odisha has the largest tribal population in India that like other tribal communities in India live on the edges of mainstream society. Much effort has been spent on trying to 'develop' them. Their homes often lie in dense forests and in the mineral rich areas of Odisha. Access to these resources has been coveted by outside enterprises, supported by the state government and has resulted in several well-publicized debates in recent years.[3] I visited two mountain villages that belonged to the *Kondh* tribe but the villages that were a part of the forest network that I was studying were populated mainly by the 'general castes,' the *Khandait, Chasa, Kumithi, Telegu,* generally low in the caste hierarchy. The villages often had *Dalit* or *Harijan* residents living in separate hamlets. *Harijan,* meaning 'the people or the children of god' was a term given by Gandhi to those who were formerly called the untouchables. In country-wide political and social movements many have chosen instead to call themselves *Dalits*, the oppressed. In my interviews, they referred to themselves as *Harijans*. *Dalit* and tribal populations are also called respectively the scheduled castes and scheduled tribes because of the schedules in the constitution that seeks to address the discrimination to which they are subjected. Both the scheduled tribes and scheduled castes are vulnerable groups in social hierarchies, not only in Odisha, but also in the country at large.

The forests of Nayagarh play an important part in sustaining livelihoods, especially for the tribal populations. They are dry, deciduous, and *sal* (*shorea robusta*) is a common species. In addition to the timber used for housing and furniture, many men and women from farming families gather supplementary non-timber forest products (NTFPs) from the forests. In varying degrees, they depend on the forests for fuel, fodder, medicinal plants and timber. Contractors active in the forests employ local villagers to log the forests for paper, pulp and timber. They have contractual rights assigned by the forest department, such as the special concessions provided to the paper mills in the bamboo forests. But, there is also considerable illegal logging.

The forests are an important part of the identity of these communities, especially since the community forestry movement began in this area. The forests are a site both of work and leisure. Especially for some of the women that I interviewed, the forests formed a social space in which groups of women went out together to collect fuel-wood. For the younger women, especially from the lower castes who worked in the forests, the forests were a free space, away from the rules of the villages and prying mothers-in-law, but a space that was increasingly being restricted by forest protection efforts. In some villages, women also patrolled the forests for its protection. Upper caste women normally did not spend much time in the forests as it was considered inappropriate for them to go to the forests on their own. In the densely forested areas around some tribal villages, at the same time as being a sanctuary, the forests were also the space where the women risked coming across aggressive illegal contractors out to log trees.

Traditionally in this area, community institutions (*in practice populated mostly by men and upper castes*) have managed common resources such as ponds, temple lands and adjudicated on village problems. In some villages, such institutions took up protection of degraded forests in their immediate vicinity. Those who spearheaded these initiatives were motivated by the need to conserve forest resources to meet their needs for forest products as well as to keep them for future generations. They linked the droughts, soil erosion, water regime disruption and loss of soil fertility to forest destruction and believed that an important way forward for village development was through forest protection. By the late sixties, sporadic efforts for protecting the forests were already present in the Nayagarh area (Kant, Singh, and Singh 1991).

Shaping the Forests: The Friends of Trees and Living Beings

It was in the village of Kesharpur in Nayagarh district that the now famous movement, *Bruksha O' Jeevar Bandhu Parishad*, (BOJBP) translated literally as the Friends of Trees and Living Beings, first began and swept over the entire district.[4] The village lies at the foot of the Binjhagiri hill, now dense with trees and foliage, but that was bare before the movement started. The river Kusumi flows past Kesharpur and is fed by many small streams from the hill that came back to life when the forests returned as a result of the untiring efforts of men, women and children in these villages. The nearest town from Kesharpur is the district headquarters (also called Nayagarh), which takes about half an hour by car. There were about 800 people living in the village at the time of the studies (1998–2000). Castes in the village include *Chasar (Khandait), Telegu, Gond, Kewat*. The women took care of the homes, backyard plantations, and village upkeep and worked on small patches of land. The men worked as small-scale farmers and landless laborers. *Dalit* women made bamboo goods for sale. In Kesharpur, most of the landless families belonged mainly to the *Dalit* and the *Telugu* caste. Of the 800 people living in Kesharpur, only 13 women were landowners. In the neighboring village of Manapur, of 650 people, only 12 women owned land and in Binjhagiri it was 1 in 250.[5] There were mainly Hindus and no tribals or Muslims in any of the BOJBP's 22 villages that I visited.

Many BOJBP men cited a particular incident when referring to the origins of their organization. The story goes that a farmer (*male*) unable to find wood for the cremation of his dead brother's body, threw the body into the river. This appalled the villagers. Not only was his action a harbinger of bad luck but it also forcefully brought home the obvious, 'if the situation continued as it was, soon they might not even have fuel-wood for their daily needs.' Then, in the early 1970s a prolonged spell of drought occurred for six consecutive years, and it was believed by the villagers that the drought was caused by the deforestation.

Narayan Hazari, one of the founders of the movement, in a book authored with his brother on the movement, writes that Kesharpur used to be "bedeviled by factionalism." "Factions (*men*) constantly ran to the police and to the court to settle scores against the enemy." Then in 1954, when he had just finished his matriculation,[6] along with a group of people (*young men*) he decided to "stop the rot" and try and bring cohesion in the village. They talked to the people (*general caste men, women? lower caste?*) and asked them what their priorities were. He writes that everyone (*in all probability men from cultivating castes/ general castes*) wanted something to be done about irrigation. Through voluntary labor the community (*men and women, caste?*) renovated their public dams. They constructed a lower primary school together in 1958, a middle school in 1965 and a high school in 1970 (1990).

During an interview, Hazari told me that one of the great lessons of the movement was that whenever you work for social reconstruction, you must go for education. He quoted a Chinese proverb from one of his writings: "If you want to plan for one year go for agriculture, if you want to plan for a decade go for a well from which you can irrigate the fields, if you want to plan for a century build up a school."

He believed that priority needed to be given to education because it created requisite human resources. A number of school teachers and other villagers (*men, general castes*) got together in Kesharpur in 1976 to decide on their future and took up the protection of the forests as an important need. These young men went on to become the bulwark of social mobilization, political organization and economic development, not only for this village but for the entire area. They began with informal discussions with the villagers (*men, women?*) and organized a series of village meetings to talk about the need to protect the hill. Finally a decision was made to protect the root stock on Bhinjagiri hill so that it was allowed to grow into trees.

The villagers (*men, women?*) decided to use a method called *thengapalli* (stick rotation). Four sticks were made and one member (*mainly male*) each from four families patrolled the hill. In the evening, they would leave the sticks on the verandah of the four neighboring families. The persons on whose verandah the sticks were placed would patrol on the succeeding day. The group's attention gradually moved to the neighboring Malati hill. The people living in the nine villages surrounding these hills were approached to discuss forest protection.

The movement based itself on the Gandhian philosophy of self-sacrifice and social equality. Men, women and children in the community undertook foot marches and hunger strikes as well as continuing their forest protection efforts. The villagers (*men and women*) were also encouraged to involve themselves in a plantation program organized with the help of volunteers of the National Social Service (NSS) unit of the Utkal University in Bhubaneswar, the capital of Odisha. The plantation program was carried out in the Malati hills with a lot of effort but was upturned by other villagers (*men*) at the instigation of a quarry contractor. Nevertheless, the movement continued to spread and eventually 22 villages joined them.

In February 1982 the NSS, in collaboration with the Nayagarh College NSS unit, organized a workshop on forest conservation. This was attended by four (*male, general caste?*) representatives from each of the 22 villages. The problems related to protection were discussed. The meeting was facilitated by social workers (*male, female? caste?*), educationists (*male, female? upper caste?*), and forest department officials (*men, upper caste?*). The need for an organization to foster activities and coordinate efforts in all the twenty-two villages was articulated at the workshop. A committee was formed with proportionate (*male*) representation from all of the villages, and the principal objectives of the organization were decided. The people (*men*) at the workshop decided to name the organization BOJBP or the *Friends of Trees and Living Beings*.

In 1984, the BOJBP was registered as a voluntary agency. By the early 1990s it was apparent that a major problem had developed in the movement. Although there was momentum among the villagers to protect the forests around their villages, they (*women and men*) often went to other areas to meet their daily fuel-wood needs. The BOJBP men tried to create greater awareness across the entire area, to find alternative means of energy. In an interview in 1994 Hazari said,

> "In any movement there is no finality. Some people still cut trees. But you have to keep working . . . I do not think a very big thing has been achieved. There are a lot of forests in Nayagarh which we have not been able to conserve. But in perspective of the progressive destruction, the movement has made a significant impact. We have covered more than 1,500 villages in *padayatras*.[7] So far 324 villages have started forest protection."

Eventually the movement spread into adjoining blocks.[8] Once an individual committee had expanded to cover a number of villages, or a federation of villages, it separated to become a sister organization (called an *anchalik* level committee) of the BOJBP, working in consultation with the main body. The sister organizations had full autonomy in management and administration and the number of villages varied from eight to twenty-four. Village representatives (*men*) were nominated by village institutions or village meetings (composed of *men*) in the respective villages.

Alhough there was no formal monitoring of the forest preservation movement, BOJBP was kept well informed through visits by villagers and members of sister organizations. The BOJBP staff and volunteers also collected information about activities in the other villages during their field visits. The BOJBP published leaflets, posters and letters that they sent to the villages and schools all around them, asking them to join their work for the environment. They wrote to villages that were also protecting their forests inviting them to link up 'for then they could be strong.' A newsletter called *Sabujima* was started where they wrote about the environment, conservation and other activities in the villages. They organized tree planting ceremonies and forest festivals.

The People in the Movement

BOJBP (*men*) believed strongly in voluntarism. There was a team of about 25 committed volunteers (men) who formally (as opposed to the women involved informally) provided their time to the organization on an honorary basis. The group of young men involved in the movement carried out *padayatras* with other men and women and motivational campaigning in the area. To follow up, they also helped the communities streamline their forest protection activities. They entered the movement with a strong belief in the cause of environmental protection and improvised their approach as the movement progressed. The volunteers were highly motivated and were accepted and regarded well by local communities and organizations.

Narayan Hazari was an important leader of the movement. Although he lived in Bhubaneswar, where he was a reader in public administration at Utkal University, he visited the village often. In interviews, BOJBP members often referred to the inspiring role played by Hazari. Joginath Sahoo was one of the first teachers to join the movement at the outset and he has become legendary among the people for his selflessness, dedication and humility. Udaynath Khatei, also known as Bapa (father), a well liked village leader in Kesharpur provided a strong link to the people of Kesharpur. He had been the president of the BOJBP for several years when I visited Kesharpur in 1993 and was still the president in 1998/9. The movement is known for the sacrifices made by the volunteers and the villagers. A story is often told about an early meeting where the villagers invited the District Forest Officer (DFO) to support their plantation activities. On seeing the goats in the village, the DFO is supposed to have remarked, "what is the point of planting trees when the goats are sure to eat them up?" This was followed by another meeting in Kesharpur where the owners of the goats were persuaded to sell their goats, for many a major source of sustenance. The *Dalits*, who depended most on the forests, stopped collecting forest produce. A film made about the BOJBP members shows Joginath Sahu speaking to the *Dalit* community. He says that he was aware of how the greatest hardship might fall on them but the only way to bring back the forests was to agree together to protect the forests.

Little is written specifically about the movement's relationship to the *Dalit* communities nor of the many anonymous women who worked to give the movement a base in the villages. Although women were never involved in decision-making, they were active in the *padayatras* and other instances of activism, in addition to day-to-day care of the families and the village during the various functions organized by the BOJBP. Many women who spoke of their involvement in the BOJBP seem to have taken part in this way. Several were wives and relatives of the male leaders. According to Narayan Hazary, when the BOJBP went campaigning, the women were often the first to come forward to take the oath to conserve the forests or to agree to bring about changes.

A *banamahotsav* (forest festival) at Tulsipur was organized on 6–7 July, 1989 in the foothills of Balaram mountain. A *padayatra*, and a workshop on forest conservation were organized to coincide with the festival. The organizers wanted the women to participate in tree plantation and the workshop. The men in the village said such a thing would never be possible. Joginath Sahu and Biswanath begged the villagers to permit them to contact the women directly. They went to every house and the women were requested to come to their doorstep to meet them. When they came to the door, Joginath Sahu and Biswanath prostrated themselves at the women's feet[9] and implored them to come out and participate in the function. The women were moved by their sincerity and almost all women, young and old, numbering more than two hundred joined the function (Hazari and Hazari 1987).

The question of women's rights was taken up whenever and wherever the women were involved or sought to be included in campaigns. In the late 1980s and early 90s, the BOJBP began to organize women's *padayatras* which were very successful. In an effort to involve more women, the BOJBP in 1987 introduced tailoring training for women as an income generation activity. A woman from the village of Asuradhipa said in an interview,*

> "A tailoring training program was established in our villages and after that meetings for forming groups among women were conducted. At the village level issues relating to sanitation, pond management, tree plantations, environment protection were discussed. . . . Once I had participated in a 3-day-long *padayatra* in 22 villages. Four women organized cultural activities in the villages to sensitize women on environment protection and women's rights."

Although environmentalism eventually 'shaded the social justice agenda' (c.f. Human and Pattanaik 2000), the BOJBP's moral appeal—for instance, to bring an end to untouchability or to exchange saplings at weddings instead of dowry or put a stop to violence against women—appealed to many women and men, and especially to women from the lower castes. Though women were not present in the formal decision-making structures, many were active in the activities organized by the BOJBP. Yet, Hazari admitted (interview 1994) that, barring a few villages like Manapur and Tulasipur, women were never involved in the planning and decision-making. He said,

> "The scarcity of fuel is especially the women's problem as they are the ones who collect fuel-wood from forests and are also responsible for making meals. No such movement will pick up unless they come to the forefront."

The teachers made a concerted effort to include children in the movement. That this had a significant impact may be seen in the membership. Many young men active in the movement spoke about Joginath Sahu and others who came to their schools to speak to them and encouraged them to join the movement. Similarly, a young boy of class 7 in Kesharpur recounted in an interview,*

> "Children are also involved in forest protection. Once, people from Sanagarada and Badagorada were cutting from our forest. When we (the children of Kesharpur) opposed them, they threatened us by showing a knife and an axe. We ran into the village and informed the elders and 40 to 50 people went to the forest and caught hold of the woodcutters."

Cultural activities in schools were an important part of BOJBP's awareness creation and schools became a focal point of environmental activity.

The Underpinnings of the Movement

Both Joginath Sahu and Narayan Hazari emphasized that Gandhian philosophy was at the core of their movement. They fell at the feet of the people (*men and women*) to persuade them to think about their own development, conservation and of the environment. They made this gesture usually when there was factionalism in a village and people were destroying the forests. The activists fell at the feet of those men who were cutting the trees 'to move their hearts.' *Padayatra* and *satyagraha* (non-violent protests and hunger strikes) were other important ways to mobilize the villagers. Apart from this there was a mix of the religious.

The religious and spiritual idiom in the movement was strong and appealed to people's sentiments. Through music and theatre and the written word, the men in the BOJBP communicated their message of environmental protection at traditional gatherings and other occasions. The strong religious and moral dimension to their work played a large part in drawing in the women. School children were engaged in the campaigns and their teachers organized planting activities with them. Joe Human and Manoj Pattanaik write about a 'green spirituality' that imbued the movement although they caution the reader not to overstate its significance,

> "There is no doubt that *Friends of Trees* have tapped into a deep vein of 'green spirituality' that lies within rural Hinduism, a spirituality which embraces all living things" (2000, 80).

The drive for environmental improvement was accompanied by the leaders' efforts to bring about social change, and give up their caste identity. Some took on new names as last names often reveal caste belonging. For instance, Joginath Sahu, called himself *shramik*, meaning 'worker,' to show that he was there to work for the people. Udayanath Khatei took on the name *Muliya* Udaya, meaning 'laborer,' and Biswanath added *Sangrami* to his name, meaning 'the one who struggles.' They spoke of their movement as the *buddhagram* movement, translated literally as 'that which brought them enlightenment.' Hazari (1990),[10] who was one of the forces behind the movement in the early days writes,

> "The Buddhagram movement stands not only for environmental conservation, wildlife conservation, ecology development and afforestation but also for total development. It stands for development in its economic, social, political, cultural, humanitarian, moral and spiritual aspects. Apart from economic reconstruction the movement has also worked for social reform, family planning, employment generation . . . removal of untouchability, settlement of disputes in villages, village reconstruction through voluntary action rather than voluntary organization (because Indian society is over dependent on the government on everything)."

Disillusionment with various organs of the state that according to the people, had abandoned these areas, made BOJBP men particular about wanting to be independent of the larger political administration of the country. They spoke about the importance of being able to solve their own disputes instead of going to the courts and to be to be able to plan their own development. According to them, the courts merely extracted money from the plaintiff as well as the defendant without necessarily imparting justice. The villagers realized that party politics creates factionalism, and that this must be avoided at all cost. Thus, during elections they took unanimous decisions on which party to vote for in order to prevent external politicians making inroads into village unity. Udayanath Khatei told me that representatives of the political parties often tried to instigate factionalism within the village so that they could be assured of at least half of the votes. He was proud that Kesharpur had managed to avoid this quite successfully. For the past 30 years, no case had gone to the police station (interview in 1993).

The dedication of those years is reflected in the rhetoric of the movement, epitomized in BOJBP reports, such as the one from which I quote below. Though these are not thoughts that are exclusive to the BOJBP, they reflect that spirit of dedication and the moral conviction that they were doing the right thing:

> Thoughts that beckon us,
>
> - What you spend years building may be destroyed overnight—build anyway
> - Give the world the best you have and you get kicked—give the world the best you have anyway
> - The biggest people with the biggest ideas can be shot down by the smallest people with the smallest mind—think big anyway
> - If you do good, people will accuse you of selfish ulterior motives—do good anyway.
>
> (BOJBP, Kesharpur at a glance, n.d.)

Figure 4.1 Kesharpur school children singing the forest song. Photo taken by Stefan Jonsson, Kesharpur, 1993.

Formalization

As the network began to get more formalized over the years, problems began to arise, some of them to do with outside funding. For 15 years, from 1970 to 1985, the volunteers survived on *gram bathapedi* (small amounts from village contributions). If any of them went to a village to organize a meeting, the only requirement was that the villagers (*women*) should feed them. Then when a fire had raged in one of the villages, the BOJBP approached Oxfam for help, who gave them Rs 75, 000 (approx. $1,422) for relief work. A few years later, they gave them Rs 85, 000 ($1,612) that was spent mainly on stationary and postage (for their postcard campaigns and newsletter). Then the budget was increased to Rs 6 lakhs ($ 11,379). According to Hazari, this was a very huge amount for the villagers. They demanded that all the money be accounted for. The BOJBP began to circulate a statement of accounts among the people.

With a growth in its activities, the BOJBP started recruiting fulltime paid workers to organize program activities and help in administrative work. The staff strength of the organization went up to 11 in 1993. This included one field coordinator, one office coordinator, five organizers, one worker each for the seed bank and tree nursery program, one office assistant and a night watchman (all men except for three field organizers who worked with a women's program). All the staff were under the direct supervision of the (*male*) secretary. They came from the younger generation in the local area who had been motivated by the inspiring work of the volunteers. The field organizers were in charge of the sister organizations and were paid partly by them and partly by Oxfam. Although BOJBP was averse in principle to being funded (in 1996, they actually returned Rs. 1 lakh—approx $1,896 to Oxfam), as the work expanded, they found that they could not cope with the accounting and thus began to employ people to carry out these tasks.

Forming the Mahasangha

By the second half of the 1990s, the state of the forests of Kesharpur and of the rest of Nayagarh had changed dramatically with protection. Bare patches became clothed in green. Springs that had dried up came to life. Wild animals began to be sighted again in the forests. The movement and the forests brought the people together. The regenerated forests gave them a new identity and they began to call themselves the forest castes (*ban jatis*), a new caste united by the forests that they lived from and among. They began to receive media attention and were awarded prizes. They became known as the communities connected to a special kind of space, the forests.

Most of the BOJBP families, especially the *Khandaits* by 1998 used agricultural waste as an alternative fuel that made them much less dependent on the forests for fuel-wood than they had been earlier. Their drive to protect the forests went beyond immediate material benefits. The forests had acquired values that shaped how they were appropriated or protected. They became resources for collective representations of the community in new ways as the 'forest castes' and a new politics of the region was produced through their webs of committees and networks. There is of course no uniform picture. The women who still collected fuel-wood from the forests belonged to the *Dalit* community and were not part of the forest committees.

In 1992, the various sister organizations and committees decided to form the *Nayagarh Jungle Suraksha Mahasangha* (the Nayagarh forest protection federation) that would span the entire district. As the *Mahasangha* grew, several sub-committees were established to deal with conflicts between sister organizations, or between committees, and sometimes also between villagers who came to them from villages that were not formally a part of the *Mahasangha*. There was one woman in the publications committee and one in the conflict management and none in the executive committee. Every sister organization was free to govern itself, with the BOJBP and *Mahasangh* playing a facilitative role. One sister organization decided to have one-third representation of women on the executive committee.

A sub-committee on legal affairs was set up to deal with the government Joint Forest Management programs. They were wary of the government's plans for Joint Forest Management as they felt that they had been successfully managing the forests without government intervention so far and their involvement might spell problems. Relations with government authorities varied from place to place in the BOJBP/*Mahasangha* areas. Several forest officials were supportive of their efforts in the early days and impressed by the way the villagers were managing the forests. However, tensions had developed with the introduction by the government of social forestry programs supported by the Swedish government. These were meant to provide fuel-wood to the villagers. But the villagers claimed that they were being used as a cover to provide cheap timber for the paper industries, at the cost of the villagers' labor and time. The villagers' experience with the social forestry program made them wary of subsequent programs for joint forest management.

Joginath Sahu, who had moved his attention to the *Mahasangha* and was helping to build up the federation, began to be looked upon by the other leaders of the BOJBP as someone who had changed loyalties. In several interviews,* men from various villages spoke of a 'lack of interest,' an ageing leadership, and a lack of commitment among the members of the BOJBP. Over the years, the organization had become more bureaucratic and had lost its widespread appeal. In an interview (1999) one man regretted that the zeal of the 1970s and 80s had disappeared,

> "Gradually BOJBP became a closed organization. Even the villagers of Kesharpur were not informed and involved in the activities of the BOJBP . . . Whenever a visitor used to come to the organization the villagers welcomed him/her and shared their experiences. Nowadays the villagers are not even told about the visits."

The younger generation within the BOJBP felt that they did not dare oppose the leadership. "Even if we did, they would not listen to us anyway" said a young BOJBP office bearer to me. Other BOJBP members felt that once the center of energy had moved to the *Mahasangha* that had its office in Nayagarh, they knew little of what was happening in the movement. "People in Kesharpur are confused about the role of the *Mahasangha*." And at the same time, there was disillusionment with the BOJBP leadership.

While I was in Kesharpur, I visited the *Harijan sahi*, the *Dalit* hamlet to speak to the women there. Noticing that I was filming the discussion, the men joined the discussion and both men and women complained bitterly of discrimination by the other castes in Kesharpur and their exclusion from forest related decisions. They knew little of what was going on in the network and had heard that some bamboo had been divided from some forests but that they were never involved.

As the center of the movement moved from the BOJBP to the *Mahasangha*, problems arose between the two. The *Mahasangha* office had moved to Nayagarh town, the district headquarters, in order to be more centrally placed. The growing separation between the two organizations was reinforced by this physical distance. Tensions between the *Mahasangha* and the BOJBP had a part to play in the working of the women's groups in Nayagarh. But before I take that up, I now look closer at the issue of 'gender' that was becoming problematic for the movement.

Gender Becomes an Issue

The need for social reform, for the abolition of dowry, and for greater involvement of women in the movement, recurred often in BOJBP rhetoric. In 1987, the BOJBP started a women's tailoring program and held women's classes in environmental education, sanitation and family planning—making little difference in the lives of the women. In an evaluation of BOJBP activities carried out by Oxfam on behalf of the British Overseas Development Agency (ODA),[11] in 1992, the absence of women in the forest networks was emphasized. Striking in these reports and accounts of the movement is that although it was pointed out that women were absent from the BOJBP management and leadership, little attention was given to the women who were already working in the movement—those who organized the *padayatras,* took part in a range of functions and were active in supporting the work of the men.

In their three year budget proposal to Oxfam for 1992/93, the BOJBP acknowledged, "Women's participation in the environmental conservation program launched by BOJBP is poor." But their proposal for change was basically more of the same: training in health and family welfare, environmental education, and tailoring, for which they proposed the appointment of a core of women workers, although under the management of a man. However, between the proposal being drawn up and the grant being made,

Oxfam insisted for the first time that there should be a gender-training workshop for the BOJBP staff (Human and Pattanaik 2000, 87).

Human and Pattanaik recognize the role played by Oxfam in bringing up this issue more concretely but they are also critical of the fact that Oxfam hitherto had carried out so little to address this issue. As a result of the ODA evaluation, funds were provided to BOJBP by Oxfam to enable them to set up a savings and credit program for women. Credit schemes and micro credit had become popular within the development community, inspired in part by the success in Bangladesh of the Grameen Bank. The Savings and Credit program was introduced in 1994 and women's savings and credit groups were set up in fifteen villages. Oxfam provided funds for field organizers, field assistants and a co-ordinator to help the women in the villages organize themselves into *mahila samitis* or women's groups.[12] This was in tune with other governmental programs on income generation for women. In 'sensitization camps' attended by more than a thousand women in the BOJBP's twenty two villages as well as three sister organizations, workshops were conducted to plan strategies for developing women's groups.

During 1994–95, in the workshops carried out by BOJBP with the women and supported by Oxfam, a four-tier structure for federating the women in Nayagarh was proposed (ibid.):

1. At the village level were the *Paribesia Mahila Suraksha Vahini* (PMSV), the 'Women's Brigades for Environmental Protection.'
2. At the village cluster level an association of the brigades or PMSVs would form an *Upamandal* (Sub-Council).
3. At the level of the sister organizations, three or four *upamandals* would form a *Mandal* (Council).
4. At the district level, once *Mandals* had been formed, there would be a *Mahasangha*.

Although this was the structure that the coordinator of the program and the women came to advocate, the idea of a women's *Mahasangha* was alien to many men in Nayagarh. I was told by Narayan Hazari, ". . . the *purdah* (veil) is a great inhibitor in our society . . ." (Arora-Jonsson 1995). At that time I took his words at face value. However, the present research led me to question the many ways in which ideas about the *purdah* are reinforced and kept in place amidst discourses on women's empowerment and independence. I go on to discuss this in the chapters ahead.

PART II: DREVDAGEN

Drevdagen is in the northwest corner of the county of Dalarna in Sweden. The scenic village valley lies nestling in the Swedish mountains on the border with Norway. In the middle of the village is a lake that joins a river further on. The houses are spread over the area on both sides of the lake and relatives tend to have their houses situated close to each other. A nature reserve starts at the northern edge of the village. This is also the beginning of a walking path that goes through the forests that the inhabitants say links up with the *Kungsleden* (the royal trail), the walking path that leads through the mountains of Norrland.[13] The path also leads to a *fäbod*. Since the forest is a nature reserve there is considerable forest cover there but just outside the village, large bald patches that have been clear-felled can be seen all around. The forests are mainly pine and fir and grow slowly at this high altitude. Much of the landscape in and around the village is covered by overgrown shrubs; an eyesore for many in the village. Women and men sighed as they told me that they no longer had animals to feed on the grass and maintain an open landscape as they did a few decades ago and that the villagers would still like to see.

Since the 1960s there has been considerable depopulation that in the past two decades had stabilized to about 115 people. The women that I spoke to in 1998 claimed that "while other villages were dying Drevdagen was picking up." Many villagers believed firmly that the place had an innate force. On one of my later visits to Drevdagen (2002), I asked a man who had recently moved to the village with his family what made him move there. He laughed and not without seriousness, said: "Drevdagen has magic in its air. It is the volcanic soil and the forests." This was not the first time that I had heard about Drevdagen's volcanic soil and its healing properties. The majority of the adult population at the time of the study was between the ages of 40 and 50, which meant that the median age was very low for a village in such an area. It was ethnically homogenous with the exception of a Swiss family that moved there to start a dog-sledding company. As I perceived it, there were no big differences in wealth among the inhabitants.

Much as in the other villages in this region, small-scale farming and forestry that used to be the mainstay of the people in these areas gradually disappeared as large-scale forestry was encouraged in the country. A few men owned their own companies in carpentry, transport, construction, some women and men worked with tourist activities (usually a family company), and for a while one woman ran the village shop. Other villagers worked for the county, municipality, or other branches of the state and with the church. A couple owned a tourist home. Many of the women working outside the home were nurses or in other forms of health care. Some of them were *hemsamarit*, 'home Samaritans,' who visited the elderly in their homes to take care of everyday chores. It implied driving long distances in the countryside to reach the people who needed their services. People joked in the interviews that some of the women who were *hemsamariter* were old enough to need care themselves. There were about 15 adults who were unemployed. Both men and women were dependent on temporary and seasonal employment, for instance in a nearby ski resort or in other parts of Europe. Some women had been able to organize childcare after protracted discussions with the *kommun*[14] and two women in the village worked as child carers. There were also the retired and those on sick leave (*sjukpensionärer*). Many in the older generation were hoping that plans for an old age home in the village that some younger women were working on, would be successful. They did not want to leave the village where they had lived for most of their lives to spend their last days at the *Särna sjukstuga* (translated literally, the Särna sick cottage—an old age home for the infirm). Many of the older women spoke disparagingly of Särna and declared that they would never move there.

Marginalization and Conspiracy

As people moved out of the countryside in the 1960s, being unable to sustain an adequate infrastructure for a dwindling population, infrastructural services were cut down in the country and Drevdagen was no exception. The village shop, petrol pump and the postal outlet were closed down in the village. A feeling of being penalized by a centralized state for living in the *glesbygd* and more specifically in Drevdagen was strong among many villagers, especially the older generation. Two narratives, one of marginalization for living in the wrong part of the country was strengthened by another, that of a conspiracy against them. Villagers felt that there was a conspiracy against them because of Drevdagen's struggle with the government authorities in their refusal to close down the village school. Since the school strike (that I describe ahead), stories of conspiracy against Drevdagen by municipal authorities abounded, such as difficulties in getting loans sanctioned, building permits or being fined unnecessarily. There was a general antipathy to the political system. Märta, (a woman in her 60s), believed that community relations were actively destroyed by state policies,

> "Voting is a game of wild cards that makes people think that they can do something . . .The government does not want the people to do things themselves. It can become a threat. It has become almost dangerous to have anything to do with human relations. Women do not have anything in common anymore. They divide themselves up in families."

The 'disarming' of the countryside that I refer to in Chapter 3 was palpable in the interviews with older women in the village,[15] who complained that all their meeting places and contexts had disappeared, for better and for worse. They claimed that with that had also disappeared a culture that was typically women's own.

Paradoxically, with greater centralization and the drawing of the countryside closer to the center, the distance between the *glesbygd* and the center seemed to increase. Drevdagen was previously a part of Idre *socken*. The municipal center then was Idre town, close to the village. After a reform in 1974, municipalities in Sweden were amalgamated into larger units. The municipal center for Drevdagen moved further south to Älvdalen, leading to a greater feeling of alienation among the people now further from centers of decision-making. Yet, although distances increased, the administrative net tightened around them with greater bureaucratic control.

An intricate system of applying for grants and subsidies was also put in place. According to Frans (a man in his late 60s), the application system for grants made co-operative action more difficult. As a result of the many small projects carried out individually, people sometimes sought money for similar projects from funders, putting the village in a state of dependency and creating discord between the people. Rut, an elderly lady in her 80s said,

> "the youngsters have become spoilt by being at home and getting the dole."

The people in Drevdagen felt that they had few choices. They elaborated on this 'administrative net' even as they tried to disentangle themselves. The villagers were perpetuating a system that they disliked, but at the same time unable to survive outside of it or feeling that they had no possibility of doing so, feelings that played an important part in the negotiations about the forests and that also contributed to disagreements among them.

The administrative system that was meant to be the same for everyone in the country, was experienced very differently by those who lived in a village compared to those who lived in a city. In light of recent scandals in the media about directors of state owned companies who retired with big bonuses, Rut dryly remarked when talking about the pension that was decided for her husband before he died,

> "One doesn't exactly get a golden handshake if you have worked in the barn all your life . . ."

Struggling for Community

Stories about the marginalization of their village went hand in hand with stories about struggle and defiance. Drevdagen is known for its long battle with the authorities to keep the school alive in their village.[16] Elsa who was newly-married and worked as a volunteer at the school in 1983 related,

> "In 1971, the school was threatened with closure. . . . Then again in 1983 the school board (*skolstyrelsen*) in Älvdalen decided a week before school start that the school was going to be shut down . . . They didn't inform us directly. We read about it in the newspaper headlines. In fact, the county board had promised us that they would give us a teacher's position here. We all felt completely steamrolled . . . There was an immense coming together in the village. We refused to send the children to the school in Idre . . . we taught them ourselves for six years."

There were times when the possibility of holding out indefinitely in this way was questioned in the village,

> "It was difficult to hold out for so long but we never gave up . . . Several women sat on a hunger strike. That was just before Chernobyl . . . Finally, in 1989 the government allotted money for four years . . ."

The first *friskola* (independently run school) in Sweden was established in Drevdagen. The villagers ran the school themselves with some financial help from the state. Parents and other villagers worked voluntarily and were responsible for running the school and employing teachers.

Village identity was linked strongly to the long struggle for the school. Although an important symbol of a collective identity, memories of the school struggle also cast a long shadow in their stories. Their identity as the village that confronted government authorities was as much a burden as a resource especially when negotiating with the *kommun* on other issues, such as childcare. The extensive media coverage during the school strike had led to everyone outside the village, including at my university, forming some sort of opinion about Drevdagen. Stories about the school were told and retold and researchers and others contributed to defining the 'place' and setting lines around village identities. Work in the school took up a lot of the villagers' time. Some spoke of being tired after having struggled for so long and that they did not have the energy to continue to fight. One woman said to me,

> "The only project that has succeeded is the school . . . people are tired . . . they want results" or that

> "People haven't really made a comeback after the six years of the school strike."

A number of older people were doubtful about the projects and activities under way, questioning if anything was at all possible in the *glesbygd*. Several younger men and women felt frustrated by this attitude. They felt that many of the older villagers were negative to so many things, including relations to the municipality, that it made it difficult to work with village development.

Differences were also nuanced by gender. In most endeavors, especially in the school struggle, it was typically a man who had dealt with the authorities, although it was the willingness of women to act as staff and support the strike that had been crucial to the continuation of the school. With respect to Drevdagen's plans for the forests, at the time of my fieldwork in 1998, it was again men who spoke for the village. In 1995, several men and women had together drawn up an agenda for village development and the forests (*Detta vill vi med Drevdagen*) and formed the village association to work with these activities. Speaking about the problems that they faced with local politicians, the women said that the men had managed to irritate the municipal authorities and made it difficult for them in their work. Meja pointed out,

> ". . . like plans for child care and so on. We have to actually discuss them with the *kommun*. It is not that easy then."

In conversations among the women it seemed that a widely shared view was that the men took actions on behalf of the village, and as village representatives, that the women often did not know about or came to hear about only later. Occasionally they expressed irritation for having been co-opted as a part of something they either did not agree with or did not know about, or one that put them in a confrontational position. As one woman put it,

> "It is actually quite irritating that there is so little information about things done in all our names. The old ones (*de gamla*) dominate. It makes it difficult for the others."

Most activities in the village took place through various village associations such as the village hall association, the school association, the sports association and many more. The villagers had several plans to revive facilities in the village by their own efforts. Such efforts were considered necessary to counter the marginalization that they were subjected to for their choice of living in Drevdagen. *The Drevdagen Village Association* that was formed in 1995 was an umbrella organization for all the other associations, to be able to coordinate development activities for the village. An information center was set up and a newsletter started. The head of the village association was the school's former principal, one of the people who had led the school strike and the school through its problems. He commanded a great deal of respect in the village especially as most of the younger inhabitants of the village had been taught by him in school at one time or another. He was also the chairman of most of the other associations in the village. In interviews and discussions, the villagers often pointed out that being a small village it was often the same people who were active in the various associations. The work was done on a voluntary basis, as was the case with most other village activities.

The Forest Question

According to the villagers, being subject to the decisions of the state went hand in glove with being subjected to the vagaries of Assi Domän, the forest company that owned large parts of the forest in the region up to 1999. As I described in Chapter 3, much of the forest around the village was taken over by the *Kungl. Domänverket*, the *Royal Swedish Forest Service* in the 1800s. It was reorganized into the *Domänverket*, the Swedish Forest Service in 1912 to manage the state's agricultural and forest land. Its administrative tasks as a public authority were later taken over by other authorities and during the 1960s it became a commercial enterprise. Through a decision in parliament in 1991, *Domänverket* was restructured yet again. It was fused with a private company ASSI AB, and the joint stock company Assi Domän was formed in 1993. The state remained part owner with 50 percent shares. Assi Domän took over all the commercially viable forest land in the country that was not protected in any way.

Because of this, 174,000 ha of forest around Drevdagen thus fell into the hands of Assi Domän. Another part of the forest previously managed by *Domänverket* became in 1992 a nature reserve reflecting the changes taking place within Swedish forest and environmental policy at the time. The nature reserve was taken over by the *Naturvårdsfonden* (a part of the *Naturvårdssverket*, the Swedish Environmental Protection Agency) and managed by the *länsstyrelsen* (the county board). The *Naturvårdssverket* is the central environmental authority responsible for protecting the forest in the nature reserve. The *länsstyrelse* at the time (1998) was managing 180,000 ha of forest and had eight men employed in administration and management. The setting up of a nature reserve initially was welcomed by the people in the area since it meant that there would be a stop to the logging carried out by Assi Domän.

Villagers not only in Drevdagen but also in the surrounding areas claim that the state had expropriated their land ownership rights beginning in the late 1800s.[17] Although they lost formal or statutory rights in the crown forests around the village, the villagers had informally continued to exercise user rights. *Domänverket* gradually restricted user rights like fishing, hunting, tourist related activities, firewood and lichen collecting and small-scale forestry and processing. Several villagers related indignantly that,

> "The only right we villages have left is one that is applicable for everyone in the country, the *allemansrätt* (the right of public access)."

Jon added bitterly that although they were inhabitants in the area,

> "We have to pay for the moose hunt . . . It is probably the most expensive here in the whole of Sweden . . . 3000–4000 crowns for the moose, 10, 000 for the land."

Many could remember times when their families treated the land as theirs and restrictions did not exist in the same way. This may also be read in a short history of the village that Halvarsson, a village resident wrote in an appendix for a report. He writes,

> ". . . . the ownership rights to the *myrslogar* included since old times, timber from the *slog* area to use for wood for hay-drying racks, the *slåtter* cottage etc. Being able to exercise this old right was tested by Sixten Emretsson in Drevdagen. . . . It could only end in one way, and after the legal trial Judge Sandgren stated, "how could you be so dumb as to think that you could win against the state?" (Byskog 1998).

Changing Forest Relations

There was also a difference in the ways the villagers viewed different generations of foresters. From the anecdotes related by some of the older men, restrictions on villagers' access to and use of the forests accompanied a generational change among the foresters in their area. A report on the forest project *Byskog* had the following quote,

> "Certain slog land could be accessed even after the great distribution of landholdings with ownership rights and the accompanying right to forest products (*skogsanslag*) that was later forgotten. Ownership rights naturally included the right to hunt. A number of inhabitants could claim these rights *vis-à-vis* the district forest officer from the early 1960s. That is why the forest owners with his implicit support could lease out the land for the moose hunt for a number of years, all the way until the general director at the Swedish Forest Service put an end to such generosities" (ibid.).

These changes came about alongside the growing antipathy between advocates of environmental conservation and those engaged in production forestry. Referring to the frosty relations between foresters and the environmentalists at the beginning of the 1980s, an official report on forest policy in Sweden states, that it was only at the end of the decade that a discussion could be conducted among researchers, nature conservation people and proponents of commercial forestry. This more open attitude resulted partly from increased knowledge, partly from a generational shift in the forestry sector—those foresters who had been wedded to the ideas of clear felling began to be replaced by people who, during their student years had been confronted with, among other, Carsons' and Ehrenvärds' thinking on environmental consequences (SUS 2001, 30). Similarly, according to a speech made by the minister for forestry at SLU on December 2, 2003, the shift in the generation of forest officers allowed a significantly different policy to emerge in 1993, making it possible to place important environmental aims alongside those of commercial forestry for the first time.

On the contrary, the villagers' view of the new generation of foresters was not as promising. Many of the older generation of foresters working in the area previously had been familiar to the villagers and conversant with the people and the customs of the area. Their replacement by a new generation of foresters who knew little about the area and with few prior ties to the place often led to a collision with local hunters and other inhabitants.

In the previously cited report, the new foresters schooled in environmental values were thought to be more open to environmental concerns in the forests, opening the door that had been closed by a previous generation whose overriding goal had been to increase commercial production. Yet according to the villagers in Drevdagen, it was the older foresters who, because of their identification with the local area, were seen to be approachable. At the same time as this generational shift, there was also a shift in images of masculinity associated with forestry as Berit Brandth and Marit Haugen illustrate for Norway (2000). A generation of foresters comfortable at a desk perhaps distanced them further from the men in the villages, and with older associations of hard work in the forests as a determining characteristic of a certain image of foresters.

In several places in Sweden, as in Drevdagen, villagers have mobilized arguments based on environmental efficacy to stop logging by forest companies. Yet the setting up of the nature reserve while restricting the space available for logging, did not automatically enable local development, or necessitate a change for the better. In neither case were local people themselves seen as actors. In 1996, the village association had approached the *länsstyrelse* with a plan detailing how they could use and help to look after the forests that had been made into a nature reserve on the other side of the village. According to the men in the association, the *länsstyrelsen* merely laughed at them and turned them away when the villagers approached them with their plans. This was the time when my colleagues from SLU became involved in the village. Debates on engagement with local communities, voluble in countries in the South have until recently, not been a part of Swedish debates.[18] It is open to question if the ambitions of small scale forestry, use for local development, and community care for the forests, in Sweden would have more in common with environmental goals than the current model of production.

Figure 4.2 Lekåsen, Drevdagen's fäbod. Photo taken by Anna Ryen, Drevdagen, 2000.

Resistance to the Forest Company

Villagers related of extensive logging of hunting grounds; of treasured partridge sites where the villagers had been promised that the company would not log; of the company not caring about the way they went about the clear cuts; of planting *contorta* pine which contravened the rules of the *Naturvårdssverket* (Swedish Environmental Protection Agency). The village association had protested against the logging of the forests by the company, which according to the villagers, had continued the management practices of the Swedish Forest Service. This had resulted in large areas bare of trees, a landscape that is of relatively long duration because the growing period for trees is extremely long at this altitude and in this rugged terrain (low *bonitet*).[19] Men and women in the village recounted stories of their struggle with the Forest Service, of trying to stop them from cutting the forests, especially in areas that are in close proximity to the nature reserve around the village. At one time when the villagers got wind of the fact that Assi Domän was going to log a forest path near the village, several rushed there and took over their machines. "We threatened to shoot their machines," said Jon.

According to Märta,

> "Assi Domän has made it ugly in the forest . . . .They have taken out timber and so on but denied it on the radio program. The film shows all of this . . .[20] We want to get back the right to care for our forests, run them ourselves . . . . No-one has succeeded in tackling Assi Domän yet and they won't be able to do that unless they don't carry on in the crooked ways that they do."

Jon spoke of the time when Assi Domän had 1½ percent untouched forest that they were planning to sell out in pieces The villagers thought that perhaps that was one way they could find a way forward, by buying some of the forest land in the area. However, he said,

> "they refused to sell to the villagers . . . then they said that they would not sell small units."

In the spring of 1997, the question resurfaced. Assi Domän wanted to concentrate its work in core areas and the Drevdagen forests lay outside of these (Assi Domän 1997). The initial plan was to sell the forests in small pieces to private buyers. The village association in Drevdagen was galvanized into action. They felt that any purchaser would be bound to further fell the forest in order to subsidize the purchase and wanted to act quickly to save the forests that were still standing. As one of the men from the village told me,

> "It started when we got to know that they had planned to log the forests . . . all the way to our doorstep . . . then it became a burning issue."

The association wanted to stop the sale of forest land to private buyers in order to avoid possible logging. They based their argument on the fact that the vitality of the entire area depended on the communities having access to a standing forest for various activities as well as a measure of control over their environment. The village association wanted the villages to be part of the process of managing the forests that they knew so well. They lobbied for the sale of the forests to the state rather than to private buyers since they felt that the state must be answerable to the people in a way that a private company is not. The men in the village association contacted local politicians, and eventually came in contact with researchers in Dalarna, and with my colleague Axel from SLU, who supported them in their cause.

The forest issue within the association was initially led by Gustav, a long time resident, with active support from Karl, a younger man who had moved to the village recently with his wife who was from Drevdagen but had not lived there for many years. Karl was a skilled carpenter, and hoped to make a life for himself in the village with his family. The plans with the forest project provided one opening for a future in Drevdagen and his interests in computers and filmmaking proved useful to the forest project. During the months that followed, discussions were held between politicians at the municipal level and Assi Domän. Colleagues from SLU supported the cause of the village by helping them lobby international environmental organizations and government authorities in Stockholm. The central authorities were informed about the importance of paying attention to local and environmental interests. Local and regional protests received media attention (e.g. in the forest magazine *Skogen* May 1998). Eventually, the sale of the forest to private buyers was abandoned and a new proposal was put forward. The forests were to be bought by Sveaskog, a state-owned company.

The Involvement of People from FTPP/SLU

As a sector university, SLU is responsible for research and education in agriculture and natural resources. It is involved also in support to farmers and local people in the rural areas on these issues. At the time, I worked with the Food and Agriculture Organization (FAO)'s Forest Trees and People Program (FTPP) office in Northern Europe that was based at SLU, at the Department of Rural Development Studies. There were changes over the years but at about the time of the fieldwork, the FTPP mandate was to support networking activities, strengthen institutions in the South, build up a Swedish resource base on questions dealing with community forestry, work on method development, and be responsible for information dissemination. It was interest and passion in questions of local management, rather than an official mandate, that prompted FTPP in Sweden to work with Drevdagen. The situation was in many ways similar to those we had been working with in the South. Those from FTPP who worked in Drevdagen sometimes worked in the village with university support, sometimes on behalf of the FTPP network, or sometimes in their own capacity as interested individuals, but the villagers made no distinctions in these positions. For them, we were all from SLU whether as development practitioners from FTPP or researchers. Thus when I refer to ourselves, especially my colleagues in the rest of the text, I write 'SLU' unless I need to further distinguish who was involved.

With the help of SLU, the men in the village association attended conferences and presented papers on their struggle. In this way, they came in contact with forest communities in other parts of Sweden as well as with local people struggling with similar issues in other parts of the world. In Spring 1998, Axel, Niklas, Kristen and Diane, all of whom then worked with FTPP at SLU, carried out a Participatory Rural Appraisal with several men and women in Drevdagen.[21] Together, they charted out what they wanted to do with the forests and the village. One of the points taken up was the need to get in touch with other people within and outside the village, and to plan for a conference attended by people from the municipality and other representatives working with rural development and forestry. Keeping in mind their ideas of partnership in what they saw as a global issue, the SLU group also arranged meetings between people from Drevdagen and those working with local forest management in India and Scotland. Individuals from India and Scotland visited the village in the winter of 1998. With the help of Niklas and Axel from SLU, some of the men in the village and from a nearby village started making a video film detailing irregularities in compliance with the sustainable forestry certification criteria (FSC) that the forest company claimed to fulfill.

It was in this context that I began my research in the village. I met Karl at SLU and was extended an invitation to visit Drevdagen. They regretted that the association consisted mostly of elderly men and hoped my presence might prompt the women to engage themselves in association activities. I was accompanied by Axel on my first visit and that ensured me a warm welcome, among both men and women. He was respected for his work and regarded as a true friend of Drevdagen.

What is Local Management?

The conference with people from Scotland and India had taken place recently. Although for many in the village it was difficult to see the connections, Sara remarked,

> "Imagine, it really makes you think and gives strength when you see that the struggle against the state for your forests isn't something only in Drevdagen or Sweden but is actually a global phenomenon . . . that one can now try and struggle for our environment together."

However, the women seemed to know little of what was going on in the association. Men and women had placed various concerns on the agenda that they had drawn up for the village association in 1995. But problems had surfaced.

Most people did not know what plans the village association had. Since most villagers did not know what local management was supposed to mean, they worried that it might cause discord and ill-feeling in the village. They knew that my colleagues were working with the men in the village association and since I was from SLU, I was asked questions about what local management really meant? Which forests were being talked about? Local management by whom? People were uncertain of how they could manage the nature reserve themselves or if it was a question of having a right in decision-making, together with the authorities?

Those who did know more were divided. According to Jon,

> "We want to take care of the nature reserve also . . . have a part in the decision-making . . . it is too much dreaming to think that we can take care of it all by ourselves . . . Local management . . . . Complete decision-making by us isn't good. . .then it would lead to discord . . . it needs to be part of the decision-making on the forest that lies closest to the village . . . a part of the profit can go back to the forests . . . maybe through some sort of village council."

Some were afraid that the village no longer had the skills necessary for working in the forests. Einar, who worked for the local forest authorities, felt that by wanting to manage the forests themselves, the association was implying that they were not doing their jobs properly. Like Jon he also thought that it could lead to *osämja* (discord) in the village. Annika pointed out,

> "Everyone is not interested in the same things, those who shout the loudest get the most."

Among others like Frans, the apprehension of *osämja* sometimes resulted in a distrust of all collective activities. On the one hand, he recognized that villagers looked out for each other and helped each other when needed but he pointed out that as far as the forest question was concerned it was different, it was more complex. It involved some men speaking for others.

There was also a fear in the village as voiced by Jon, that they might be getting out of their depth. Kerstin cautioned,

> "The forest is a thing of the future . . . One knows so little . . . are we capable? It isn't easy . . . are we ready to take responsibility . . . because then one is tied down."

My initial interviews revealed questions that kept coming back: in this effort called 'local management,' who was going to take over, who was going to make the decisions, and who was going to do the managing?

Formalization and Outside Pressure

These fears, I realized, arose partly because the villagers knew little of what was happening in the village association. Those closely involved in the association, and from the university who were dealing with this issue had increasingly lost touch with the rest of the village. As the negotiations and lobbying were carried out outside the village itself, the scene of action moved further and further away from the village. In the village, only a handful of men remained involved. All the activities that they had worked with since 1997 gave them a new standing to argue for their cause. However there was not much change in forestry practices and village rights to the forests remained unaltered even after the sale of the forests to Sveaskog. As they sought to negotiate for local management outside the village, the interests of the group of men most active in the forest struggle drifted away from those of the rest of the village, and became distanced from the issues which the women in the association had wanted to take up. Most of the villagers, especially the women, no longer attended association meetings. Many women felt that the association was inhibiting,

> "It feels so overwhelming," sighed Alva.

There was a frustration among some others who had been involved in various ways with the 'projectification' of yet another issue. Cecilia pointed out,

> "We would like to see the village as a unit even if different people are working with different projects it belongs to the village . . . like with the tourist activities."

It seemed that the need to ground the activity that was being done for the village, in the village, or in the local community itself, had been overlooked or by-passed in the increasingly complicated process of negotiating with politicians, bureaucrats and forest company officials. The feeling that the village association had become reduced to a small clique of men was exacerbated by the fact that they did not always announce their meetings, and gave out information only sporadically. There was little communication with the rest of the village.

For example, several spoke about the film on the forests that only a few had seen and that the villagers did not feel a part of. They felt that by giving priority to the strategic decision not to show the film in the village, the village had lost out on an activity that they all needed to be involved in. The men in the forest project had chosen not to show the film as they believed that it might reduce the value of the forests on the stock market and thus there would be less chance of them being able to sell the forests to the state-owned company. They also had a fear that it would jeopardize negotiations with politicians and others.

For many, the forest struggle became another 'project,' led and managed by a few, and that did not have much to do with the others. On the other hand, unlike other projects the forest project purported to speak for them all and for the village: for the local people. Although the association may be said to have espoused a decision-making model based on consensus, and that made it important for everyone to attend the meetings, not many people always attended in practice and not all villagers were part of the association.

Gender and the Practices of Power

The women who had taken the time, and who had tried to take part in association meetings, said that the formal rules and the procedures of the association's meetings, such as a pre-set agenda, were inhibiting. It left little time for them to talk about their work. They claimed that the insistence on a formal protocol, like being able to speak out only when called upon by the chairperson and other such strict procedures, all contributed to a great deal of formality and were time-consuming. According to Cecilia,

> "At the meetings, the agenda and so on takes a lot of time and at the end when one wants to discuss important questions. . . . the AOB—any other Business . . . then it is time to go home. The association works but it is not visible in the village. Not even half of the village is part of the association. It is the association's board that works here. A small group with six people is active. The others support but are passive . . . but nobody is negative."

Because many women found the protocol inhibiting, they stopped going for the meetings. For other women, practical considerations such as responsibilities at home and the care of children gave them little time to attend. It is interesting to note that when I spoke to some of the women, they told me that not even half the people in the village were members of the association. In my initial interview with one of the men in the association, he had told me that more than half the village was part of the association. I did not check the figures but found these perceptions significant of how people experienced village participation in the association. One or two women were more critical. Sara believed that it was a battle for women to be active,

> "Old habits persist . . . women are quiet in big groups. Women don't get much of a chance to talk at the meetings. I know two women who stopped going to the association because they felt that they were always expected to make coffee and bake buns for the meetings. I refuse to do that. The forest has always been the men's domain and many women think that it is not really their concern or that they don't understand what is going on. I wanted to find out myself what was going on regarding the forest. Now I know. But it takes so much energy. I have been strong and continued but not everyone can do that. I don't have any small children at home so I can spend time on that."

The idea that the forests have always been the men's domain seemed strong in the village. However, as I describe in Chapter 3, it seemed to be more a reflection of the present and existing gender relations in the context of resource governance than of the past.

Karin felt that women were mostly silent at the meetings, but were still expected to make coffee and help at conferences. According to her, although she herself was the chairperson of one association in the village,

> "There is a feeling among the men that women are not good enough or not so knowledgeable when it comes to running the different associations. Yet they expect that the women volunteer and organize the food and coffee for meetings and conferences."

Both she and Kerstin felt that many men did not think that women were capable of running associations. While I was sitting and talking to Kerstin in her kitchen, her husband joined us. He spoke about how they had always had to rely on their capabilities and resources in the village and that was how they were going to succeed in the future,

> "We have always done it on our own steam. We must all do our bit . . . then things will get done."

Kerstin was indignant,

> "Own steam? . . . It's the women who end up doing it. Women actually have jobs now . . . they can't carry on and volunteer all the time."

According to her, their own steam or force that he spoke of was based on the assumption that the women would do much of the organizing and practicalities of the work, even in support of ideas that were not necessarily their own. She said that although she had tried to work with the men in the association, her efforts had been disregarded. It was only the support from her husband that had kept her going,

> "The men don't let anyone in. I sit in the municipal council in the *kommun* . . . but nobody cares about that. As it is now, the village association is a club for mutual admiration . . . I have said at some point that I am interested in working in the association but nobody has taken it seriously. Men are afraid of strong women . . . It isn't enough just to invite women to the meetings. More is needed. The men must show interest in letting them in. This is also true for now when one is building up the council of villages (*byarådet*) . . . I hope that more women will dare to come to the association meetings."[22]

Although Kerstin hoped that more women would come to the meetings, she also speaks here about the contradiction of being at the meeting but not really being let in. The presence of more women might influence proceedings but they were still subjected to the same structures and strictures. Their opinions apparently counted for less and, if they were there, they would be bound to decisions that they did not necessarily believe in. In this situation a number of women found it sometimes strategic to work to get their views across in other ways. One option was to put their issues up through their male partners and relatives who attended meetings. According to Yvonne, it was often easier to influence decision-making in the village association in these informal ways rather than by attending long meetings. She said,

> "I don't go for the meetings. But I have influenced through Thomas. They have planned to build a small trail around the village. I suggested that they could make a little path where one could ride, take a carriage . . . not around the whole village but there we can make a path at least till we lay the trail. I talked privately with people . . . whenever someone came to visit . . . in this way I can reach out anyway. It was the same thing with the bridges. I spoke to people that they should be wider so that one could take a carriage and so on instead of building more bridges later. One talks to one's husbands and then they put it forward. One influences others also at the coffee table."

This was one way that some women put forward their issues but it was not always feasible. And it was not only a question of getting the issues of concern to women put forward, as later developments in the village indicated.

Talk and Little Action

Cecilia had moved back to the village and had restarted the village shop that had been closed for a long time. She saw it as a way of reinvigorating village life in the *glesbygd*. It also had a special emotional attachment as several years ago her father had run the shop. Re-starting the shop had not been an easy task. Her determination and endless negotiations with authorities for loans made it possible for her to keep the shop open for a brief while as a private concern. She had discussed the possibility that the village association eventually take over the shop, and hoped then to be employed by the association to run it. Sitting in her shop I tried talking to her about her involvement in the project for local management of the forests, but she found it difficult to connect this issue with her own everyday life,

> "Men have always been dependent on regular meetings. One wants so much but it isn't always that so much happens . . . Earlier the idea was that the shop would be run by the association. They talk a lot but not very much happens. Then one loses the spark."

Many women I interviewed felt that the men in the village association were involved in planning for the future. The women were often concerned with issues that they felt needed to be sorted out immediately and that needed to be 'acted' upon even if only in part. They claimed that action was better than only "talking about them."

> "Sometimes it feels that nothing really happens at the meetings. That is why it was good to see the film that the village association has made on the forests. At least it is some sort of action," said Sara, once they finally had a screening in the village.

The women also spoke about how they needed to link up with the forest project without losing sight of other priorities in the village. The idea had been to work in the forests locally,

> "But what are people to do when there is no attention to housing for the young people who want to move here and maybe work with the forest, for day-care for the children, a shop and other services. Especially women can't do anything about their ideas as long as there is no proper day care for the children."

Cecilia spoke about the need for holding on to what she called the larger thought, the self-governing village where all the different activities in the village needed to be seen in relation to each other. This is a thought I come back to in Chapter 8. Even within the forest project, according to Kerstin, activity was focused on the economic part. In a conversation at Kerstin's home, her husband spoke about all they were going to do with the forests as he stretched out his arms expansively. She interrupted him and turned to me,

> "Do you understand now why we women are not a part of all this? *Gubbar!* . . . it all becomes so pompous when they sit and talk . . . The question is . . . how does one tie up the whole together . . . does one have the capacity here in the village?"

Searching for New Forms

The women said that they preferred to start from where they thought they could make a difference. Some of them had been active in organizing a cattle-grazing association and were active in the sports association. The women who were active in village activities chose to work in ways where, they said, they were not constrained by the formal atmosphere of the village association's meetings.

The meetings of the village association seemed to be a forum of importance for some of the men in the village. There was no comparable forum for women, not formal or established. Some of the older women in the village thought that it was sad that so many of the older ways of meeting had disappeared and wished that there were spaces for them to meet more often. Hillevi, one of the elder women in the village sighed,

> "I wish that we met more . . . earlier we used to knit in the evenings . . . now it is only TV that counts." Others felt that they needed something together, "something that would bridge differences between us."

But at the same time a lot of activities seemed to be taking place in the village. Kerstin had been active in starting a group on spirituality and a meditation circle in the village, which in a way formed the initial core group of the inquiry process that I describe further. Her big project was to start a healing and recreation center in the village where people could come and relax in the peace and quiet of the beautiful mountains and the forests. She had lived in the village previously and had now come back to live in Drevdagen again.

Although the interest in spirituality was considered a little dubious by some in the village, several women started meeting and taking an interest in getting together. Many said that it provided a space for them as women. Others in the village thought this talk of spirituality could be harmful or even dangerous. But it had led to a new sense of togetherness among the participants and they felt strengthened by it. Marie who had always been interested in these questions thought it was a way to come closer to nature, and to realize that people, animals and plants are different parts of the same nature, and can get energy from each other. Here was offered an alternative way of interacting with the forests that one did not find in projects and programs. She believed that this view helped one to be humble in relation to the nature around you.

Some women spoke of trying to find other forms through which they could work, some sort of village network perhaps, so that they were informed about what was going on as well as to be able to influence activities and to take up issues that concerned them. The catalyst to such a network became a meeting organized in June 1999 by the village association and SLU to try and set up a council of villages working for local management. I had accompanied my colleagues to the village with a report that I had put together from my first round of interviews with the villagers. The women wondered if I knew what the meeting had been about. Some were upset that they had not been informed about it while two other women had been told about it but only to be asked by the committee if they could arrange the lunch and coffee and take care of the dish washing. The issue of having a space of their own came up once again among the women, precipitated by the latest omission. Several women told me that they could identify themselves in my report and were excited to see that others had similar thoughts and also to see other issues being raised that they had not thought about themselves, but considered important none-the-less. They were interested in sharing their feelings and experiences. While I was visiting Sara in her home, we were joined by some of the other women in the village and they brought up the question of having their own network. We decided to meet in a few weeks time when it was convenient for the women in the village.

Sara said,

> "We could find ways of functioning other than these meetings. . . . Not follow the men's patterns."

Sara's words presage a process in the village that became the focus of my research and that I analyze in the rest of the book.

CONCLUSION

In this chapter I track environmental politics on the ground when villagers in both countries sought to establish a common sphere of action around a common material space, that of the forests and their villages. Discourses on local governance and forest management found expression in the particular physical contexts of Drevdagen and Nayagarh. Apathy with the political system in their countries and a determination to take charge of their own development characterized both communities, especially evident in Drevdagen in their feelings of active marginalization by various parts of the state. In both places, the forests were an important part of village identities but became even more so, with the development initiatives that wove in around the forest issue. Clear in both accounts however is that headway with forest initiatives was possible when it was an essential part of a wider agenda of social change, and where a large part of the community was either involved or supportive and as in Nayagarh, where religion and the spiritual were the foundation for political action. Although in both places, the forest issue was spearheaded by the men, women engaged actively. In Drevdagen one woman defined it as part and parcel of 'the larger thought, the self-governing village.' Protecting the forests from disappearing was important for reasons that went beyond the material.

The struggles for local forest management symbolized an assertion of rights *vis-à-vis* recalcitrant political authorities. It was also a reassertion of their place and a wish to engage together in governance of everyday life that especially in Drevdagen, villagers claimed, was becoming increasingly atomized. The difference that typified the two contexts was most apparent in how they expressed themselves in relation to the political system in their countries. While in Drevdagen, the villagers felt marginalized, their relations to the state were double edged. Their efforts were directed towards securing a space for exercising agency for themselves within the political system. The forest movement in Nayagarh on the other hand was a step away from the larger political system. By choosing to solve their own disputes rather than go to court and to organize their own governance of the forests, they sought to bypass what they perceived as corrupt and unjust government authorities.

The attempts by the communities existed in tandem with current neoliberal discourses on the need for new organizational forms and responsibilities (decentralized, privatized or deregulated) for the governance of natural resources and for development. As the village and forest organizations became formalized and the outside world impinged on them, they became enmeshed in new state practices and tended to become complicit in them. Certain relations were privileged while women in particular were marginalized. While this occurred in relating to the world outside the villages, it was also in relation to outsiders that 'gender,' translated to mean the absence of women, became an 'issue' that needed to be dealt with. Women and men's actions in Nayagarh and Drevdagen were shaped powerfully by images of forestry and farming as a male domain, setting nominal space for what is ideally permissible for embodied real men and women to do within larger gender and power relations. In both these places gendered hierarchies were grounded in an interdependency. The forest network in Nayagarh and the village association in Drevdagen marginalized women from decisions and political power but at the same time depended concretely on women's labor for their routine functioning. But, as the women sought to organize in new ways, in their acceptance and/or challenging of current images, they brought to bear new and changing subjectivities that were central to their lives in the countryside. It is to this discussion that I now turn in the next chapter.

5 A Politics of the Possible
Gendered Subjectivities in Collective Organizing

The women's groups in Nayagarh and a women's forum in Drevdagen came into being in somewhat different circumstances, but both in the context of struggles over local development and forest governance. In this chapter I discuss how the women's collectives came about through a telling of their stories. The focus in the stories is on the complicated ways in which the women negotiated personal and collective experiences while building up a collective space for themselves. Rather than claiming a generality for the accounts, I explore the conditions and contexts in which the stories were produced and the women's experiences of living and working in the countryside. In studies of group organizing, individuals are often ignored in the analytic focus on the collective that is seen to act as an organic whole. Understanding subjects and conceptions of subjectivity are important for understanding politics, not only for understanding how subjects are produced through power relations (in a Foucauldian sense) but also the place of subjectivities in shaping the political.

Subjectivity refers to how we as individuals construct and give meaning to our experiences as we dynamically position ourselves in relation to others and within discourses (Henriques, Hollway, Unwin, Venn and Walkerdine 1984). That the formation of subjects is a social practice is evident in the stories and practice of the women as they reimagined and reconstituted themselves as subjects and built up an intersubjective space, a vantage point from which to act. Experiences are structured by expectations, norms and values, in short by the dominant culture.[1] Although cultural norms act like magnets, "drawing the self in certain directions," we do not simply internalize them in any straightforward fashion (Blackman, Cromby, Hook, Papadopoulos and Walkerdine 2008, 20). Interpretations of experiences can change. Subjectivities are thus contingent. There is nevertheless a continuity and historical specificity, as individuals draw upon prevailing spaces and discourses. While "subjectivity . . . is always a part of an assemblage in which it is used," its contingent qualities, "as unfinished, partial and non-linear" make it an active agent of social, political and cultural analysis and change (ibid. 2008, 14, 16).

The chapter is divided into four parts. Part I deals briefly with how the groups came into being. In Part II, the women's stories provide glimpses of their subjectivities and of how 'communicative acts such as their narratives depended on previous acts and how they creatively interacted in the task of making and inferring meaning' (Jaworski and Coupland 1999, 4) as they built upon and negotiated the past. In their stories they drew upon a stock of tradition and connected to wider notions and meanings that existed outside the particular individuals. New discourses on modern women and women as income generators and entrepreneurs played a part in the form taken by their collectives. Subjectivities for some women in Nayagarh were shaped by their experiences of living in *purdah* (veil) but also in relation to new responsibilities demanded of them by the forest movement. Appeals to spirituality and equality on Gandhian principles evoked new and different ways of relating to the present while drawing on the past. The discussion on gendered subjectivities is weighted in the case of Drevdagen, since I also played a part in the women's collective and in its inception.

How the women built up their groups inter-subjectively forms the core of Part III. In Drevdagen, through discursive practices they established their subject positions and constructed the notion of the women's forum despite an ambivalence about it. The women spoke about themselves as strong, able to do things that men could not or as working women, as stubborn and impulsive. In Nayagarh, the *mahila samitis* that were active were set apart from the rest of the program by the action they took. Action became the basis of a shared intersubjective space. In Part IV, I analyze how in both places, the women's subjectivities were productive of a new politics and of new possibilities of being.

As I deliberate on whether the women were in fact reproducing and/or challenging discourses and how the women's subjectivities changed in the course of the inquiry, the aim is to learn what affects or empowers social groups (in this case the women's groups) in their (our) capacity to act and (that I take up in the following chapters) its relevance to social, political and environmental concerns. The point is to recognize women as gendered subjects and active in their environments rather than as objects of development initiatives or as a missing category in development work.

PART I: DIFFERENT WAYS OF BEING—BEGINNINGS

The women's collectives in Nayagarh and Drevdagen came into being in familiar ways, building on past networks and caste groupings. Yet, for many they became the grounds for different ways of being. This section is about how the women's collectives came into being and the social conditions that determined their relationships to each other as well as to the others in the villages. In the following sections I examine how their collectivity gave rise to something different and new.

THE WOMEN'S ENVIRONMENT PROTECTION BRIGADES IN NAYAGARH

Women had been active participants in the BOJBP movement, especially as the male leaders advocated 'total development,' social reform and greater involvement of women. As the movement began to get formalized into a network of forest organizations, women who had never formally been part of the decision-making groups, became conspicuously absent. The forestry networks came to be dominated by elderly men from the general castes. Oxfam began to provide funds for a 'women's development program' as a means to involve women in the organization. The 'training' for this took the shape of classes in tailoring, family planning and sanitation and eventually in 1994, in assisting the women to set up women's groups, the *mahila samitis* to carry out a micro-credit program. Funds were provided for a program coordinator and for field organizers in the villages to help the women set up the *samitis* and to network with one another.

The *samitis* varied in the number of women involved and also in the issues that they wanted to work with. In some places the efforts to organize the women did not result in any groups. One of the women who had tried to organize a group in her village spoke of how difficult it was without support,

> "BOJBP has sometimes tried to involve women. But, there is no continuity of programs for the women. Whenever they organized any program, there used to be interaction among women from different villages. They used to make friendships. The sphere of interaction was really spreading out."*

On the other hand, sometimes in a single village there could be several women's groups. A savings and credit group normally comprised fifteen to twenty women. Several groups were named after famous women, as the *Lakshmibai Upamandal* (the Lakshmibai Sub-Council after the queen who led the 1857 revolt against the British), and the *Madame Curie Paribesia Surakhya Vahini* (the Madame Curie Environment Protection Brigade after the famous scientist). Each group had a president, a secretary and a treasurer who took turns in maintaining minutes and accounts. The coordinator of the program, Anita was a university graduate and had come to live in Kesharpur to work with the women's program. The field organizers lived in the villages for which they were responsible. In some cases this was also their home village.

Anita and the field organizers formed the link between the various groups and kept everyday contact with the women in the villages. Several *samitis* applied for funds from the government's DWCRA program.[2] Although there was a difference in the staff employed by the BOJBP, that is, the coordinator and the field organizers and the women in the villages, in terms of education and their roles in the *samitis*, when I refer to the 'women' in the *samitis*, I include them as well. They played an important part in the direction taken by the groups and in several instances they appeared to identify themselves with the women more than with their employers and the program.

AN INQUIRY WITH THE DAMMIGA DAMER

The women's collective in Drevdagen came into being in a somewhat different way and in a process where I was closely involved. In preliminary conversations and interviews with the men and women in Drevdagen in 1998, I had understood that there were few women in the village association. The women pointed out that they did not talk much when they attended village meetings. "It feels so intimidating," said Alva. These gatherings appeared to be a forum mainly for a few village men. My coming to the village at the time, wanting to do research on rural development and local governance that would be relevant to the villagers coincided with the women's desire to build up a women's network to work with local development. In the spring of 1999, after one meeting with 12 women and a second meeting with 10, it was clear that the women wanted to work together but it was unclear how to proceed.

As I looked for ways of structuring our gatherings, I chanced upon accounts of cooperative/ collaborative inquiry (Reason 1994), a form of participatory research. This involved the idea of taking action as individuals and then coming together as a group to reflect upon it. I wanted to create a meeting place for reflection, the form and content to be shaped by the women, a meeting place between the academic world and their everyday lives. I insisted on calling us co-researchers. This was received with jokes and some suspicion. As Maria was finishing off relating her life history at one of our first meetings, she had paused and had said,

> ". . . and then . . . of course . . . . I do research in my spare time"

and was greeted with gales of laughter. Research on the whole remained a suspect activity. What is life to some is research to others.

> "Research sounds so big . . ." said Ingrid, ". . . To us, the important thing is what we want to do in the village, what are the problems that come in the way of our work and what it is that we can strengthen."[3]

The inquiry was a small part of the women's organizing and activities in the village. Its purpose was twofold. First, for the women to be able to choose the questions that they wanted to pursue and for us to design the inquiry together. Second, for me to be able to leave the conceptual frame of the inquiry open to their (our) categories. The collaborative inquiry opened up the space for negotiating the research question that was of relevance to both the women and me. My role in the inquiry was to share facilitation, document the process, interview individual women, and contribute with examples and theories to discuss together. I kept a record of the stories, minutes, and discussions and wrote reports of our get-togethers. The implication of opening up this space was that the research process was unpredictable and the framework for understanding and analyzing changed as the process unfolded.

At the first three meetings, the discussions centered on the women's ideas and projects. We met at different locations in the village. The women divided themselves into working groups to address different village matters such as the school, the shop, the running of a goat farm, the *fäbodar* (summer farms in the mountains), as well as a tourist camping site. It was not entirely clear what the purpose of the new group or network would be. Practical plans were discussed, such as screening films and having photo exhibitions and documenting village history with elderly villagers, planning the Christmas fair and organizing village get-togethers. One question that arose was whether the network should include the entire village or only women. "You need to have women as well as men who work together, even though the initiative comes from the women" some pointed out. It was important as a social event as much as a place to decide on village activities. Sara called us the '*dammiga damer*' in the village newsletter,[4]

> "Our latest meeting at the pond hut resulted in an upcoming theatre in the village. I agree with Eje, we shouldn't just meet when there is work to be done, we also need to have a good time together."

Eventually our get-togethers crystallized into a *kvinnoforum*, a women's forum that I describe further in the chapter.

In both places the women built upon past activities and projects that they already worked with. Apart from discussing their projects, the women continued to use the space to plan village fairs and other joint activities. The *mahila samitis* in Nayagarh planted trees, cleaned and maintained village spaces, made backyard plantations (discussing what would be planted and how), planted trees at the outskirts of the forest and cleaned village commons. Apart from the savings and credit activities, they also carried out small businesses like making snacks as part of a government sponsored income generation program. The women claimed that they did many of the same things individually anyway. But it was in the groups that many found the openings for working in the ways they chose and negotiated among themselves. For the women in Nayagarh their work within other spaces such as within the family were more difficult to negotiate on their own, especially for the younger women where custom was reinforced by mothers-in-law and husbands.

PART 2: BROKERING MODERNITY AND TRADITION

The women's (our) subjectivities and the inter-subjective space they (we) created was already conditioned by social and power relations. We were never outside of those relationships of power and ways of thinking (c.f. Foucault 1990, Butler 2005). Yet, it was from *within* these 'oppressive' social relationships that dictated how we thought that new ways of thinking and acting arose. In this part of the chapter, I focus on the discourses and prior social relations that structured the women's thinking. The emphasis is on the women in Drevdagen who spent considerable time debating their place in the village while I hold up the case of Nayagarh as a mirror to their discussions to bring them into greater relief.

BEING RURAL

Rurality and their marginalization from national centers was a recurring aspect in the narratives of women in both places. As opposed to Sweden where policy in the past had actively planned to diminish differences between the urban and rural, in Nayagarh their distinction from the urban was tangible and incontrovertible. Access to urban spaces was often contingent on class, caste and gender. In the perception of a majority of women, not being educated made them different and disadvantaged compared to women in the city. Other more mundane things like clothing and food were physical markers of difference. I was asked questions especially by young girls in Nayagarh if girls walked around in jeans in Delhi, or what people in the cities wore at night when they went to bed, for they had heard that people had different clothing for night and day. Being rural and living close to the forests was linked to a responsibility to the environment—the forests and village, that they felt made them different from others without forests.

In Sweden the stories told by the women and shared with the others provided insights to the group about how women who had moved to the area (even if it was several years ago) experienced themselves in the countryside. Kajsa and Sara spoke of how it was to be seen as the ones who had moved to Drevdagen from the city. They had decided to set up a goat farm together.

Sara: We were advised by an EU project to go and have a look at a goat farm in another village in Älvdalen. An elderly couple ran it. . .

Kajsa: I called them to see if we could come and visit their farm. It was then that I realized, how wrong my accent was.[5] The man who answered the telephone was not too happy about us coming there. It was my accent and that we were two women who wanted to start a farm on our own that sounded suspicious to him. I finally persuaded him to let us come and see the farm. When we were there, we knocked at the door. . . .

no one answered. . . .then Sara saw a little note stuck on the door. It said, 'you are welcome to come in and take a look at the house and the barns. The doors are open.' They did not even want to meet us. They knew from the telephone conversation that we were two women and what is more we were from the city. We had the wrong accent.

Sara: But then as we were leaving, he came back. . .First he was really irritable. . . . but then he realized who our grandfather was and then he began to talk and talk . . . He himself knew nothing about goats before he started the farm . . . it had all come gradually

Towards the end of the conversation it was with relief that Sara and Kajsa discussed how one did not have to be born as a farmer to become a farmer, although that feeling was strong in the countryside. The story by Sara and Kajsa was about doing two things wrong: being two women and starting a goat farm on their own and secondly not sounding as if they were from the area itself. Both often mentioned that they were 'going to be a farmer,' a *bonde*, the connotations of which were still very much male.

On the other hand, Cecilia related another story where being from the city and speaking with a Stockholm accent had been useful. A couple of women in the village had been working to get day care facilities in the village. Yvonne had been trying unsuccessfully to negotiate with the municipality. Then Cecilia came in and called the man responsible for it. "All I had to do was to speak my Stockholmska and it worked." The others in the group nodded and I looked a bit puzzled. You see, she explained to me,

> "When a woman from the area calls them, they think they can put them off somehow, that they don't really expect much. But when someone who has lived in Stockholm calls, then they think, oh . . . no . . . she expects child care facilities . . . we can't put her off so easily. . . . Besides which, they treat the women here with such disregard, which they don't do with city women."

This story also shows another side to the accepted notion within Swedish local development that it is often women who have moved into the area who start things off. It is perhaps not only because these women come with energy and a willingness to change things as is often implied but also because of the ways in which they are treated by the authorities. This attitude on the part of the authorities underlies an understanding that rural women were not necessarily capable partners in development activities in the *glesbygd*. To relate to the people living in the area, it was good to be able to speak the local dialect, but to work with the authorities, a Stockholm accent often had more effect. In the ordering of power and gender in this little incident, having an urban background gave Cecilia a certain amount of power and leverage *vis-à-vis* the official.

Despite the lack of services that they often spoke about, the women also felt that the countryside gave them a freedom that the cities did not have. In part, by wanting to live here they were also challenging modern life in the city and those whom they saw as trying to wield power over them from the center. As Sara once said,

> "We are different when we are here in the countryside . . . but it is not only us . . . our men are different too . . . from the men in the cities."

This again is an example of distinctions being forged in dialogue. In this case unequal subject positions were turned into an advantage, of having something (like the women who spoke of the forests in Nayagarh) that was absent from urban areas, that was rooted in the place but also importantly in the people when they happened to or chose to live in the rural areas.

WORKING WOMEN, MOTHERHOOD AND OTHER DISJUNCTURES

Many women in the group spoke of themselves as *yrkeskvinnor*,[6] working women. It emerged in conversations as an important aspect of their lives, especially for those who had moved back from the cities. Their involvement in the workforce gave the women an important identity as independent, modern women. There was a certain pride in that: being modern working women provided a sense of liberation from what they saw as the drudgery of the past.

When the group discussed getting the village together for a theatre, they realized the organizational problems they actually confronted. Comparing themselves to the older women who had organized a play a number of years earlier, one woman remarked,

> "We are all working people (*yrkesarbetare*) now. We are not in the village in the daytime, it makes it difficult for us compared to them."

An understanding of being different from their mothers, of being working women, contributed to the forming of their subjectivities. In their perception, this was also what made them different from the women in other countries when the topic of my research with the women in Nayagarh came up. I spoke about how the women in Nayagarh had organized themselves and how some of the issues were similar to Drevdagen. This prompted a discussion on what it meant to be a working woman and being engaged in the formal workforce. I discuss this further in Chapter 7 and take it up here only to show some aspects that were part of their definitions of themselves as working women (*yrkeskvinnor*). Their views on *yrkeskvinnor* also stemmed from differentiating themselves from the earlier generation. Märta, in her late 60s commented with some sadness that it was easy for the younger generation to forget the toil of the older women and to take things for granted. She and Hillevi (in her 80s) spoke about the hard work of the women in the past who had established the village and made it possible for everyone to live here.

Working life notwithstanding, women's responsibility for children and the home was clear, something that is often associated with the (discourse on) 'traditional woman.' Several pointed out that they were also family women and/or mothers. They said that as women, they always had to choose (or make trade-offs) on living where they wanted to and to work in ways that they would like to,

Kajsa: I have to be available at home. Björn (her husband) works all the time . . . It is quality of life to be able to do this . . . to live like this and have the children grow up here . . . to be close to them during the day.

Yvonne: We moved here after our children were born. . . I don't work outside anymore . . . it is difficult when you have children . . . It is difficult with childcare here.

Alice: I have three girls . . . At the moment I clean in Idre. . .but I would really like to be here and work here . . . I want to cook . . . maybe the school kitchen or something.

Ingrid: I wanted to educate myself as a *syokonsulent* (study advisor) but waited till Olle finished his ninth grade.

Birgitta: People should be able to live on here and have work, especially women . . . because of the children.

On reading their stories, contradictory images abound. There were tensions in how the women regarded their working lives. They were proud of their careers outside but at the same time they wanted to live in, and work in, the village and be close to the children. Some of them believed that they were primarily responsible for childcare. Perceptions of mothers as mainly responsible for children in Sweden was at the same time in tension with ideas about themselves as working women and gender equal. The women in the forum were however insistent on pointing out that motherhood, in comparison to work, was often one of those relationships that was rewarding, where they could be cherished by their children especially in comparison to their work outside.

In Sweden opportunity to work is regarded as a milestone in women's liberation, but many spoke of not being able to do what they wanted, on their terms, feeling trapped in the jobs they had. Some worked within health care that was constantly being reorganized or rationalized. Being and working in the village meant that negotiations over the use of their time was for their own benefit rather than for their employers, that is, they felt that to work in paid jobs was not always worthwhile. They spoke about wanting to leave those jobs, especially as in the health sector, where they claimed they were "used in strange ways during bouts of rationalization." Plans and dreams for the future often involved seeing themselves as entrepreneurs with their own small companies, as farmers in their own right, or as working for the village so that they could be in the village in the daytime. But they were also daunted by the uncertainties of being a woman and starting something new, especially if one were a single mother like Linda,

> "One doesn't leave a permanent job . . . In that way you are stuck. You don't dare to do that."
>
> *Yvonne, agreed in support*, "If one doesn't have permanent employment . . . one is a little scared . . . indecisive . . . don't know what would become of it."

The bureaucracy associated with this was equally daunting. Kerstin who did have permanent employment in a school in the nearby town and wanted to start her own firm said,

> "I was at the employment agency to see if I could get some help to start my project here in the village . . . but then she said to me, 'I could help you if you were unemployed' . . . but as it was now, I had a job so I did not get any help. It is difficult to give up a job and then one doesn't know how things will turn out."

Fragments of discourses on motherhood, and on work, were interwoven in the discussions around these topics as the women struggled to re(articulate) the meanings of experiences which made sense in village life and politics. They did not see their own nurturing and caring roles as mothers or wives as conservative (as they did when they discussed women's past roles). They wanted to build on these visions for freedom over their time and bodies and not having to be in a place they did not like. This is specially so because their involvement in the workforce—that in some respects provided them with economic freedom and an identity—also made them prisoners of a system over which they had little or no control. For example, mobility or the fact that they could move around was a freedom, but also a curse. Their movement to a new place was often pre-empted by the fact that it was difficult to find employment that gave them the freedom to work with what they wanted to do in the place that they were. They moved often because they had to, not necessarily because they wanted to.

THE MYTH OF THE MODERN WOMAN

Discourses on development and being modern were ubiquitous in both places and in very direct ways in Nayagarh with development programs that promised a better and developed countryside. The savings and credit program was accompanied by discourses on women as entrepreneurs and brought prospects of linking up with wider economies and being drawn into the modern world. But in the one place that the women were most successful with their savings, that is, in Manapur, their collective activity was minimal. The women sat in *purdah* in my meeting with them (since the BOJBP secretary who was a village elder had insisted on being present). The women had complained about not having meeting places for larger groups and for having to work individually at home. Being small time entrepreneurs in the home did not necessarily imply an improvement in everyday life as they tried to reconcile contesting discourses on being homemakers and working as small-scale entrepreneurs in a group to increase family incomes.

Despite the presence of women who did work outside the home, especially in the *Dalit* communities, women in Nayagarh appeared to have different pressures, and less anxiety to meet competing norms of working outside the home and being good mothers. The gendered division of labor was clear although in practice the women undertook many 'male' activities. The management of the home however was their responsibility. Mobility was restricted and it was mainly men who travelled in and out of the villages. The women who were educated and worked outside their homes, such as the coordinators of the women's program, had an uphill task but working outside the home was often regarded as an individual choice to which the women had to 'adjust.'

In Nayagarh talk about women's incapacity was often attributed to their illiteracy. Although being educated, one of the signs of being modern (and urban) was something to aspire to, for the women it was also dangerous. One of the women told me proudly how she cycled to work to a neighboring village where she worked as a school teacher. She was supported in this by her husband who also an office bearer within the forest federation. But this independence did not mean an escape from violence at home. As some women in Talapatna pointed out, 'being advanced' had its own dangers. It could lead to accusations of disavowing tradition and of immorality in the face of what was regarded as modern influence.

. . . Remains of the Past: Low Self-esteem

Being incapable recurred in Drevdagen as well, internalized more obliquely in ideas about women as passive and uninterested in village affairs and old-fashioned or traditional, the latter much to the irritation of the older women. The older women who were acknowledged as strong were looked upon as aberrations to the norm. Tradition, in this sense, was considered to be all that was left behind after modernity. References to tradition also help to pacify uncomfortable practices in an otherwise modern world (clear in the next chapter).[7] For the younger women and some men I interviewed (aged up to their 50s), traditions or vestiges of the past made women hesitant to take part in village life and for men to accept it as a matter of course. Women's absence from village association meetings and activities was attributed to women's low self-esteem (*dålig självkänsla*).

This changed over the course of the inquiry and I discuss this later in this chapter. The women spoke about the importance of increasing women's self-esteem, though nobody spoke of themselves as lacking self-esteem and when asked, the term was always used to describe someone else. In the contexts in which I met them in the village, none appeared to be suffering from low self-esteem. And I had interviewed almost all the women in the village. Yet, in conversations, the image of the old fashioned, shy and traditional woman came up. In their discussions, needing to go beyond images of traditional and passive women opened up new spaces for the women in the *kvinnoforum* that they felt they needed to occupy.

The counterpart to this image of the rural woman was the rural man. This was clear as Jan, a man in his 50s who had lived in the village for most of life, put it to Karl, who was a few years younger and who insisted that the women attend the village association's meetings,

> "There would be hell if the women were at the village meetings and food was not on the table when the man got home."

Here it was not merely older men but also rural men that Jan was referring to. Karl had moved to the village from the city and Jan and Sara were trying to explain to him that things were different here. Sara said, "Old habits die hard."

Corresponding to the shy, retiring rural woman was the rural man who expected to be served his dinner on time. Unfortunately, I do not know how the other men in the village would have described themselves or if they would have identified themselves with this description. Although 'such men' were mentioned once more in reference to a discussion about a woman in the village, there were in fact few discussions of men in the family in the forum or otherwise. The focus throughout was on the women when it came to explaining their absence from village activities, or on men in their positions as heads of village associations.

A SAFE SPACE FOR A *SJÄLJAKT*: THE QUESTION OF SPIRITUALITY

Spirituality was a theme that often came up in discussions in Drevdagen although there was also unease about it. Karin and Kajsa pointed out that though some of them might be interested in spirituality, it was a theme that could alienate some others.

> *Karin:* There could develop two groups with differing positions . . . We must make sure not to slip into spirituality. We can meet in a women's forum but not when we meet about spirituality . . .

This decision was prompted by wanting to include other women in the village who had other religious beliefs and would object to the more eclectic style that many of the women in the core group had. Most of the villagers were Protestants and a small but devout group belonged to the Pentecostal church. The women at this meeting wanted all women to feel that they could come to the get-togethers. It was decided against discussing this theme further although in their language spiritual metaphors were not uncommon.[8] Spirituality recurred in the discussions, often in reference to the forests and nature around them. At the time of the annual moose hunt when most of the men were away, Kajsa said laughingly,

> "But we are also on a hunt of sorts, a *själjakt*"

translated literally, as 'soul hunt.' Later, during the process, I accompanied the women on a boat trip to Finland called the 'Harmony Wave' where the theme was spiritual practices. Like Kathleen McPhillips, I believe that "This 'New Age' could be read as a product of consumerist logic, but I also think there is some evidence to indicate there is an authentic and conscious search for new ways of being, new understandings of self" (2002, 188).

For Maria the group enabled her to talk about her work with handicrafts, nature and the spiritual. But as she pointed out, she did not want to be seen as the village idiot. It was within this group that she had felt secure enough to be able to talk about relating to nature differently, of talking to beings in the forests, hugging trees to get energy, of being part of nature and exploring a more sensual approach to nature without being ashamed, "where inhibitions do not have to come in the way." Hers was a different, affective way of relating to nature and being in the world than the one that dominated forest practices, transcending the neat divisions between nature and humans. This way of being however also opened her to ridicule.

Spirituality, and the need to talk about it, was linked to women. There were some men who made references to it in conversations and interviews but they declared they would not admit or be a part of discussions about it in public. Harding writes, "Women and men do not have the same relation to cultural metaphors, models and narratives precisely because these frequently carry sexual and gender meanings" (1998, 99). While this is true, here, it was also a question about it being permissible for men to be seen to have a relationship to a spiritual narrative at all. For both men and women, talking about spirituality associated them with what was considered by most villagers as the dubious 'new age' trend. While it was considered odd for the women to talk about spirituality, for men, in addition, it was considered unmasculine. Interest in spirituality in Sweden is gendered (evident in the almost all female participation in the 'Harmony wave') and a trait associated closely with femininity, not only with women. The stigma of the feminine was associated to whoever chose to pursue it, whether a woman or a man.

Spirituality was more taken for granted in Nayagarh and did not have the subversive feeling that was associated with it in Drevdagen. It was in fact, a way in which many women were drawn into the BOJBP's work by its leaders during its initial days. The BOJBP's recourse to the spiritual and references to nature struck a chord with many women who were often custodians of rituals within their communities.

In Drevdagen, the spiritual although taboo in a hyper secularized society may be seen as an effort to 're-enchant the world.' Talking about their relation to the spiritual felt important for the women perhaps because as McPhillips writes, subjectivities created within modern rationalism do not—or cannot—contain the generation of hope for a new ethical social order (2002, 178). Women's discussions of how the forests were a salve for their souls (see Bergelin, Emretsson, Halvarsson Lundgren and Ryen 2008) provided transgressive spaces in an otherwise rationalized discussion of employment opportunities or the environmental benefits of standing forests and of the close links of scientific forestry to male foresters.

The changing landscape of the forests in Nayagarh through protection reconstituted not only the environment, but also the men and women. The men and women in the forest organizations began to call themselves the new forest castes while the women also spoke of their need for a separate women's federation.

Appeals to modernity and rationalism may appear at odds with spiritual traditions. Although there were tensions, allusions to modernity, allowed the women in Nayagarh to adopt new ways of being, of repudiating dowry and to speak of women's rights. But as I show further, recourse to Hindu morality and responsibility on the other hand also made it possible for them to challenge men's violence and harassment.

MEETING ACROSS DIFFERENCE

Such conditions and relations of place, age, education, motherhood, work and the spiritual were used by the women to define themselves within discourse and they formed their subjectivities. In Nayagarh these were further complicated by relations of caste. While their narratives were embedded in these prior structures, I now shift attention to how they cohered on the basis of these but also met across their differences.

Small, Small Threads Make a Big Piece of Cloth and Small Tools Make a Big Factory

The *samitis* in Nayagarh were normally organized along lines of caste. In a few villages, the women organized themselves further according to age, though this was not something they wanted emphasized. In Abhimanpur (1998), I met several groups together. Some of the women belonged to more than one group. They explained how they had formed their groups,

Manjulata (Lakshmibai Upamandal): We started with 5 women and then came 30. People used to joke about us but now we have 30 members. At that time we had to drag them to the meetings but now we just have to say there is a meeting and everybody turns up. The men used to laugh but now after seeing the work we are doing they encourage us, they even eat themselves . . . look after the children while we have our meetings.

She was interrupted by Kunni, an older woman,

> "Let me tell you . . . first there was one committee, then we formed another one and only *bahus* (daughters-in-law) were members of it. Anita called it the *bahu* committee . . . The last time talk about these things came up was when somebody visited us from outside, I told the others . . . this will go to the foreign country and these people will say . . . look at them . . . they have a separate *bahu-saasu* (daughter-in-law / mothers-in-law) committee, so I told the outsiders that there was nothing of the sort."

I suppose I was doing exactly that, going to a foreign country and writing about the *bahu-saasu* committees. But that makes it all the more important to point out that they seemed to be conscious of wanting to be able to work across the *bahu-saasu* divide. Norms regarding hierarchical family relationships were being put to test by the groups. In their relationships, the *samitis* navigated a heterogeneous terrain. Differences in age were complicated by caste and class differences. The women worked together and younger women had the sanction of the program to leave their homes and come to the meetings and speak out in front of their mothers-in-law. The relationship between the women in the *samitis* and the BOJBP staff was not necessarily an equal one. Most women often referred to Anita, the coordinator as *didi* or older sister. Relationships of hierarchy did not disappear in an idea of equals within the *samitis*. Despite these differences, they were conscious of the strength they derived from the presence of each other's groups. Annapurna, (whom I presumed fit into the *bahu* committee) said,

> "First we had a 30 member committee. We saw it as a good organization, then . . .we started a second, then . . . *ka, kha, ga* (a, b, c). Small, small threads make a big piece of cloth . . . small tools make a big factory . . ."

The notion of 'entrustment' presented by de Lauretis in her reading of an Italian women's writing group is appropriate in this context. Like the women in *Non credere*, the book published by the group, the women in Nayagarh engaged in relationships—not in spite of, but rather because and in full recognition of the disparity that may exist between them in class or social position, age, caste, level of education, professional status or income. This is perhaps as de Lauretis writes, the most controversial aspect of the *Non credere* feminist theory of practice. The recognition of mutual value was made possible by their inscription in a symbolic community, a 'social contract' among women (c.f. 1989a, 22–23). Although not all women were involved in these particular groups, they were here as female-gendered subjects and not neutral equal citizens. The notion of entrustment (with references to the symbolic mother in *Non credere* or as in Nayagarh practice in deference to *didi* and *saasu*) permitted the exchange between women across generations and the sharing of knowledge and desires across differences. In Drevdagen the appeals of wanting to learn from the older women by the younger generation was also a desire for an affinity. But this affinity based partly on difference was more difficult in this formally more egalitarian context. It tempered the ways in which the women spoke about themselves, also making it more important for them to justify the existence of their collective as may be discerned from the following narratives.

Meeting as Women in Drevdagen

The need for a women's forum was justified by some of the women because they claimed that they were different from men. The village association, they felt, did not have place for that difference. Not everyone shared this view,

Sara: We women are different in that way, we are also used to being more nurturing.

Kajsa: Women and men speak different languages. It is nice for women to have their own group so we can talk about what we want.

Sara: Women are different from men. We have different needs. But then different women are different. We want to get to know each other better . . . Socialize despite our differences . . . be diverse and be able to accept it. We want to learn from each other . . . learn from the older women.

In response to Frans who had spoken about the women's projects as impulsive, the women attributed new meaning to the word. In their view, being impulsive meant taking action, getting work done, rather than merely talking about it.

. . . Being Stubborn

The women narrated stories about how they worked hard for their projects to get them going despite all odds. These were stories that most women and men in Drevdagen would recognize, stories about being obstinate and not bowing to authority (as I relate in Chapter 4). Or as Lina told me when talking about the municipality, "if you don't put your foot down, then you are done for? (*säger man inte ifrån då är det kört*)."

When the women told these stories, it was women's agency that was revealed in the stories. Cecilia, for example, had arranged for bank loans and permissions and crossed several economic and bureaucratic hurdles to open the village shop,

> "At every step, there was something or someone telling me it was impossible . . . that you can never get the loan sanctioned, etc. But finally I did manage to do that . . . The man at the *kommun* told me . . . you know the only reason that you have managed to achieve this is because of your months of obstinacy."

The others said the same about their activities like the goat farm, the ski lift in the village, the cow cooperative. The shop did not last very long and the goat farm proved difficult to start. These were problems that willpower alone could not change. Cecilia's perseverance had resulted in the shop finally being opened when she returned to the village in the mid 1990s. However, it was impossible for her to compete with the prices that the big stores were able to offer. Loyalty and village solidarity notwithstanding, the household economy played an important part in villagers' decisions on where to shop. The thrust of measures to promote entrepreneurship in rural areas that forms the basis of much of rural policy these days runs counter to large-scale enterprise and forces that do not favor rural areas. These efforts were small moves upstream in a larger flow in the opposite direction. The odds were stacked against enterprise in these areas.

The women had to relate to a largely masculine world of male foresters and farmers, the municipal authorities and bankers. The physical place was a part of their identities as much as their sex, forming ideas and norms about how the women from the countryside as opposed to urban woman are supposed to behave. However, the rural space also implied that if they did indeed want to get anything done they needed to be stubborn. They spoke of themselves as strong women who were not just passive and who dared to live in these areas and dared to dream. At the same time, there was another side to the matter or, as Karin said in a conversation with me,

> "One cannot be too strong . . . it rubs people off the wrong way . . . the men approach me instead of Sara, if they want something from the association, because they think that Sara has too many of her own views."

Sara, who had become the chairperson of the association, found that there were many small ways of circumventing her authority. But this is a story that I take up in the following chapter.

Regardless of what justification they used, the women were adamant they needed a separate space to be able to acknowledge the differences between women and men (which they sometimes explained in terms of biology and at other times as social differences) and to be free to work in ways, which felt liberating and useful. Then, of course, they pointed out that there were differences among the women also, that depended not merely upon their background or education or village. They acknowledged that not all women wanted to or had a need to meet.

. . . *Not Oppressed*

The initial coming together of the women was perhaps sparked by a sense of the discrimination created by the structures of the village association, but it was not a sense of overt discrimination that kept them together. They were apprehensive of being defined as oppressed. They had the potential to be doubly so. They were women and they were rural. These labels denoted backwardness. As some emphasized, what brought them together was not a problem, it was a vision they wanted to build upon. This was reflected in Ingrid's response to Gunilla, a colleague from the university who had accompanied me to one get-together. In speaking of other groups, Gunilla mentioned that they often got together around a common problem. Ingrid felt that the formation of their group was being seen as a response to 'their problem' of being rural women,

> "For us it is not a problem . . . We need to start with thinking about together what it is that we want to do . . . in the village . . . then, what are the problems in the way . . . what do we have that we can build upon?"

Ingrid's response reflects an apprehension among many of the women to being defined as a problem and oppressed. By resisting being called oppressed they were also denying being slotted into one single conventional category, a passive category.

They preferred to regard instances of what may be discrimination as old habits that needed to be changed among certain men and also women. Speaking about the gossip in the village about a woman who had been active in relation to a number of development activities, Lena said,

> "Often when a woman is able to do something, then they say, 'she has been able to do this . . . the reason she can do all these things is because she has a good husband'."

In other words, women could be as oppressive as men. In discussions that recurred often when we met, the women emphasized the importance of recognizing difference among women in the village and within the forum as well. According to bell hooks in her writing about women's movement in the U.S.,

> ". . . the idea of common oppression was a false and corrupt platform disguising and mystifying the true nature of women's varied and complex social reality . . . This meant that women had to conceive of

> themselves as victims in order to feel that feminist movement was relevant to their lives" (1991, 29–30).

It was demoralizing to bond with other women on the basis of a shared victimization, for one, because not everyone perceived discrimination in the same way or perceived it as discrimination at all. It was a matter also of self-respect. They bonded on the basis of shared strengths and resources. This was important for the politics within the group. There were women who came to the forum who were unemployed, there were some older women whose lives were very different from those who were younger and from those who had moved to the village.

. . . Building on Strength

The women mobilized arguments about gender and sexual difference to build upon what they saw as their inherent strengths as women as well as to justify their separate space. They pointed out how the village needed these qualities to survive, qualities which disappeared when women were not part of village activities,

> *Sara:* Things get done when women are involved . . .Women do things differently . . . We handle things better.
>
> *Kajsa:* We need this to get going[9]. . . things happen when women take charge of things . . . but we need each other also for our own projects . . . for support . . . backing . . . as a sounding board for our ideas. We support each other.

The reference to the 'we' in Kajsa's statement had a double meaning. She was referring to the group of women but she was also referring to the village following on from another conversation earlier. Such statements reflected the women's convictions that Drevdagen's chances to (re)create a living village rested very much with the women, at least as much as it did with the men. As they looked upon it, not only were the women outside of the discussions in the association but that it was detrimental for the entire village that women did not come; important issues vital for the village were not always addressed in their common meetings or not considered relevant. And there were not any other forums for them either.

> *Kerstin:* There are many who do not take part . . . if women were to engage themselves in village activities in their own ways, other issues would come into the open.

The women spoke about women being dynamic, that things happened when they took up something, and that men just got together and talked. They said that it was easier to get going with things if the women had support from one another.

Lena: Women are more nurturing. Power is important for politicians. They work in devious ways . . .withhold information . . . It is important to be open . . . to create the space . . .

Here politics and power are associated with men. Were the women reproducing binaries?[10] I take up this discussion in the section on reproducing the discourse. I have so far focused on women's practices in building up a space for themselves within discourse and language. I now turn to analyze how the women went beyond language to action that brought the groups into being. I begin with the more obviously embodied practices of the women in Nayagarh where they made claims through action. I then go on to analyze the different kind of action that characterized the coming together of the women in Drevdagen. Although innocuous in comparison to the overt action in Nayagarh, it was all the more challenging in the village in the long run.

PART 3: SUBJECTIVITIES IN ACTION AND IN TALK—DEFINING SELVES IN STRUGGLE

While some *mahila samitis* were groups only on paper, others became informal credit centers. Although the women themselves were not consulted when it was decided to begin with the savings and credit groups, in certain villages they became successful as a form of organizing that enabled the women to carry out collective activities. Some went beyond the agenda of the formal program and transformed the collectives into a space from where they could take action for the village and for themselves as 'women.' The *samitis* in different villages had links to each other through the program and were conscious of the strength this provided. Though most of them were active in their own villages where they felt they could make the most difference, the different *samitis* had acted together successfully and recognized the power in that. There was a marked difference when one spoke to the women in the villages where they had carried out activities other than savings and credit, from those that had kept largely within the program. It was evident in their spirit and confidence when they sat together and talked about what they had done and what they planned to do. They challenged how funds were spent and decisions made by the forest organizations.

STORIES FROM NAYAGARH

The following stories are illustrative of the spirit and energy of some of the groups and where the women had created a space for themselves.

The Road to the Village

The story of the road is one that involved several women's groups spread over neighboring villages. The four smaller villages of Talapatna, Abhimanpur, Chaddiapalli and Telapada make up the big village also called Chaddiapalli. Talapatna did not have a road going to it. It is a community of bangle makers and sellers and they had to endure great hardship to go out and sell their wares by passing through cultivated fields that used to clog up with mud in the monsoons. The village could not be reached by bicycle so the men had to leave the bicycles as well as the bangles in other villages in the evenings. It was not just the economic aspect that bothered the women; it was also a question of honor. As Kalpana put it,

> "Not having a road was a great shame for us. Because we didn't have a road, people from other villages said, why should we marry their daughters . . . they don't even have a road."

The problem, they told me, was access to the village was blocked by private land that belonged to five landowners and moneylenders and who refused to cooperate with the villagers. The men had had innumerable meetings about this for the past 15 years without much success. Congress party leaders had promised to help if they came to power but they had no control over private land. The *mahila samiti* felt that this was an important issue that needed to be resolved. It was discussed at the level of the *upamandal* (sub-council) where several women's groups from different villages were involved. They decided to take more drastic action. As the women put it,

> "One day we decided to take the pain . . . we will die one day anyway . . . we decided to lie on the Chaddiapalli road and fast."

It was May 26, 1997, the time of the year when temperatures go up to 45 degrees centigrade and more. Beginning at 4 o'clock one summer morning, the women went and lay down on the main road of an adjoining village and refused to let anyone pass through. There were 42 women from five villages who joined the action. The women in the neighboring villages (who were familiar with Talapatna's problem) heard about what was going on. Many were higher caste women and hesitant, but once they saw that the *Dalit* women had joined the others, they followed almost immediately. It was only the women's group from Telipada that did not take part. In fact, when I spoke to the women of Hariharpur, which lies at a little distance from Talapatna, they were unhappy that they had not been able to help as they heard of the incident only later and would have wanted to join the fasting women.

The men from the villages offered the women a drink of water which they refused as they lay there in the hot summer sun. Finally, three of the landowners agreed to donate their land for the road and the other two agreed to sell their land to the villagers. Once the land was acquired, the women told me that they themselves built the road to the village (though another researcher working there doubted if they really built the road on their own).

When I asked the Talapatna women why their *samiti* had been successful in doing so many things while others were dormant, the women gave varied explanations. One important reason they cited was,

> "We have one caste . . . it is a small village and our men are good . . . that is why. In other villages, the men are afraid that the women will get more advanced than them so they don't help them . . . our men . . . they are proud of their village."

Malathi believed it was because,

> "Telegus are more advanced . . . we are from the Dohra caste."

or

> "we feel good about all this. We have got so much confidence that we can do other things now."

and

> "all the men have respect for us."

Several women agreed that they had 'good' men. For instance they had helped them dig holes to plant saplings, put up a fence around their herb garden and even now they helped them by keeping animals out of it. Neither were they, according to the women, very 'jealous.' Their success, they felt, was a result of the cooperation between the women and men. The explanation based on the perception that their caste was more 'advanced' needs to be qualified. The women who took part during the road incident were actually from several different castes who had met previously in the meetings of the women's groups and had decided on this action. When I met the women from the other villages in Chaddiapalli, I asked them what had made them take part in the cause of the women of Talapatna,

> "It was a problem for the women and the village of Talapatna . . . Besides even others could use the road . . . We had talked about it once at the women's *upamandal* meeting . . . We didn't tell anyone, even the men didn't know about the plan. In fact, the Ratnamala (forest) committee president said . . . why didn't you tell us?"

Also, as another woman explained to me patiently, "what is the point of meeting and having a women's program together if we can't support each other?"

Shaming the Men: Protecting the Forests in Hariharpur

In the village of Hariharpur the women had another story to tell. Political wrangling had made the forest protection committee defunct. Taking advantage of this, people from neighboring villages began looting the forest. Stone-cutters began quarrying in the forest. Since the committee was inactive, the women decided to do something about the situation. They started by taking away the stone-cutters' implements and began protecting the forest by *thengapalli*.[11] The police came and threatened them because they were not letting the men quarry. The women then took the *Tehsildar* (revenue inspector) with them to the District Forest Officer (DFO) to discuss the case and the matter was finally resolved in their favor.

In the meantime, the women had patrolled the forest for 22 days until the men, 'shamed' by their inactivity, agreed to take on their responsibility. After a joint meeting attended by the men and women of Hariharpur to which the officials of the BOJBP and the *Mahasangha* were invited, the men took over the protection of the forest. Although they handed over the responsibility for patrolling the forests to the men, the women still wanted to be a part of the decisions on the forests.

After this incident, the BOJBP helped them to form a *mahila samiti* in the village and become a part of the women's program. The women spoke about wanting to link up with the other *samitis* working in Nayagarh. They asked me if I had heard what the women of Chaddiapalli had been able to do. "What the men can't do, the women can do," they told me with a great deal of satisfaction.

Like some of the other groups they had taken up various issues besides savings and credit, especially those concerning women. One important area of work was to try to put a stop to dowry. They told me with pride that the president of their *samiti*, who had recently got her son married had refused to take any dowry from the girl's family.

The next time I spoke to the women of Hariharpur was a few days after members of the *Mahasangha* had been there to tell them about their new policy where they wanted to have two men and one woman representative from every village in the *Mahasangha*. The women in Hariharpur said that they were confused because more than merely two women wanted to go for the meetings. They needed the support of each other and did not want a representative system. They wanted to attend meetings as part of their group as is also clear from the following story. This is also an issue that I return to in Chapter 8.

Dealing with Violence: Making a Difference in Nayagarh

Several groups addressed questions of male violence against women, issues of dowry and using the English term, what they called 'women's rights.'

Anti-dowry campaigns were an important part of national debates that had been prompted by a spate of murders and suicides of women in relation to dowry. They had gained media attention due to the urban women's rights movement. These reflect national discourses purveyed in part by Anita's university education and contacts to the outside world.

A woman in one village told me,

> "Earlier we didn't do all this . . . no courage . . . the men used to do everything. Because . . . slowly we have been coming out . . . we started resolving our problems ourselves . . ."

Similarly, in the village of Binjhagiri, several women told Manoj Pattanaik in an interview*,

> "No woman is harassed in our village by their family members. If any member opposed participation of the woman in any activity of the women's associations, then all the other members go to the person's house and challenge him."

The women 'named and shamed' the offender by drawing on the moral authority of norms. They drew everyone's attention to the problem, one that most people knew existed, but that was now made public and hence something on which villagers needed to take a stand.

As the stories indicate, a number of groups together challenged local elites like male landowners, while others resisted the oppression of the police when they sought to protect their forests. The groups also became a forum for women to take up domestic disputes. The men who did not let the women in their households attend meetings were 'peacefully' approached by the whole women's group and an appeal was made to let the woman to come to the meeting. This was often effective since the group had the sanction of the village and the BOJBP. The women also pointed out that now if a woman was beaten, the perpetrators knew that it was not only the woman they had to deal with, but the whole women's committee. The BOJBP's references to discourses of Gandhian and Hindu morality played an important part in the women's subjectivities and possibilities of action. These examples show how the women drew on existing social relations, yet produced something new.

A TURN TO ACTION IN DREVDAGEN: THE *KVINNOFORUM*

"Has everyone been invited to this get-together?" read one of the notes scribbled down at a brainstorming exercise at an early gathering in Drevdagen, and this became a signpost for the group. As we continued to meet, a need grew for a *kvinnoforum*, a women's forum, in which all the women in the village would feel welcome.

As they met, the women created an alternative village space where their own ideas came forth. They wanted a forum where women could take up important issues, such as the need to work for community spirit, that did not find a place in the formal village associations but were vital for the functioning of the village. Discussions also focused on how social life in the village for women was disappearing as their jobs outside and everyday work at home claimed all their time.

"It is not about prestige but about developing together and taking the best from each other, to be open and to create space for one another," wrote Sara in the June 2000 village newsletter when she reported on the forum to the rest of the village. At our get-togethers, the women often stressed upon the importance of informality, for the need for an unstructured space for the group. It was a rejection of what they considered to be formal and stilted routines of the village associations that did not have place for their concerns. This 'rejection' was symbolized in the language used and the places where we met. Our get-togethers were never called *möten*, 'meetings' because that was how the village associations referred to their gatherings. Ours were in fact *träffar*, or 'get-togethers' or the '*kvinnoforum*' (implying a collective only when we met), in their language creating a distance from formal village spaces. Informality, felt the women, gave space for unexpected ideas.

A wish for an informal space was a way for the women to be there on their own terms and where regular power relations did not prevail. This did not mean that power was absent but it was to some extent negotiable. Because the group chose to be informal and the women attended only when they could, they did not feel pressured to attend. They arrived and departed at times that suited them. They did not feel tied down by claims of being accountable to or responsible for the existence of 'a group' independent of themselves.

The number of women who met varied and the boundaries of the group were flexible as women came when they could and new women joined in. This way of organizing, however informal, was nonetheless chosen with care. The women reiterated why they needed the forum, not only because there were always new women present, but also because there was no 'one' answer to the question. Women from outside the village got to hear of the *kvinnoforum* and wondered if they could join. Since the aim was to encourage all women, they were welcomed to attend the gatherings by the women in the village.

We used story telling as a method at our get-togethers. In the beginning, many found it hard to talk about themselves. They did not believe they had much to say. "I haven't done anything special" was a regular rejoinder. However, once we started talking, people were pleased to discover that so many others were interested in listening. Fascinating stories of itinerant lives unfolded. Whether they were born in the village or not, everyone had done some travelling. The prevailing Swedish media portrayal of a backward-looking and unchanging countryside certainly did not apply here. The women told stories of struggles and disappointments, of hope and success and their dreams for the future of the village.

> "We must get the countryside to live" commented Yvonne and this came through in many accounts.

The stories brought the collective closer together.

> "Though you think you know one another, you don't usually get to hear these things," said Sara.

It was therapeutic, Cecilia said, to be able to talk about yourself and listen to the others without being embarrassed.

> "It was cozy and nice to meet like this, to hear about the others but also about oneself. You surprise yourself . . . that you are willing to share so much", mused Sara.
>
> Kajsa explained, "It is usually so that you rarely talk about yourself . . . you know . . . you say, why would I? Who would be interested in me?"

To be able to express dreams and emotions, to experience being heard and understood provided an energy that was in many ways the most important outcome of the group. The discussions became a kind of 'active theorizing' about life in the village and put many village and forest activities in context for both me and other participants.

Although every get-together demanded a certain amount of organizing, the *kvinnoforum* did not have a formal structure. It took shape and came alive every time that the women met. The form it took on each occasion could be different depending on who was present. Nevertheless, it held an underlying meaning for the women. Whenever they met, they reaffirmed its' importance in strengthening them in their work and social life. At one get-together, Cecilia traced the group back to the time when she and a few other women were part of drawing up the village agenda,

> "We had a women's group when we wrote in the social issues in the plans for the village (*Detta vill vi med Drevdagen*). That was in a way how some of us started working with these issues."

Earlier they had spoken of themselves as individual women who had helped to broaden the agenda in the association. Now they spoke about themselves as being part of a group. Was Cecilia recovering a past as she traced the history of the women's group back to an earlier point? She was also conscious of building up something new and making a break with the past.

I had started the inquiry with an idealized image of how research and the everyday life of the women would interweave. I imagined that we would discuss village issues and the women's activities and reflect on them within the space of the inquiry. And we did do that, but in a way different from what I had pictured. The women reflected by acting. The focus of the group became, in constant dialogue, to organize a women's forum, and to think about why they felt that they needed this space. From a research (methodological) point of view, it was difficult to reflect on one specific research question. To impose a structure on the forum might have meant that we moved further in analyzing one main issue. However, it would have meant that everyday life and emotions were kept out of the discussions and that new participants were excluded. The inquiry would have become *my* research tool. For the women, widening the circle and creating the forum became the most important activity and, in many ways, the research question that engaged the group.

By taking action, the women understood what they could or could not do. In this sense, action and reflection were indivisible. Forming the group was one way of dealing with unequal gender relations in the village and the inquiry, though not designed as such, became a kind of feminist praxis. The idea that action would take place outside the group and reflection within was a theoretical proposition that was untenable.

Gemenskap: Giving Meaning to the 'Community'

As the Drevdagen women put it, working in the village was not something they were doing only for themselves. Actively choosing to work with uncertain projects in the village instead of in employment outside the village was an expression of a commitment to revive village life, "for the village to be able to survive." These were actions beyond those only for themselves. They linked this commitment to the need for activity in the village. Social activities, but also the everyday independent functioning of the village (for the villagers) was felt to be needed for the village to be a real village and "not" as Elisabeth put it, "just a tourist village." However, working on this agenda was neither easy nor simple.

Gemenskap, came to mean variously a sense of belonging, community spirit and relationships and became the overriding practical concern of the women. In their discussions I detected two different yet linked ways of talking about *gemenskap*—as needing to work for *gemenskap* in the village but through *gemenskap* among the women. Conversations in the forum were felt to be vital for village survival and in many ways a precondition to be able to work. Attempts at integrating projects were an aspect of wanting to work in a different way.

Sara: What I would really like to do . . . to work for *gemenskap* . . . is to write a history of Drevdagen together . . . Organize a play

> around it . . . get to know each other . . . act out our inhibitions . . . We don't have anything in common that . . . to create *gemenskap* . . . so that everyone could participate . . . children . . . the men, the old and the young . . . everyone. When we know each other well, then we can support each other.

Their approach was a desire to work in new ways with village development. They spoke about the importance of an open forum and worked hard to involve all the women who wanted to. They spoke of community relationships as vital for the village and the importance of being able to have fun together as the basis for working together with village issues.

It may seem a contradiction in terms. Why work for *gemenskap* and community relationships for everybody from an all-women's group, not a mixed group? But to be able to work from their forum was important for the women to be able to work at all if they were serious about including as many women as possible.

A SPACE OF THEIR OWN

Through their words and actions, the women built up a notion of a special space for themselves that reflected accountability to one another. A material, physical space was important for this in both places.

The Herb Garden

The village of Talapatna in Nayagarh had a vibrant village *samiti*. It started when the BOJBP helped the women set up an herb garden. The idea was for them to grow trees and shrubs for medicinal purposes. It brought the women together and gave them the confidence of having their own project. The women related how they had set up the garden and looked after it,

Seema: What made you form the group? What were you thinking of?

Savitri: What could we have in our minds? We did household work, then Savita [12] came and called all the women . . . talked to us . . . asked us what we thought about the idea of organizing ourselves . . . First we had self-introductions . . . discussed what we should do since alone one can't do much but together we could do a lot. Then a committee was formed, the *Jyoti Prabha Paribesia Suraksha Vahini* (*Jyoti Prabha Environmental Protection Brigade*).

Anita: They got training in savings and credit.

Kamali: . . . after a while we started saving . . . Re. one. . . . Then Mamata and Anita came. Five or seven of us sat down . . . they gave us saplings to plant.

Prahlad (the BOJBP secretary who had accompanied us to Talapatna on this trip): Did you get plants?

Savitri: No, we got seeds to plant . . . and polythene. We packed them with soil and manure and put them in our backyards and watered them for some time. After some time saplings came out and we fixed a date in *Asada* (in the first month of the monsoons—July) and . . . planted them in the herb garden on the day of the '*vanomahotsav*' (forest festival) . . . So far the BOJBP hasn't done this sort of thing . . . This is voluntary work which we women have started. We also renovated our tank . . . The government was not giving money for the renovation of the tank . . .

Anita: And then I said . . . Can we afford to wait for the government? It is in our own hands.

The women's groups had got help from the men in the village to fence the garden and dig the pits. The garden provided the women with a public geographical space that was their own. I asked the women about their other meeting places, and they spoke about their other social networks—husking rice together, exchanging utensils, but this was different, Sujatha said,

> "Earlier only the men resolved conflicts . . . even those concerning women in the families . . . but now we come to the trees and discuss."

Making Space for a House of Dreams

The third joint gathering of the *kvinnoforum* (that I was unable to attend, having fallen sick just before) was held in the building that housed the old shop in the village. It had been lying empty since Cecilia had been forced to close it down because of financial difficulties. The women decided to give it a new name instead of calling it the 'old shop.' They told me at the following meeting,

Ellenor: We renamed it the 'house of dreams' . . . where we are going to make our dreams come true, both old ones gathering dust and new dreams.

The forum was a space that the women wanted, as they expressed, "to feel safe and to be able to be creative" and to bring forward their hidden talents. It was a space where for the moment at least the women did not have to conform to any special procedures. They designed it as they willed and came if they wanted to and could take up questions not permissible in other forms of association. The other women in the group were surprised to hear each other's stories and wondered why they had not heard them before,

Kajsa: One rarely talks of oneself . . . it is usually work, the children . . . Why is that? One thinks, 'who would be interested in me?' We don't have such dangerous secrets . . . We are not so open . . . we shouldn't be afraid to make a fool of oneself.

By giving a new name to a deserted building, the women tried to revive a physical place, much like the herb garden in Nayagarh. It was also the place for making dreams come true and bringing in their soul and spirit in their work.

Constructions of gender were embedded in the physical landscape. The herb garden in the village of Talapatna was one of the few villages where we walked around and I sat and talked with a group of women *outdoors*. Normally, the women refused to meet outside in full view, wanting to sit inside or at least under a covered verandah, unless the purpose of the activity was related to a household or village chore. On a cold day in the village of Manapur, the women insisted on having their meeting in a cold and dark windowless room instead of in the warm sunshine outside. The BOJBP secretary, who accompanied me to Manapur was firm about that and told me that it was inappropriate for women to gather in a public place. However, in the herb garden in Talapatna, it did not seem to matter as it was the women's space, although public. The importance of a physical meeting place for women was evident when compared to the women in Manapur. The Manapur women's groups complained that they were unable to meet as a large group because they had no place big enough to meet and had to do their group work of packing and cleaning the snacks and mixtures, in their own homes. Strangely, although not restricted by social norms in the same way as the women in Nayagarh, the naming of a space (the house of dreams) by the women in Drevdagen, if only for themselves, and the resistance to it (detailed in the next chapter) makes clear how so called neutral spaces were gendered constructions.

The affinity among the women did not imply that the processes did not have its discontinuities and undercurrents that were brought in from the broader village context. An increasing congruence of views and amicability over the course of a process does not obscure the prevailing power relationships or other differences among participants. Especially in Drevdagen, there was also discomfort in not knowing if this was the right way to act and that it was unusual. Although for the most part, the women chose not to take up these questions of discomfort, tension and power that their get-togethers occasioned in the village, feelings of ambivalence characterized their togetherness.

AMBIVALENCE

In Nayagarh, the formal structure of the *samitis* did not inspire the kind of soul searching that the women in Drevdagen did. Nevertheless, participating in action outside of the activities designated as income generation were not devoid of dangers for them as individuals. Retribution could come from within their own families. A story often told by the *Mahasangha* staff was about a president of one of the *mahila samitis* who had gained in prestige in the village due to her work against dowry. However this prestige resulted in violence and eviction from her own home by her husband who felt she was putting on too many airs. Women meeting in public spaces, eating together outside of each other's homes was not the norm in Nayagarh. Yet, because these activities took place in the aegis of a development project, the women managed to tread a fine line between activities that in fact challenged the norms but within a frame that was sanctioned in the villages.

In Drevdagen, there were recurring discussions about why they wanted a women's forum. The women's reiteration of why they needed a forum conveyed a sense of discomfort at having a forum at all and thus the need to keep reinforcing why indeed they wanted it. For the most part this was because new women joined in who needed to be introduced to the history of the group but this did not seem to be the only reason. Although there were other all women's groups in the village such as the sewing bee, the forum was seen as offering a different kind of space.

Ambivalence *vis-à-vis* the forum among many women was evident in the efforts to involve the village men in the early meetings. In fact, at the first two meetings, the question of whether and how they should involve men and the things that might interest them enough to come to the get-togethers cropped up now and then. Britta had suggested at an initial meeting,

> "Maybe we could organize a get-together in our group on a Saturday and play bingo-lotto together.[13] The men like doing that . . . we could all do it together . . . that might get them to come."

However, nothing was done about that. Interestingly, many women pointed out that the men would not be likely to come to a women's get-together. I tried to ask why but never got a satisfactory answer, other than they would not come to a *kärring träff* (a hags meet). This was confirmed by Karl in a conversation in Sara's kitchen in October 1999,

> ". . . if you were to invite the men and have meetings together, the *gubbar* would not come."

As I understand it, they would not come if it was a women's collective that organized a meeting on village affairs. On the other hand if it was an *advents marknad* (advent market) or a party, it would be alright.

PART IV: REPRODUCING THE DISCOURSE OR INTERRUPTING THE NORMAL?

Drawing on past understandings of themselves as women, rural, mothers or nurturing as well as acting on them in the village, the women used language to articulate into being a *kvinnoforum* for the times that they met.

If one were to follow Michel Foucault and Judith Butler who contend that subjects are made in discourse, one can say that the *kvinnoforum* could not fully stand apart from or help being conditioned by prevailing norms. Were the women a part of reproducing the norms in the village that played an important part in shaping gender and power relations? In many ways the language they used while working with village issues reflected this. But how well did these processes conform to the actions they took? What about the discrepancies in their language itself and their sometimes, what may be considered as radical questioning of the norms, that existed side by side, with (what may be seen as) attempts at normalizing the situation? By looking at the issues they took up and how they spoke about them—of needing to take responsibility, their use of an essentialist discourse, the need for informality and their role as guarantors of the social—I analyze these contradictory aspects. I do so by examining their language, their changing subjectivities and the challenges they posed to established norms.

NEOLIBERAL STRAINS?

The women's stubbornness in wanting to keep the village shop, start small-scale enterprise in Drevdagen or appeals to carry out income generation activities in Nayagarh, resonated with current neoliberal ideas, with "ambitions of modernity (that) require human subjects capable of picking themselves up by their own bootstraps and making something of life, with no rationale beyond the market-driven imperatives of constructing, shaping, defining, transforming" (Elliot 2002, 13). Anita's rhetorical question in Nayagarh, "can we afford to wait for the government to renovate the water tank?" and her own answer "no, it is in our own hands" reflects this acceptance. Individualized qualities such as being stubborn and 'training' whether in self-esteem or income generation activities, provided a path away from tradition with a promise of future certainty. The rationale that enterprise and income generation would automatically solve gender inequalities remains however a promise and "a certainty always tantalizingly out of reach" (ibid.).

Women were implicit in these discourses, but not necessarily passive or oblivious of its consequences. Savitri's reply to me in Talapatna when I asked her why they formed their group, "what could *we* have in our minds," reflected commonplace discourses on rural women as illiterate and not particularly capable. But their own experiences did not always correspond to these discourses. These very women also went on to point out that they did what the men had not been able to do for years. There was a disjuncture in a Sweden that had changed. The women in the countryside happen to be better educated and support families with work from outside. They have a status outside of their villages that sometimes corresponds poorly with their social status in the village or even in the family, contributing to tensions. For example this was clear in Kerstin's frustration (previous chapter) of how her role in municipal politics was not recognized in the village and in Nayagarh in the reprisals faced by the president of a *samiti*. The abiding theme of power is present in the ways subject positions were made. *But the women's material practices also structured their thought* as they re-imagined spaces for themselves that went beyond the village associations and activities beyond those of micro-credit program prescriptions. In the following sections I will examine how through their language and action, the women sought to affirm their strengths and position themselves as *active subjects, not passive objects of development*. As the women in one *samiti* remarked at a meeting, "we are doing development but nobody recognized us."

WOMEN ESSENTIALLY?

The actions taken in the process of forming the *kvinnoforum* in Drevdagen and the language used in the discussions and conversations offer conflicting accounts of how the group negotiated its identity as a women's group. By taking on norms that are normally associated with the feminine and with women, they may be seen to be inscribing themselves in dominant values. They often justified themselves in ways that are considered 'essential' in much feminist theory, claiming that men and women were different and bound to act in different ways. Feminists have pointed to problems in such an approach. Such a stance locks women into a uni-dimensional category determined by their sex. One objection has been to point to the differences among women and among men and look at commonalities that can be found across groups of men and women.

Schooled in these debates, I often found myself disagreeing with the women in the group about these differences. I pointed to how we were perhaps not so different from men, that there were more differences among us. But as I saw later, that was not the point. Their emphasis on the affirmation of women's qualities did much to counter the image of the rural, retiring and backward woman that they sometimes relegated to the past. At other times they also spoke of strong women from the past to justify themselves. It was on the basis of their strengths that they found affinity with each other. They stressed that women are active, sociable, nurturing, using these statements to create space to work in ways that felt comfortable and to justify their choices for acting in new ways. Like Biddy Martin, "we cannot afford to refuse to take a political stance 'which pins us to our sex' for an abstract theoretical construct" (cited in Bacchi 1996, 140).

Spivak notes that we may have to differentiate between the category of political mobilization and an analytical category and that essentialism may not be rhetorically right but it is strategic (1990). Carol Bacchi puts it in another way. According to her, it is the acknowledgement of the political character of categories like 'women' that takes the sting out of accusations about essentialism. She writes that such categories seem essentialist only because those campaigning on their behalf have felt impelled to define their groups and that makes them appear essentialist. They have been impelled to do this because they are positioned as outgroups, inhabiting the borderlands of power and influence. "Hence appeals to 'women' . . . are practical and strategic, not ontological. There are no similar debates about the ontological status and content of 'men' because men have seldom been asked to justify their privilege" (1996, 11).

Taking a cue from Bacchi, I focus my analysis from talking about who 'women' are or are not or what they are like, to the practices that made this question *appear* to be one we needed to answer. The answers to this lay in the context that they (we) found them(our)selves. I believe that (for the women) the question of women's special qualities was more than a question of it being a strategy and a belief in difference in nature between men and women. It was a question of solidarity and of affirming themselves. It was also, in the case of the women in Nayagarh, a 'politics of the possible.' In Drevdagen, the women's claim to legitimacy depended upon community attitudes (of which they too were a part) that positioned women as different, as unwilling to get involved in associations while at the same time there was a strong notion of everyone (men and women) being the same (I discuss these contradictions in Chapters 6 and 7). The women in the forum took places in a gender order that framed them as different from 'men' but then used their relationships and friendships in the forum, in part, to construct themselves as diverse 'women' with diverse meanings. This women-centeredness was tenuous and context bound but it gave them strength. The women played a part in upholding the norms that they were challenging. Their subjectivities were mutually constitutive of the discourses around them.

CHANGING SUBJECTIVITIES

Self-Esteem

The women's stories may be examined for the "ways they are produced, the ways they are read, the work they perform in the wider social order, how they change, and their role in the political process" (Plummer 1995, 19). Working for women's self-esteem was one of the themes that the women defined in the beginning as an issue to work with within the inquiry. It was well known that it was difficult to get women to gather for meetings and get-togethers. That self-esteem was an important area to work on was confirmed by the women's encounters with individuals outside the village. In my early efforts to be useful, I had given the women the names of women's resource centers in their area they could turn to for help when working with development activities. When Sara contacted a woman who had worked with other rural women's networks for advice, one of the first activities she suggested was a training course to increase women's self-confidence. Her suggestion of such a course in Sveg was received with little interest in the group.

The topic was dropped quite quickly after that meeting. On looking at my notes from the meetings, I saw how the emphasis on self-esteem changed over the course of the inquiry. Sam Paldanius writes that the relation between confidence (*självförtroende*) and self-esteem (*självkänsla*—what the women often cited) may be understood as that people start out from their actions. The worth those actions are given is important to achieve a feeling of self-esteem. An example is that someone who carries out legitimate and positive actions is rewarded by the existing system of norms and so achieves confidence. When there is confidence in actions, it may be possible to speak of good self-esteem (2000, 153). Paradoxically, then, to attend a course on confidence-building would suggest an identity of little worth. What the women were seeking was a re-valuation of the worth they recognized in themselves and in each other. This was in fact also clear in Nayagarh as the women strove to show how they too were doing important work for the village, that was not recognized (see Chapter 8).

Although most of the women had lived in the same village and many had done so for years, the stories that the women related about their lives were seen anew. In each other's stories, they recognized incidents in their own lives, which they had attributed to personal shortcomings. To see that others seemed to have similar experiences provided the "possibility of interpreting difficulties, problems and inadequacies not as the effect of individual, personal failings, but as the result of socially produced structures" (Weedon 1997, 81–82 in Treleaven, 1998, 132). This had political implications. An initial desire to increase self-esteem in order to be able to participate in public spaces in the village changed during the course of the inquiry to focus on wanting a separate space for themselves, because entering in to the existing structures did not always change their situation very much (see Chapter 6). From looking at women's individual failings, they turned to find collective solutions that were beyond one individual. Being in the group helped to locate wrongs in social relations rather than in interpersonal psychology.

Disturbing Heterosexuality

Ellenor had moved to the village recently with her husband and small children. They had many ideas of what they were going to do and plans for setting up tourist activities. She hastened to point out,

Ellenor: I cannot do it without my husband.

Kajsa: Of course we do things together, we depend on each other. Besides which, even though I am working on it, it is both our project in a way. I need my husband to be able to work with my project.

Sara: It doesn't always have to be like that. I know of a woman in Jämtland who set up a whole farm all by herself. It is possible.

Doubts about the forum among some women in initial meetings reflected an apprehension at the radicalism of some of the others. There was a sense that being part of the group meant that they were putting the men down, that women were somehow positioned against men, that it challenged the normal. It offered a challenge to the gender *status quo* in the village, which not all women were sure they wanted to take up. These doubts often surfaced in statements that stressed how they were not trying to take all the credit or the control, "Of course, we depend on each other."

The women called attention to how men and women were dependent on each other, to how it would be impossible for them to carry out their projects on their own, especially with small children whose main responsibility rested with them. For the women, the need for inter-dependency and ingrained notions of the nuclear family and sex and gender roles were in part disturbed by conversations about taking control of their lives in the village and for the village.

A discussion of this lingering sense of discomfort was never taken up in the group. But conversations among some women, especially in the initial phase, indicated an underlying assumption that forming such a group might be seen to challenge the notion of men and women working together.[14] An intimacy or friendship between the women at the village level was uncomfortable since it was unusual in this form. Over the past 20 years, work on gender by rural scientists in Europe has drawn attention to the importance of the nuclear family and to the acceptance of stereotypical gender roles within both the rural household and rural economy (Little 2003). The organizing of relationships according to heterosexual nuclear family norms is strong is Sweden despite the increasingly wide range of family configurations in practice. In some ways the *kvinnoforum* was destabilizing for the ". . .nuclear family as the dominant. . .model of social and community organization in rural areas" (ibid., 401). However, research also indicates that changes in patterns of intimacy are impacting upon the wider organization of sexuality (Roseneil 2000). So although there is one overarching discourse, there are also others, as is clear from Sara's interjection towards the end of the exchange.

By suggesting that it was possible for women to act on their own, Sara was complicating the narrative. By drawing on other situations and narratives, she was providing alternatives to the repeatable, identifiable ways of talking and describing lives and projects. In this particular instance she was drawing on another, perhaps a 'reverse discourse' (c.f. Foucault 1990) to provide other meanings to their experiences. This added to the ambivalent nature of the forum and created tensions that were productive of change.

A Diffuse Identity (Discovering the Same Difference)

The coming into being of a *kvinnoforum* did not really take us by surprise (when I think about it in retrospect). Neither was it something that had been planned in advance. The initial hesitation in having a women's only group remained as an undercurrent in the forum even as it grew. Paradoxically, it was also its strength. As the group grew and changed and new women came in, it became important to explain, discuss and keep alive the discussion of why a women's group was needed. Opposition caused ambivalence but it also helped in the process of generating a collective identity.

The very idea of the *kvinnoforum* was thus the result of a changing subjectivity. From thinking of ways of trying to include men in the group to articulating a need for a *kvinnoforum*, was a change. However, including men was not an option as some men themselves made clear. Within language, the women tried to build up a space for women, a space which they felt was lacking in village life. It became important to stress that women were different and that 'men and women speak different languages.' It was perhaps the experience of a shared language among them but also the apprehension, within the forum, of a gendered subjectivity, that gave new meaning to certain parts of their (our) lives in the village and beyond.

Parallel to this was a change in my ideas about *collaboration* for local management. It was clear that the men in the village association and at SLU, as well as myself and the women in the forum believed in the need to collaborate and work together. I learnt from our time together in the inquiry that the idea of collaboration hides within it relationships of power and says nothing about how men and women are supposed to collaborate or complement each other (see next chapter). The need for a women's forum and the discussions about it, as well as the reactions from the village association, made it clear that complementarity and collaboration in local development were value laden terms and norms that needed to be negotiated. Patricia O'Connor writes,

> "The very existence of friendship between women sits somewhat uneasily in capitalist patriarchal societies where the 'reality' is the pursuit of power and profit in the public area and the existence of a heterosexual family based unit in the private area." (O'Connor 1998, 131)

If this is indeed the case, seen in a larger societal perspective the women were challenging dominant ways of organizing in both spheres. They spoke of co-operatives and of co-operation for work in the village and yet they wanted a women's forum. Organizing in the way they did, gave them energy, but its nonconformity also made the *kvinnoforum* fragile.

SOLIDARITY

The women focused on what brought them together—the need for company and *gemenskap*, wanting to work together for the village and themselves, of their being in a different situation because they were women. By highlighting what they believed were feminine qualities, they were reclaiming the worth of experiences handed down from history and perhaps taking some parts of their 'life as the starting point' (c.f. Mies 1991, 66). They spoke about how 'things are different now,' 'we are career women,' making discursive interventions in how they regarded themselves and in their language made a conscious break with a (imagined?) past.

They did not discuss having an unequal position that disadvantaged them, when they were in the large group. When they did speak about discrimination in interviews, it was often directed at specific men who could exercise agency as they wanted or more general references to how they had a more difficult time in getting money to finance their projects. The problems that some of the women had spoken about in the interviews, that is, male domination in the village associations were not discussed in the larger circle (although this changed towards the end when one of the women brought up this matter in public, after my inquiry with the *kvinnoforum* had ended). This was a group of women in a village where many of the inhabitants were related to each other or had lived together for many years; taking up such questions in public was far from easy.

The strength of the group came from its being open—by the fact that most women in the village had passed by it at least once. It was inclusive but also ambiguous. It was open enough for women to define their own reasons for being there and to work in the way they chose to (or rather they chose not to) be defined. They built up an identity on the basis of strength and self-respect and not as I write earlier on oppression. By expansion and inclusion, they recognized and bridged differences among themselves. Their appeal lay in fact in that they did not adopt what might be seen as a radical stance as a group in terms of challenging unequal gender relations. The collective included women who wanted to preserve their way of life in the village, to protect the place and its gendered norms. Seemingly contradictory, these women's presence helped to give the forum its' strength. Differences among the women, in opinions and ways of action, were accommodated as the forum provided a space for them. It made the forum more tolerant to difference. The women did not claim to speak on behalf of the other women in the village nor indeed of the collective. However, there was at least one occasion where critique of some of the men in the association by one woman in public was seen as being possible because of her belonging to the forum. Many women in the forum would have perhaps themselves baulked at taking such a stand. Women's activism within the group was heterogeneous and complex, both individual and collective.[15]

INFORMALITY AND GUARANTORS OF THE SOCIAL

The women's insistence on an open forum and inclusive meetings appears to conform to research in Sweden and in other parts of Europe, where rural women's activities lean towards a preference for the informal and overtly apolitical. This corresponds to the fact that formal institutions have little place for their concerns and tend to disadvantage women. Due to their informality rural women's groups are not considered to be political pressure groups nor to have any specific interests.

Within the forum, the women chose to take up a myriad of activities. Many had to do with organizing social occasions for the village. These included small, everyday activities necessary to maintain community relationships. They often spoke of how other questions came up when women involved themselves in village affairs and that women often worked with 'social issues.' They contrasted this approach to the dry and boring meetings of the village association where there was more talk and little action. The emphasis on the social was also noticed by the men in the association. Karl told me about the time that the association drew up a development agenda for the village. He spoke about how they had spent several meetings in discussing various issues but not made much progress. It was only when some women joined the association and took over the writing up of the agenda that the social issues were raised. A document was put together to take to the authorities and then things began moving.

The discourse of the feminine epitomized by informality, maintaining social relationships, doing the groundwork, might seem to be cemented in contrast to the formal, the official and the masculine. While it brought to light the work that the women did, this division of work was also problematic. The exclusion of the women in the work for the forests was justified by the men in the association by women's lack of interest in the forests and their preoccupation with the 'social.' It was expected that women would maintain social relations in the village as appears to be the case in rural areas elsewhere (see Little 2002). In a case study of a Swedish workplace Eva Magnusson (1997) writes about office assistants, who by conforming to expectations to maintain a cheerful atmosphere, became complicit in reproducing their own subordination. But in Drevdagen, it could be said that the women were also exercising agency and mobilized other villagers for what they wanted done. They also made a difference to the physical environment, for example by developing the ski slope.

By emphasizing informality within their group and the importance of different ways of working, the women were changing the forms in which meeting places were organized in the village. The informality of their own meeting places enabled them to meet on terms decided by them, to decide if they wanted to come at all and what they wanted to talk about could vary from time to time or they could just choose to socialize. These challenged the ways in which village activity was ordinarily organized.

On the one hand, the informal spaces made it possible to act in new ways. On the other as research has shown, it is often only when a system is formalized, that women have been able to enter into public areas since it is the informal networks that work to keep them outside (Reskin and McBrier 2000). As I show in Chapter 7, it was the formality of rules that provided an opening for the women in Nayagarh to put forward their claims and in Chapter 8, I discuss the tensions in acting from different spaces.

No Single Activity

The collectives both in Nayagarh and Drevdagen were organized around a range of issues. In Nayagarh much of the official business was recorded in minutes from meetings but these spaces also served as an important semi-formal discussion forum. The women often took up this space to discuss what was important just then. It was when they took up activities outside of these boundaries that it began to cause unease among the men in the forest organizations.

In Drevdagen, discussions did not center on any one issue and various questions wove in and out of each other. The coming of new people to the gatherings made it necessary to repeat what the women wanted from the group and the needs that the newcomers had. The efforts of the group also became more action oriented in order to try and create a forum open to all women who wanted to come. That the women's activities could not be predicted or known in advance contributed to making it uncomfortable and controversial. These aspects made the *kvinnoforum* different from other conventional forms of meeting. The women's argument, that they needed their own group was not new (there were already sewing bees, aerobics groups with only women), but the reasons for the *kvinnoforum* were new. It was not to sew or only to plan the Christmas fair. They were meeting because they were 'women' by occupation, by bodies, not for example because they were people who wanted to sew. The men in the village association felt that they had no idea of what the women in the forum were doing (as I go on to show in the next chapter)—the women did not specify what they were doing in ways in which group activity was normally understood or justified.

When Talking becomes Dangerous

The ambivalence towards a *kvinnoforum* challenged assumptions of the 'naturalness' of gathering as women. If it was indeed so natural for them to meet as women, would it have been so difficult and necessary to justify it all the time? Yet it seemed that they had enough in common to come together and seek each other's support. They were aware of the disapproval of some others in the village but also of the strength they got from each other. When we spoke about why the existence of the group felt uncomfortable to some men in the village who had been critical of the get-togethers, or what had begun to be known as the 'women's group,' Anita said,

> "Women are used to men getting together and talking . . . but women . . . it becomes creepy (*läskigt*) when women become strong."

Kajsa agreed,

> "It becomes dangerous when one talks too much."

The formation of the forum had been questioned by others in the village association. By putting together a women's-only group, they were presumed to be making themselves out to be different, and to have withdrawn from 'common spaces' that mattered in the village. Yet, in practice, many women had become much more active in the village association as compared to the past.

As Sara's intervention shows (in a previous section on pg 141), the impetus for change is already in the discursive. It is perhaps therefore that it is the 'talking' that is dangerous. Furthermore, the *kvinnoforum* went against the idea of how village gender relations were supposed to be organized, surfacing a fear of the women 'trying to be too important' even though the women themselves were not questioning their interdependence with the men in the village. In fact they often emphasized the mutual dependence of men and women. They were apprehensive not so much of undermining mutual dependence with men but because they knew that they were perceived as doing so by the men in the association. One reason the association was uneasy about the forum was because it was difficult to define what it was that made the collective come alive.

The women in Drevdagen were disturbing the norms of gathering places-being only one sex (or rather only female since many neutral spaces were in effect mainly male).[16] They had no clearly defined activity, though they were convinced that meeting each other and talking was in itself an action that would lead to the benefit of women and the rest of the village. In contrast, in Nayagarh, single sex gatherings were the norm rather than an aberration. But here, the women who took on activities outside the program became disturbing for the village and forest committees. In both places the women had appropriated an in-between space that straddled the public and the private and that was hard to define. They sought to retain a shifting boundary between the permissible and the not permissible, both in their relations with the village and within the group itself.

REACHING OUT TO THE VILLAGE AND BEYOND

The inquiry had multiple results for the women in Drevdagen and for me. Several women became active in the village association. Some found it easier to engage in its work when they saw other women taking part. Sara became the chairwoman of the village association. She and a few other women worked hard to ensure that the association involved more women in its activities and in the forest project.

A few women from Drevdagen and nearby villages also attended the 'rural parliament' in 1999 and other such gatherings.[17] When she returned, Lena shared the following comment with us at an inquiry meeting,

> "One realizes that even small people like us, can raise our voices, we can affect rural development in Sweden."

And then Sara added,

> "It feels that things are happening now, this with the rural areas (*landsbygden*) and the *glesbygd*. That is what gives you an injection. It strengthens confidence for us women when you see that what you are doing isn't so crazy."

She was struck by the atmosphere at the parliament where all the different groups wanted to revitalize the countryside,

> "It struck me then . . . there were different problems that people worked with in different villages. . .Villages have found twin areas (*vänort*) and are collaborating around a number of questions . . . doing good work . . . trying to find something . . . and then I think . . . of the authorities . . . why not give people the trust?"

The fact that the women met and discussed these issues and that they needed their own forum to do so was disturbing to the village association. Their doing of *gemenskap*, of 'support' was at the same time a 'doing of gender.' The group came more into the public eye in the village perhaps because I was there as a researcher and because what was said was put on paper. In village public life, they thus came to acquire interests and values as women, contrary to 'the tendency among women not to think of themselves as women in the public arena or as having values and interests other than those deriving from their connections with men' (O'Connor 1998, 121). As the women, especially those most active in the *kvinnoforum*, worked to create a space for the women in the village and extend the participatory space, they may be seen to be exercising power generatively. This process was clearer to see in Nayagarh.

SPILLING OUT OF THE FRAME

The *samitis* began to question decisions regarding the funds spent on them. According to women, they had no idea about how the funds that the BOJBP got for them from Oxfam were being used. The group in Chaddiapalli said that a number of women were taken to Andhra Pradesh for a couple of days and they did not have to spend a paisa. One woman asked rhetorically,

> "What is the BOJBP money used for? Where is the money that we have been waiting for the latrines or sewing machines, saplings for an herb garden? There is money to go to Tirupati, Puttaparti and Gadpa . . . but no money when it is needed. We never get information beforehand . . . staff members come and spend money and we never know what is happening. The women's groups are never consulted when it comes to planning the programs."

Some of the groups began to demand that they be accepted in the forest committees in their village. Reporting from a youth workshop, Mamata Tiwari, a field organizer wrote in her report,

> "women should not only conduct environmental protection work, they should protect themselves build awareness in the society."

She placed this responsibility on both men and women, as she writes,

> "Women atrocities have been on the rise because of the dowry system. What role does a male have in putting a stop to all this?"

The Oxfam officer responsible for the program told me in an interview much later (2004),

> "Some of the women's groups eventually decided to stop with the savings and credit and continued to meet as a women's group . . . and then in Chaddiapalli itself, they demanded that we should be part of the village committee. At least secretary . . ."

The women were taking the groups far beyond that of savings and credit or environmental protection. They were also speaking of linking up in a wider network, much like the forest federation. These changes were not welcome everywhere and the idea of a women's federation became cause for unease.

A Federation of Their Own

The *samitis* spoke about forming an all-women's federation for women's rights because they felt that their issues would not be taken up in the forest federation. They could not wait for them to be considered important enough by the men in the *Mahasangha*, to be acted upon. These issues included violence against women, "demand" (dowry) problems, problems that women faced in the *panchayat*. Anita said,

> "We do not want to go the court and have long drawn out cases but want to be able to solve our problems ourselves."

Women from a number of villages attended mass meetings where they had been discussing the idea of a women's *Mahasangha*. They had also organized rallies and conducted meetings with other committees. At that time (1998/9), they had village *samitis* and four zonal *samitis* consisting of 20–25 village *samitis*. The possibility of forming a women's *Mahasangha* depended on how everything progressed. All the *samitis* put together comprised approximately 5000 women,

> "At the moment we lack funds or organizers. Eventually we may even link up at the state level. We have only a token presence in politics (*panchayat*). We want to be a part of law-making. Even in the BOJBP or the *Mahasangha*, we have no place in the decision-making. They just want to make us 'statues' and not really involve us in meetings."

In 2000, Anita and the field organizers of the program organized what they hoped was the first of several big meetings of the women's federation. All the women's groups met to draw out a strategy for their continued work. There were some aspects that had become quite clear. They wanted to form a women's *mahasangha*. The meeting was supported by Oxfam. However, the *samitis* were already becoming a point of contention between the BOJBP, Oxfam and the *Mahasangha* and the meeting became a catalyst for a crisis that overtook the *samitis*. Tensions rose when they began to take up questions of violence and dowry and to speak of the need for a women's federation parallel to the men's committees. The *samitis* and especially the staff of the women's program active in coordinating the groups began to meet with resistance from the men in the forest organizations.

As the women met and spoke about their experiences of living in the villages, looking for work and managing families and for the women in Drevdagen, also working outside and travelling, they were building on their experiences and using them constructively. They did so not to step out of their relationships with each other and with the village but to transform them. They were constituted through relationships of power and discourse but were also self-constituting. They recognized that the village and forest organizations were constructed as masculine and it was difficult for them to be a part of these activities. While they made an effort to become involved in them, more importantly they also questioned how village development and forest governance was being defined.

By stressing the need to have their own space the collectives were "productive of new configurations of social relations rather than reproductive of the behaviors that instill dominant values in us" (Lather 1991, 96). Though not all actions were seamless or non-contradictory, the very act of forming the *kvinnoforum* and dreams for a women's federation were an "intervention in dominant practice" (Haug 1999). It interrupted the normal although in neither place had the women challenged the men overtly as a group. The rupture took place in a dialogic context amongst them, in language but also in the actions they took.

CONCLUSION

While discourses on modernity and development promise a future, what the women created in the *kvinnoforum* and the *mahila samitis* was the here and now. Discursively, they reimagined qualities such as being social, nurturing or impulsive that were otherwise seen as producing their inadequacy. The production of reverse or counter hegemonic discourses is necessary but not sufficient. "What is therefore needed is something that works, additionally, at the level of affect" (Couze 2002). The 'social' space that the women created in their groups, a space that several in Drevdagen had lamented had disappeared, and one where being together went beyond making snacks for income generation in Nayagarh, provided for the women, the springboard for change. With a base in affect and anchored in their enviroments, the women created an intersubjective space for an alternative politics and for new ways of being.

The women's theorizing and practices around organizing themselves illustrate how their subjectivities were fabricated through relationships of power in which they found themselves (c.f. Foucault 1991). But they also illustrate how subjectivities can effectuate and promote social and political change by putting new alternative forms of sociability in motion, construct new materialities (for example by naming a physical place or constructing a garden), how subjectivities materialize in new relations of intimacy and finally how subjectivities contribute to the emergence of new political engagements and collectivities.[18] Importantly this illustrates how power can be both generative and non-coercive and not only subordinating. By collective action in both public spaces and public-private spaces the women had created, they were able to interrupt certain norms and transcend their ascribed status in the public space. This interruption or rupture was enabled by the dialogic context and the creation of an alternative space that made this possible. It was the same language and yet a 'new poetics' and new ways of being in the world.

After Sasha Roseneil I believe that giving analytic time and space to counter normative practices—at the same time as casting an old-fashioned critical lens on normativities and dominant practices and discourses—is vital to opening up the possibilities of alternative futures. But this opening up also requires acknowledgement of the suffering and oppressions, the troubles, and pains which coexist with, are part and parcel of, these counter-normative practices and new ways of living (2011, 130) and it is to these that I turn in the next chapter.

6 Micropolitics of Rural Development and Environmental Governance

Resistance, Maintenance and Outside Intervention

When gender is not specifically mentioned, processes and events are considered gender neutral. This is true of rural development and environmental governance that in its terminology of the 'local' and 'people' conceal gendered differences in power. The village association in Drevdagen, and the BOJBP or the *Mahasangha* in Nayagarh, had visions of a different countryside which they were active in constructing. In the vision lay greater rights and responsibilities with the people and the community. The exclusion of women from organizations for local forest governance and village development was acknowledged and regretted, and by some their inclusion was desired. Beyond their obvious absence, exclusion or discrimination in formal forums, what were the processes by which women were kept outside or chose to stay outside these organizations? The focus of this chapter is on the everyday, small incidents, trivialized as village politics, the discourses and actions that construct the idea of what is 'local' in development and environmental governance. These played an important part in gender relations in the villages but also reflect normative assumptions about development and environmental governance.

In Part I of the chapter, I focus on the response to the women's organizing by the men in the village and forest associations that makes clear how the women disturbed norms for working with village activities. According to Benhabib, a "norm—is a rule of action, interaction, or organization, while a *principle* is a general moral and political proposition. Principles permit a plurality of normative organizations; the same principles may be instantiated through different norms and institutions" (1992, 107). Norms are continuously reproduced in routine practices, often without much thought given to them until particular practices and relationships change. "Power functions through creating norms but norms can be ambivalent" (McLaren 2004, 224) and susceptible to change. Examining the women's organizing and the new relationships they engendered, makes it possible to think about the ways in which social relations were constitutive of the women's efforts in the villages and yet, how they challenged norms of how development and environmental activity was meant to be organized. Part II shows how the men were forced to defend and sought to maintain what they believed to be the principles (and assumptions) according to which local development needed to be organized. Power was not a privilege that the men in the organizations automatically possessed. It was 'exercised in the form of a strategy, "a network of relations, constantly in tension, in activity" (Foucault 1979, cited in Butler 2004, 183). The doing of these relations were however hidden until they needed to be defended. In the third (III) and last part, I analyze the role that my colleagues and myself played in the events in the villages. Struggles over meanings of rural development and environmental governance included not only the women's groups and the formal associations but also development practitioners and researchers who were never outside of the relationships of power in these places.

PART I: THE GENDER OF LOCAL DEVELOPMENT

By taking action in what appeared to be an unconventional way, that is, by organizing within their groups and carving out an alternative space for themselves (see Chapter 5), the women had interrupted the normal in 'local development.' These norms, taken so much for granted otherwise, became clear when the men in the village association had to defend them. This brings into focus the ever present and yet unseen gendered processes of local development and environmental governance. Turning to the micro-politics and everyday practices in the villages, I analyze illustrative reactions from the men in the village and the forest groups and the arguments that they deployed to justify their support or resistance.

THREATENING HARMONY

By meeting in their own group and sharing dreams about the future, the women disturbed norms in the village that confirmed that activities like this were meant to take place within the confines of the formal associations. The women believed that they were working for development. Instead, they were seen as threatening the harmony in the villages. In Drevdagen, the villagers were not indifferent to the women's forum.[1] The reactions varied from an attitude of understanding, to benevolent expressions about the *dam träff* (the ladies' meet), to jokes about the *häxmöten* (*witch meetings*), to irritation and annoyance expressed by the members of the village association who perceived women's organizing as a threat to the harmonious working of village life.

The women's critique of the village association and of its' sole attention to the forests that surfaced in the first round of interviews that I conducted, was not perceived as a threat in itself.[2] But it became a threat when that critique became the basis of their self-organizing activities. The women in the forum discussed everyday life and how to work with village activities. As compared to Nayagarh, for instance, where some of the groups took up what may be seen as specifically 'women's issues' (violence, women's rights, representation in village bodies), the women in Drevdagen did not do so. Their activities could include planning a pub evening or a theatre in the village. They spoke about working on relationships inside the village so that the village together could work effectively with the authorities and agencies outside.

Although every get-together in the group was reported in the village newsletter, not having one definable activity made it difficult to know what the women did when they met. This feeling of not knowing caused discomfort, apparent in the interviews that I conducted with Gustav and Tage in October 2002, both active in the village association at the time of the collaborative inquiry with the women.

> *Gustav:* There was no insight . . . Because we had no insight into it . . . we thought that it would have effect in the general village association. There was curiosity. We got some women in the village project. The group lay a bit on the side. There was no insight.
>
> *Tage (was more forthcoming):* We got to hear that we only had the forest on our brains.

Gustav's reference to the village association as the 'general' may be regarded as an effort to show that the association was open to all and was meant for everyone. By meeting outside of it the women were seen to be thwarting this common space. Without necessarily meaning to challenge the village association, that is in effect what they did do. The women's organizing in the village became political although every effort was made, both by the women's group and the men in the association (for different reasons), to make it appear apolitical. Ideas about equality and the proper way to go about working for the village through 'village' associations with their constitutions and protocol were disturbed by the women's choice to meet in an informal women's forum and discuss everyday life in the village.

A chance meeting in the village between Karl, Sara, Jan and myself, resulted in a discussion about the resistance to the women's group within the village association and about their understanding of the group as discordant in relation to the village association, 'village development and environmental governance.' I quote excerpts from the conversation in the following sections to show how they positioned themselves in relation to each other. The arguments capture the uncertainties, disagreements and the conciliatory attempts between the speakers and reflect different positions adopted by the men in the village. The fact that they were having this conversation indicated that both Sara and Karl, who were the main speakers, were looking for solutions. Critique of the women by others was otherwise normally veiled and more difficult to respond to, as I show in the following pages. Sara and Jan started the conversation by asking Karl about what was happening in the village association. In contrast to the time when several men and women had all founded the association, Jan and Sara pointed out that after the initial meetings with the people from SLU, there was a sudden silence and the rest of the villagers had no idea of what was going on.

Sara: In the beginning the women were a part of the activities . . . but then there was a shift . . .

Jan: There was a lot of hope at that time. It felt that Drevdagen had come far . . . but then it became very . . . quiet.

Karl: . . . maybe . . . but . . . I don't believe in a women's group.

Jan: But if the women were at the village meetings, there would be hell if dinner was not ready at home.

Karl: Earlier it was always . . . Cecilia who was at the meetings and I was at home.

Sara: It is difficult to get the women involved and interested. They are so busy with housework when they are not working outside.

There are several issues being worked on here in this exchange. Some become clearer only when the conversation continued, but I take up a few here. First, it shows how individual men positioned themselves differently as regards the women's forum.[3] In this particular exchange, while Karl expressed his displeasure at the existence of the women's group, Jan and Sara begin by pointing to the impracticality of expecting women to attend village meetings and being at home at the same time. Jan pointed to the costs arising when men as opposed to women, attend meetings, what Agarwal calls the 'transaction costs' of attending meetings (2003). As she points out gender inequality dwells not only outside the household but also centrally within it although as Karl shows there are variations within this. But the inequality in the power to shape the agenda is reflected also in the formal settings,

Sara: Maybe it is just that it's the issue . . . for example forest logging that they are not interested in . . . the women in the village.

Jan: Yes, that too.

Karl: It's good with women's meetings and so on but it's a ridiculous solution to the fact that the village association is not working for them. It is not the ultimate solution. You are doing the same thing that the village association and the forest project did.

Sara: Karl, you are unusual. It is easier to create projects when there are only women.

Karl: That is a lousy excuse . . . To be able to develop the village, we must be able to collaborate.

Sara: Our network for me is contacts, to find out how other villages are working and so on . . . And for women to dare to go out and collaborate.

Karl: I don't think a women's network is the solution. It's good to have networks, contacts.
Sara: But this could be a good way to work . . . dividing up the women and men . . . they may be interested in different things.

Karl believed in openness and of working together and he admitted that the association and the forest project were not doing that. Yet he wanted the women to follow that ideal. He believed that the women were doing the same thing as the association. The difference was, however, that in the *kvinnoforum* the women were speaking for themselves, often as individuals, and not professing to do so for the entire village. According to Karl, by placing themselves outside of the village association, the women were placing themselves in opposition to the village associations. Sara pointed to how this might be a way to activate the village association and prompt women to join it. Sara did not challenge Karl's belief in needing to work together but unlike Karl she did not see the existence of the forum as being conflictual. She justified it by saying how this was a good way to involve the women in village affairs. Karl's reaction to the group was not based on the issues that the women took up but on the existence of the group itself. Both wanted men and women to collaborate but Karl did not want that to happen from within a women's group. It is possible that women, being the ones who had employment outside the village compared to the men, had experiences and a status associated with it that was threatening for many men, especially when they chose to organize together.[4]

Karl also shifts between various positions in the conversation. On the one hand he believed that 'it is good with women's networks,' but at the same time not because women are dissatisfied with the village association and not in this particular case. This is a recurring aspect, of how gender is believed to be important, but not in one's own case. Earlier he had told me about a successful women's network in Äppelbo that was doing a lot of good work for their area. These contradictory positions are reflective of the different discourses in society that find form as fragments in such conversations. The importance of gender equality and the need for women's networks in working for development in Sweden, find place in the same conversation with ideas about the gender neutrality of societal institutions.

In Nayagarh, since they were a part of the women's program, the *mahila samitis* were formed with the support of the forest networks. Their success was considered to be the success of the movement. There was, however, dissatisfaction among individual men who wondered if it was worth spending the money and effort on women's groups. But the program, funded by outside agencies was not open for discussion. It was not the formation of the *samitis* but instances where the women took over the agenda and pushed it beyond that envisaged by the program that discomfort with the groups became apparent. The activism by some of the *mahila samitis* was not anticipated by the official program. Talk of their own federation was considered unnecessary and foolish. When I asked one of the *Mahasangha* functionaries about the federation the women wanted to form, he put it eloquently,

> "We do not have so much contact with the women. Once the *Mahasangh* is stronger we can support the women in what they want to do. Without guidelines or ideas there is no point in women gathering. They need the *Mahasangha*'s/BOJBP's support."

It is significant that he says that "we do not have much contact with the women." In their own groups the women took on another identity. 'We' in the *Mahasangha* was a collective identity that was different from their identities as individuals in the village and family. This was also the case in Sweden. When in their collectives the women took on a different identity. They became women and not only mothers, sisters and wives and other men's relatives that the men knew in everyday life at home and in the villages. They were regarded as a unity from the outside. In Drevdagen for example they were referred to as a women's 'group,' making them into a category, which they resisted by the flexible nature of their organizing. The forum for the women in Drevdagen was a place where they could express their individual subjectivities. But they were also a collectivity and the women sought to resolve this dilemma (of a collective and individual subjectivity) by not calling themselves a group but a forum or a meeting place. That it was so ephemeral made it more suspect for others.

Both in Sweden and in India, the need for a women's group or federation was questioned by men in the forest committees, albeit for different reasons. In Sweden, it was questioned whether there was a need for a women's group when there were other village associations. In India, a women's federation was considered unnecessary as men felt the men's organizations were capable (and better) at taking decisions for women as well. In each case, women's efforts to reshape spaces reveal the presence of asymmetrical gendered orders. Yvonne Hirdman (1990) argues that it is when women step into men's territories, (in these two cases exemplified by attempting to define community projects and as in Nayagarh to have a say in decisions over the budgets), that the gender power order becomes apparent. It is this transgression of boundaries that reveals the power relationship between men and women. However, although in both cases the women spoke of their nurturing roles in the village, which may be seen as 'traditional' they were opposed all the same. It was not only a question of where they were stepping, but also one of *how* they were stepping. The imbalance caused by this transgression prompted several men in the organizations to attempt to restore the order.

MAINTAINING AN ORDER

Gender relations are not static and do not just exist but are kept in place by dynamic processes and deliberate efforts. Just as gender relations were being challenged by the women's activism in Nayagarh and Drevdagen, there were also constant negotiations to maintain the *status quo*. In this section, I write about some of the ways by which this occurred.

Veiled (and Veiling) Confrontation

Although the women's forum in Drevdagen evoked opposition among the men working with forest issues, for the most part, resistance was veiled and indirect. Karl, although opposed to the idea of the women's forum, was seen in a positive light by the women. His willingness to discuss his opposition gave hope (at the time) for some kind of understanding of each other's positions. As some women said, "It was good to have Karl in the association, whatever he may think . . . one can at least talk to him." It was better than feigned indifference and silent disapproval.

At SLU, my colleagues believed that I had questioned their actions in the village and that my writing could jeopardize the forest project. However, they did not voice this critique to me. Instead they spoke among themselves and with Karl in the village. Veiled confrontation might seem like a contradiction in terms but there was a sense of conflict or tension about the women's organizing and my research on it that was veiled because the underlying reasons were not discussed. For example, in general it was considered good to have networks, but not in this case or as at the university, instead of talking to me about my research, there were ambiguous discussions about "what research was for?" or "the point of research that divides people."[5] Unlike Karl, to talk about their dissatisfaction was also to admit the challenge posed by the women, to recognize the women and the group and the critique that the research presented. It was to recognize a position. But by choosing not to do so, there was an effort not to acknowledge that any gender question existed. One way the effort took shape was by trying to depoliticize the groups.

Depoliticizing the Groups

The challenge that the forum was seen to offer the village association was met by attempts to depoliticize the group by making them out to be 'different.' The men in the association initially sought to maintain order in the associational life of the village by choosing to regard the women's forum as a group that had been formed for the purpose of interesting women in the conventional associations. It was not regarded as comparable to the other associations in the village. Similarly in Nayagarh the women's groups were seen as the space where women discussed women's work, saved money and carried out income-generating activities and 'got training.'

As a result of the initial critique by the women and others in the village, the association in Drevdagen sought to include more people in the forest project and Kerstin joined the forest group. During the course of their work, the association wanted to write a letter to the authorities about the forest issue. Although it was important that the letter got written, the men in the association felt that writing such an open letter might jeopardize their position in further dialogue with various authorities. The chairperson then suggested that perhaps Kerstin could write it. Better still, since she was a part of the women's group, she could write it on behalf of the women in the village. This aroused the indignation of the women in the forum as they related the incident to me,

> "They have been very bad at talking to the village although they talk for the village. Kerstin is in the committee now but it is a struggle. They decided that she should write a letter to everyone about the forest[6] . . . But then it was hu and ha . . . And then they said . . . but maybe you can send it out from the women's group . . . maybe . . . then it wouldn't be so dangerous . . ."

The women felt affronted by this. The assumption behind it seemed to be that the association was working for the main cause, for which the women's group could make itself useful. Whether it would jeopardize the women's chances for dialogue with authorities for their projects, or if the women even wanted to write such a letter was not considered. It was not exactly how the women had envisaged themselves as partners in village development. The women's forum as a collectivity for itself was not respected. It was an attempt to depoliticize the forum as far as work in the village was concerned. "The obverse of the refusal to image women as political actors is the bestowal on them of a social role" (Tharu and Niranjana 2001, 520).[7] While, on the one hand, as I write in Chapter 5, women derived their strength from their 'gendered responsibilities' (nurturing, as mothers, the social), on the other hand, these could also be used to justify unequal relations. By taking on the authorship of the letter, the women were expected to make a point for the village (or more precisely for the men in the forest project) and at the same time to rescue the men in the association from the embarrassment of making the statements that the letter contained. Women both in Nayagarh and Drevdagen were 'mobilized' to work for the activities of the associations and committees. But it did not mean that they were automatically part of the decision-making. In Nayagarh, the women were supposed to keep within the framework of the women's development program charted out by the BOJBP and Oxfam. In both places, their activities outside of that frame were regarded with growing apprehension. Talk about women's incompetence in running development programs and their illiteracy was an effort to depoliticize this space.

In being part of the *kvinnoforum*, all the women were expected to be in agreement with each other. There was disagreement between some women who had joined the village association about a trip they were to make outside the village. The men scoffed at the women who had organized themselves together and yet could never get along. The assumption was that the presence of what they saw as a women's group meant that all women thought alike. Although the women in the forum resisted being seen as trying to represent all women, differences between them were seen as a sign of their weakness. The village association that was working with the forest project was marked by conflicts between the men. While for women to have differences of opinion was because of their nature and inability to get along, the men's disagreements were considered to be a difference of vision. As one of the men said in an evaluation of their work regarding disagreements in the village association about local governance, "we don't really have the same vision about what it would lead to."

The resentment to the naming of an empty building, the 'house of dreams' by the women offers another example of how the forum was seen as political and how efforts were made to depoliticize it. Towards the end of the conversation that I cite in the beginning of this section, Karl said,

> The name . . . house of dreams . . . how could you just name the place like that . . .
>
> *Sara:* It was at the women's meet . . . we spoke about organizing a film evening, a coffee day, bingo for everyone in the village . . . the nurturing work the women do . . . nurturing relationships in the village . . . It also needs to be brought out. That is what we feel needs to be done . . .
>
> *Karl:* The name . . . none of the men were part of it . . .
>
> *Sara:* Because all the men were away for the moose hunt . . . and that was the theme we were working with . . . talking about our dreams for the future and the village . . . and then we thought, let us christen this place where we are meeting.
>
> *Karl:* But you are painting the same picture as the men.
>
> *Sara:* What does it matter what we women want to call it? . . . maybe all this is threatening for the men..

On the one hand, to be provoked by 'this small thing' as he himself admitted, revealed perhaps the perceived threat a women's group posed to the existing gender and power relations—the women had appropriated the right to define a specific place in the village. Gender and power relations were sought to be maintained by denying the women the right to name a building in the village without going through the right channels, without the legitimacy that came from within an established system. At the same time, this resistance was illustrative of the threat that they felt that the women's forum represented.

A Resort to Tradition

Tradition in the form of shy, passive women, who were difficult to motivate, was seen as something that could come in the way of working together for local development. But it was also tradition that excused men from being individually responsible for an exercise of power that discriminated against others.

Karl: Nobody has said that the women cannot be part of the forest project or the village association.

Sara: But look at what happened to Kerstin when she tried to be a part of the forest group . . . the letter . . . There was resistance from the men all the time.

Karl: That is tradition. It isn't contempt for women. And Gustav . . . isn't all men.

Sara: But how many women and men dare to do that . . . to question established authority?

Karl: It is easier for us who come from outside.

Sara: Gustav is not used to working democratically . . . Kerstin is already run over (*överkörd*).

Karl explained Gustav's omissions and disregard for Kerstin within the association as tradition or culture that made some men behave in certain ways; that they did not mean purposively to marginalize women (although they did so nevertheless). References to tradition are double edged. Gustav did not mean to be insulting. He may be seen as enacting certain 'traditional' values but what is not expressed is his exercise of power. These were everyday practices expressed as tradition. A resort to culture or tradition is often used to justify gender inequalities when biology, such as women are passive, is no longer a justification. "Conflicts are mistakenly characterized as between isolated individuals, when they are actually between richly enmeshed sets of interests and meanings" (Cuomo 1998, 102). Karl may not have subscribed to them but by accepting them as tradition, he was in fact 'reinventing tradition' and reinforcing the maintenance of unequal power relations. "Power is thus difficult to locate as it runs through notions and practices, can be enacted by individuals who may even be opposed to it, and is localized through its expression in everyday practices. Individuals adopt discursive and embodied articulations of power that become readily accepted as cultural norms. In this way, power and inequalities become normative and thus often remain unchallenged" (Cooke and Kothari 2001, 144–145). This was more straightforward to see in Nayagarh as it was tradition that kept women indoors, with their heads covered and subservient to older men.

Opposing Individual Women by Making Them Abnormal

One way that resistance to the forum was expressed was by focusing on individual women. They were seen to be aggressive and not like other 'normal' women. Women who were most active and vocal were seen to be assuming too much importance. In Tage's words,

> "Some of the women took too much place on the stage with what they wanted to do. It led so easily to too many words and talk that was more or less unrealistic. We experienced that from some parts of the women who were active . . . Some persons got too much space because of that. That colored it (the forum) too much . . ."

As he saw it, the inquiry had created the space for some women who would not have that space otherwise or would have been restrained from being so vocal within the existing framework. Karin was one of the women who had also joined the village association along with other women. According to her, some of the men in the association often called her instead of Sara who had become Chair because they claimed that Sara had too many opinions and they did not to know how to relate to her.

> "They felt that she was too strong, not like other women."

In BOJBP, it was Anita, the coordinator of the women's group who became a source of irritation. During my stay there, I attended some BOJBP meetings. Anita often brought up women's issues at those meetings. At one such meeting, she refused to form a group of only women as suggested by the Chair once the plenary was divided up into smaller groups. She felt that the women and the issues that the women wanted to take up then tended to get marginalized to just the women's working group and could not enter the main debate. An older man at the office complained to me that Anita did not always listen to them. He felt that she was trying to be too 'professional' and was not doing her work in the volunteer spirit that characterized the BOJBP.

Anita was seen as trying to take over control. "A consistent argument of the men who control all the power centers of the world is that the oppressed who rebel want to exercise power" (Mies 1991, 62). But it was a power that was unacceptable. The power that the men exercised, on the other hand, was regarded as different and legitimate.

Shifting the Arena

Discussions around the women's collective and women's feelings of marginalization from the *Drevdagen Village Association* resulted in conciliatory attempts by some men (especially Karl) in the association. Some women joined in administrative positions and Sara had become the Chair. The men's exercise of power became more apparent with this change. Some men who had previously led the association consciously tried to keep the women, especially Sara, out of village decision-making. They organized meetings without her knowledge, invited people from outside the village and did not inform her, although as Chair she should have been part of these interactions. Although women came into the decision-making body, the arena for decision- making shifted elsewhere.

The right to talk for the village came not simply from the arena or the office which is formally thought to have the trust of the people. That some of the men had the option to exercise agency not available to the woman who became Chair (despite her office) was not a random event.

> "While not all men choose to exploit this advantage—to exercise power—an individual's abstention does not make the advantage disappear. Neither men nor women can simply 'opt out' of gender's organizing framework,[8] although both can find ways of disrupting it" (Cooper 1995, 10).

The men in the association had complained about the women not taking an interest in village meetings. But when the women did involve themselves and were active in trying to involve other women, decision-making shifted elsewhere. By organizing themselves, the women in Drevdagen resisted being made into "the problem, the recalcitrant category" (Bacchi 1996), a passive category whose non-participation was irresponsible. Once some women involved themselves, they were resisted all the more. The contradiction may be seen to reflect dominant relations of power (or "hegemonies") that are themselves "nothing but elastic alliances, involving dispersed and contradictory strategies for self-maintenance and reproduction" (Berlant and Warner 2000, 317).

Not Only Women and Not Necessarily Gender

It was important for the men in the forest project at SLU to show that the divisions lay not only along gender. Criticism of the village association was positioned by Axel and Niklas from SLU as personal politics in the village. By trying to make the criticism a case of personal issues or coincidences, the focus shifts from looking at the normative order to personal relationships or a series of coincidences. Karl pointed out that there were men who were also opposed to the association's disregard for openness and that this was not a man-woman issue. Rightly so, gender was not the only way in which power relations were organized in the village and not the only basis for exclusion. At the same time, gender was one axis and could not be disregarded. It was when the women organized as 'women' that this axis became evident. According to Eduards, by taking action separately and collectively, women challenge men's privilege of setting boundaries for gender/sex. That women take action together implies, therefore, not only that they reconstruct the category 'women' but that they also name men. Men are forced to position themselves as men and in relation to the construction of masculinity. It thus becomes a reversal—from what men *do* and women *are*, to what women *do* and men *are*. Men were defined as having a sex, the onus of which normally lies on women (2002, 149–150).[9]

The efforts made in maintaining the order—the veiled confrontation, the depoliticization of the women's work, shifting the arena of decision-making and questioning gender—though small on their own, were instances which questioned the existence of the forum, although the women had made no claims to being an established group. They sought to have a forum where women could meet. The gender and power order in the village was thus not one that was maintained automatically but effort was invested in maintaining continuity just as there were attempts to bring about change. "Change is taken to be a mark of activity or endeavor, whereas continuity is not. Yet change and continuity depend on each other to demonstrate their effect" (Pringle 1997, 81).

PART II: SOME ORGANIZING PRINCIPLES OF RURAL DEVELOPMENT

The opposition to the women's forum made visible the norms that the women had disturbed. When challenged, these norms were defended by propositions and discourses about how action for development and environmental governance needed to be organized. In this section, I examine these organizing principles (with their subtext in parentheses) that recurred in both places to varying degrees. The point here is to explore, "what were the most immediate, the most local relationships of power at work? How did they make possible these kinds of discourses" (on how women are, issues that interest men and women, what work is important, the forums that are acceptable) "and how were these discourses used to support power relations?" (Foucault 1990, 97).

WOMEN AS PASSIVE AND THE NEED FOR TRAINING *(REGULATING WOMEN'S PARTICIPATION)*

The reasons for women's non-involvement in 'neutral' organizations and institutions are often explained by the fact that women are either too shy, passive, illiterate or not enterprising enough. Even among those who supported the women's groups in Nayagarh, several believed that 'there was little that a group of illiterate women could do without guidance from the men.' However, not all the women were illiterate, just as not all the men were literate. Also, the women thought differently, "We can't keep waiting for them to decide when they feel that our issues are important to take on."

In Drevdagen invitations were sometimes extended to big village meetings—which the women often refused.[10] The women were encouraged to be more proactive. This notion of passive women is prevalent both in Sweden and in India, prevalent within development, in policies and in their implementation, despite extensive research on the presence of women's networks and entrepreneurs in Sweden and the many rural women's movements in India. In Drevdagen, individual women were seen as being strong and able. Having recently carried out a Participatory Rural Appraisal (PRA) with men and women in Drevdagen, Axel had responded to my intention of having the women guide the course of our research together, "Yes, you certainly can't run them over."

But as a group, they were still spoken of as passive. When I had first interviewed people in Drevdagen, both men and some women had explained the absence of women from the association by women's passivity, lack of interest or lack of self-confidence, ideas that were internalized and accepted regardless of experience. Like all norms it was not only men that worked to keep them in place and not only women who disrupted them. There were also women who believed that women (other women) were passive and scared. Cecilia who had returned to the village from a city had said at the time,

> "Women here in the village are not so conscious of what is going on in the *Drevdagen Village Association* . . . Not very many women are active. Most of them are passive. They have lived here for a long time. Maybe it is a lack of self-confidence?"

This understanding was prevalent in the wider arena of rural development especially about women who had chosen to stay in the village and not travel outside, although very few women fit into that category in Drevdagen.[11] Courses to raise self esteem such as the one mentioned in the previous chapter are no doubt constructive attempts to help women overcome some of the problems. They are efforts to accommodate women within existing structures.

In my interviews with some of the BOJBP male members, several spoke of 'educating the women,' 'making them conscious' and 'empowered.' Statements like 'lack of women's awareness on sanitation and childcare,' or 'the decrease of interest by women in developing the community,' 'ignorance of women's rights' recurred in BOJBP reports. Educating the women or giving them courses to enable them to enter into extant structures was a thread that ran through, in different ways, both in Sweden and in India.

After having met several *samitis* in Nayagarh, I was somewhat surprised at BOJBP functionaries' conviction in the importance of training. The initiatives taken by the women were regarded as extraneous or irrelevant to the women's program. The BOJBP president complained about the inadequate funds allocated by Oxfam for the women's training programs. He believed that there was no point in asking women to attend meetings and take part in activities if they were going to come there and sit with their heads covered. They needed to be trained so that they could gain the confidence to be able to speak out. In his own home, his daughters-in-law told me that they always kept their faces covered and dared not speak in his presence. His son told me laughingly that, even they, his sons, almost did not dare to express a conflicting opinion. 'Training' notwithstanding, this was culture and tradition!

This was different from the Oxfam project officer's account (in an interview in 2004) about Joginath Sahu, a leading figure in the movement,

> "A lot of people don't know but Jogi babu's wife played a major role in this . . . although she is very shy. . . . that is where Jogi babu got gendered . . . He said that if it doesn't start from my family . . . then how can I do anything."

Despite efforts like those of Joginath Sahu, bias toward 'training' for women's empowerment was widespread in the BOJBP. As another BOJBP member claimed in an interview, "We are educating women to participate in the movement." The onus lay on the women to conform to the procedures laid down in the training, to save money and to tailor or to participate in an appropriate fashion. Both the funds and training for women were double edged. On the one hand they provided women with resources and the means to organize. On the other hand they were used to regulate and keep their activities within program boundaries.

While illiteracy is often used to explain women's lack of self esteem, women would be unlikely to be motivated to take part in organizations or to form their groups for forest protection if they feel they have no influence themselves. It was the freedom of being able to take up a range of questions in the *samitis*, and to then take action on them, which proved to be crucial for the women in advancing their interests.

In both countries, forming the women's groups brought questions of self identity and status to the fore for both men and women. While men were identified as a group, it also became possible to ask, which women are passive or with reference to what are they passive and why?

WOMEN ARE INTERESTED IN DIFFERENT ISSUES? (A QUESTION NOT ONLY OF 'WHAT' BUT 'WHO')

It was generally assumed in Nayagarh and Drevdagen that the women identified with some kind of issues (the social) in the village and the men with others (forests). Although it was true that many women wanted to take up issues that differed from those of forest management, it was not only a question of different issues. Neither was it a watertight boundary between the men and women involved in village activities. Not attending association meetings was not only a question of 'what' issues were being taken up but 'who' had the space to take them up. In some cases in face of the women's critique, neglected issues like, for example, housing that some women had been arguing for, were now brought onto the agenda. But when these questions were taken on board, they were not always accompanied by the women who had been speaking for them. As Sara remarked,

> "If I happened to make a suggestion at the meeting in the association nobody said anything. About 15 minutes later, when Leo said the same thing, it was discussed with great enthusiasm."

Yvonne claimed that she managed to get her ideas through in the association without ever going there but by getting her husband to take them up at the meetings. In these cases, it was not the issues but the social position of the speaker that was decisive.

Sometimes an assertion of interest in different issues may be seen as a strategy by the women. By maintaining their 'difference' at the level of 'issues' rather than in terms of power and gender, they attempted to open a dialogue with the village association. This aspect recurs in the conversation between Sara and Karl, where Sara said that the women needed their own forum because they were interested in different issues. In the long run, however, it also made it easier for the association to talk about the issues and not the asymmetries of gender and power that were often the crux of the matter (explained further in 'the right forum'). Differences in 'issues' and interests became a way to mask unequal gender relations.

Being a more gender-differentiated society there was more explicit talk about women's work and men's work in Nayagarh. The women's groups were meant to take up women's issues. However, the groups that were most active took up a range of issues that seemed important to them just then. They were not specifically those that were considered women's work, as the example of the road or the forest protection by the women in Hariharpur shows. The division of work had been sought to be resolved by having a woman's program and women's groups, but that too had spilled out of its frame.

A HIERARCHY OF WORK (SOME QUESTIONS ARE MORE IMPORTANT THAN OTHERS)

By consistently trying to make work different and incomparable, the men working with the forest question continually recreated a hierarchy between the women and themselves where the women and their issues were subordinated. References to the 'important issues,' the 'larger question,' as compared to those taken up by the women, recurred often. One of the men in Drevdagen said after a June 1999 meeting on the forests, when speaking about the women's criticism of the village association,

> "The forest is a men's thing . . . it is okay to sit at the kitchen table and complain and air opinions but one must show commitment . . . one must be prepared to work like we do. . .it is actually we who take on way too much."
>
> *Seema:* But what about the cow-cooperative and the sports association . . . ?
>
> "Yes, yes but I mean this, the bigger work."

This was not all that different from the view expressed by the man from the *Mahasangha* in Nayagarh who believed that once the *Mahasangha* was stronger, it could then support the women in what they wanted to do. In other words, once the important work was done, the smaller questions could be dealt with. The men in the association and the *Mahasangha* had assumed and acknowledged the privilege of defining what was more or less important. This may be seen as a judgment made on the basis of the assumption that the men had the right to define what public village life looked like. In this way, men were seen as the ones active and taking initiatives, while the women were 'passive.'

In Nayagarh, in conversations and interviews, the women articulated their identity as strong women who found their strength together in the groups and in their work to bring about change in their villages. That much of this work was looked upon as women's work and 'different' or not as important as the larger issues was clear for many men. I was constantly reminded of this. One such occasion was when I had filmed our discussion in Chaddiapalli and the women in the *samiti* wanted to play the video back to see what they had said. The villagers finally located a small black and white television set that belonged to a young man in the village. He was a migrant worker in Andhra Pradesh and had been able to buy the television on one of his working trips. At the moment he was back in the village and he agreed to let us use his television. However, as about thirty women and some men crowded into his little hut, he was not entirely pleased with the situation and confused by what I was doing there.

Finally, he came up to me, "Why exactly are you wasting your time on them? What would they know of anything important?" he asked rhetorically, waving at the women sitting around and all talking at the same time as they waited expectantly to see themselves on television. I was also a woman but, in our hierarchy, this was mitigated by class, the fact that I came from a university and because I had access to modern equipment like a film camera. And here I was wasting my time with the women about what they wanted to do. The villages in Nayagarh were famous for their attempts to develop and manage community forestry and especially so among people working professionally with development activities. It was not uncommon for researchers and development workers to come and speak to the men about their movement. But for someone to speak to the women about their work in the village was considered dull and not serious enough.

The reaction of the young man in Nayagarh, was in fact similar to some of the reactions that I encountered in Drevdagen (although in a very different setting and among people in a different gender/race/power relation to me). Now and then when I met some men in the village, they greeted me and said, "oh, so you are here for the ladies' meet" (*dam träff*) or "what are you going to do when you grow up and stop 'studying'"[12] and I suppose wasting my time with the women. Unfortunately, this was not so different in the academy. At the university, by working on gender, I felt forced to reiterate and make a case for why this was also an issue of local environmental governance and rural development, not merely a story about a group of women getting together to work and socialize.

THE RIGHT FORUM (THE NEED TO CONFORM TO EXISTING STRUCTURES)

Women both from the *kvinnoforum* and the *samitis* were eventually expected to integrate themselves into the 'village' association or the *Mahasangha*/BOJBP. The understanding was that there existed structures into which 'women' needed to be brought. In Nayagarh it was considered self-evident that the BOJBP and the *Mahasangha* or the village committees were the right forums to deal with village questions. The BOJBP's reservations concerning a women's federation were based on the understanding of women's inability to deal with bigger issues because of social restrictions and because of 'the way women are.' The women's groups were seen mainly as a tool to organize the women so that they could join the forest committees. Nevertheless, the fact that the women were beginning to organize themselves also made them interesting allies. The groups thus became a bone of contention between the BOJBP and the *Mahasangha* and further limited the space for women to take action themselves.

The legitimacy of the 'neutral' and the right forums in Drevdagen was so taken for granted that the formation of the women's forum was experienced as puzzling and then threatening. In September 2000, I accompanied a class of master students with faculty members from our department to Drevdagen for a study trip. Gustav and Karl spoke to the students about the school strike and the forest project. Sara was asked to speak on the women's forum. She chose to speak about the difficulties for women in working with rural development,

> "Men dominate associations. One doesn't get so much information either . . . Traditionally women were not involved in it but now there are women who want to be part of it. But we are excluded . . . it makes it difficult."

But Gustav brought this decision back to the women choosing to stay out of the village association,

> "The women have been outside the forest project . . . or to put it correctly local management. But local management includes everything . . . not just the forests . . . they have misunderstood it. Women . . . they draw back. When Seema began to talk to the women, in my foolishness, I thought . . . that now the women and men could work together. But it did not happen."

He shifted the question from one of exclusionary practices to women not wanting to join hands with them. The women's need to work with local development from elsewhere was not considered an option. According to him, there were established ways of working for the village through the association and the correct way was to join them. The association that professed to work for the democratization of forest governance resisted the efforts of the women by trying to re-establish accepted relationships.

There is also an interesting discursive shift in Gustav's expression from the forest project to 'local management.' It reflects how the question had changed as a result of the women's views that the forests could not be seen in isolation. It might be seen as a cooption of the women's arguments or as neutralizing their claims, but also alternatively as an opening of the space for defining the forests and governance.

Who Joins Whom?

In the conversation that Karl had with Sara, Jan and myself, when Sara had suggested that the men could come to their meetings, Karl had said,

> "if the women are to meet together, the men (*gubbarna*) are not going to come to that."

Jan retorted by saying that the women might feel the same way, that they may feel that the association was irrelevant for them, "And then the women are going to say . . . I'm not going to get into this . . . and its back to the stove . . . if you continue to discuss only those things that you want to and in the ways you do."

Karl made it clear that it was expected that the women would collaborate with the men but also that it was 'natural' that symmetrical behavior could not be expected of men. The same demands could not be put on men. Which self-respecting man would join a women's group?[13] Here too it was the discursive neutrality that set the norm. The women were expected to join an association that was not called a men's association although it was in effect that.[14] Karl complained that the women were not being inclusive by forming a women's group. At the same time the men did not want to be included in what they saw as a women's forum. The asymmetry in what was expected of women as compared to men in the village became clear in that collaboration did not include the men joining the women, but meant that the women joined the men. Neither was anything in-between possible in this scenario.

COLLABORATION (UNDER CERTAIN TERMS)

In a conversation with me, Karl acknowledged the role that the women played in actually getting Drevdagen's village association going. He said this in response to Sara's words at the meeting with the students. He attempted to show that men and women do in fact work well together. Didn't the women write up the agenda in the association that the men had been talking about for so long? That was the normal way of working. He implied that by separating themselves the women were disconnecting themselves from power that was theirs to take. And herein lay the difference in understanding the situation. Was it theirs to take? This understanding fails to take into account lived experiences that tied the women and men in the village in relationships of power.

By organizing on their own, the women disturbed the notion of complementarity. Although they discussed everyday village activities that the women in the village organized anyway, they were held to be doing it in the 'wrong' ways. The women's companionship was seen to be directed against those in the association. For example, despite remonstrations to the contrary from Sara, in their conversation Karl was assuming that by having a women's network or forum, the women did not want to collaborate. He felt this way despite the fact that Sara had become Chair of the *Village Association* and that several women had joined other village projects. In principle or theoretically at least, women were not excluded from village associations. But the question was, collaboration on whose terms and how were the terms negotiated? Did tradition not come in the way? Collaboration was meant to take place in one direction only.

The women's development program in Nayagarh was meant to empower the women in the villages by eventually bringing them into the *Mahasangha* as individuals. In conversations some of the *Mahasangha* staff spoke warmly of including the women. They wanted to make sure that the men did not just come and sign their female relatives' names on the attendance sheets or pay their membership fee for them. One of the men suggested that the women should instead sign with their thumb impression to guarantee that they had been there in person. But how this was to be done, or whether that is the way the women wanted to work, were not central to the discussion. Neither was it considered the women's concern to decide how the funds were spent.

The micro-credit groups that were meant to form the basis of women's organizing did succeed in savings in several villages. But the fact that the women chose not only to be integrated in other committees, but also to form their own federation, was seen as circumventing the norms of development, of gender relations in the villages and of what women were expected to do. The question that is often put in relation to women's groups is whether women's organizing gives them a voice in other forums. This question does not take into account the active (though not always overt) resistance by the actors in the structures which they are supposed to join. The women's ability to raise their voice depends very much on the resistance to their organizing and the social context in which they organize.

My colleagues considered the research with the women in Drevdagen dangerous because it had opened the possibility of giving voice to differences (or causing divisions) that could jeopardize the larger question of forest governance. The problem was that the women's organizing was a piece of the jigsaw that did not fit in. I had a role to play in this view on 'collaboration' which however I was seen to have jeopardized by writing about the conflicts in the village. I now analyze the role played by outside development practitioners and myself as a researcher in defining the field and constructing what rural development, empowerment, or local governance meant in the two places.

PART III: THE OTHER SIDE OF DEVELOPMENT: THE OUTSIDERS

Village Politics in Drevdagen

At one of the early get-togethers of the women's forum in Drevdagen, I arrived in the village late in the evening, having been delayed on the way. The women had started already and were in the midst of planning events in the village, including a film evening. Märta had a collection of several films taken over the years by her family in Drevdagen and the other women planned to complement this with films and photographs assembled from the others in the village. It was to be a called a nostalgic film evening. This exchange of ideas was interspersed with anecdotes about the village and stories about various attempts at working for the village over the years. The conversation turned to the plans for the forests and the villagers' lack of information on the project,

> *Britta:* In the beginning we discussed the forest together but then things changed . . . it became a man's club.
>
> *Sara:* Axel and Niklas probably don't understand that they don't inform us or care about telling us anything.

This was not the first time that I had heard this statement from the women. It felt uncomfortable hearing this view expressed in the light of my own conversation with Niklas at SLU a few days earlier. He had said,

> "My role is to help people negotiate with more powerful people . . . I don't like village politics . . . I work with real questions. Not these issues."

The background to this conversation was a draft of a paper that I had written on the basis of my initial interviews in the village. I had cited the women who were critical of the forest project because of the lack of information from the association and because of the women's absence from discussions that were carried out in the name of the village. I had also written about the activities that many women were working on, which were of a more immediate nature and which had direct consequences for the village. This paper caused a great deal of discussion within the FTPP group at SLU. Some of them believed that by writing in this way I was endangering the process of community forestry or local governance. They felt that by writing this I could cause potential divisions between the men and women in the village and make it difficult for them to work together. Besides, they felt the paper could be used by local politicians (and others) for their own purposes. The politicians could use it against the village association to thwart the association's leadership in the forest struggle,

> *Niklas:* You bring out the problems but not the collaboration. Who is it helping? What is the real problem? They are going to start felling next month. What is the point of talking about these things?

The heated reaction to my paper at SLU was not necessarily the cause, but it did contribute to the strained atmosphere between the women's group and the village association as the men at SLU discussed my paper and the perspectives it had brought to light with men in the village association. The position of the university reinforced the notion for the men in the village that the critiques offered by the women were personal matters and not necessarily something that needed to be brought into the working of 'the real issue.'

Although Axel and Niklas were apprehensive about engaging in 'village politics' seemingly unconsciously, that is what they were doing. In 2000, a researcher from SLU interviewed the people in the association on their work for local management, as part of an evaluation of SLU's support to the forest project. In response to a question about whether there was a clear division of roles between SLU and the village regarding the forest project, one of the interviewees answered,

> "Maybe it would have been needed in the sense that they should have been more neutral towards the others in the rest of the association, because now there has been a lot of 'let's ask . . . (him) . . .' I feel sometimes that they call and talk with me instead of the chairperson, which has both advantages and disadvantages. Sometimes it is better to be formal, at the same time as the informality is important for commitment."

Axel and Niklas spoke to the men in the village whom they believed were interested in the issues that they themselves were interested in, rather than to someone in the association who might not be. At the same time they took some of the men to be representative of the village, gave them their support and by doing so engaged directly in village politics. By supporting the men, they strengthened the *status quo* in the village in terms of gender relations. Their relations with the men in the village association also affected the relationships among the men in the village. Despite being a newcomer to the village, Karl was active in the association and especially in the forests, a role that had been difficult for most women even as long time inhabitants to achieve. His position was nonetheless that of an outsider and his importance in the forest project that arose partly from his relations to the outsiders was also challenged in the long run.

Dividing the Village

According to Niklas, by writing about what the SLU group felt was the criticism of the village association by a few women, and by speaking of the activities initiated by the women as 'women's projects,' I could divide the men and women in the village. I was skeptical that an academic report would have this effect given the complex webs of gender relations in the village. By highlighting the differences that the women spoke about, my research may be reinforcing the differences. Making visible these relationships may not always be so desirable for the women concerned. Niklas' argument was that bringing the differences into the public space could jeopardize the forest issue. My concern was that perhaps I had jeopardized the women's chances to work with the issue in other ways?[15]

Shortly after my conversation with Niklas, I met Karl in the village. At that point, he was not perturbed by what was written in the paper. This was partly because he had already read reports that I had been giving back to the women (the argument in the paper was not new and was in fact an English translation of the reports I had sent earlier), and probably also because he did not give much importance to an academic paper. However, in the months to come he became one of the vocal protesters of the idea of a women's forum.

The view that the research would divide the men and women in the village came up once again in another interview conducted during the SLU evaluation,

> "One thing that I experienced personally was when Seema worked with the women's bit here. A report was to be written and it was written in English but it was never translated. When I read it I was upset by the division that had been made, women's projects and men's projects. For example, the ski slope was labelled as a women's project, yes . . . it was the women's idea but it wasn't the women who cut the trees. I think it is fatal in a small village like this to begin to talk about women's projects and men's projects because it creates yet another division. The result was that people said, yes, yes they can have their women's project, instead of seeing the positive side to it. To call it specifically a women's project creates bad blood, damn feminist society. No-one talks of pub evenings as men's projects. To create such a situation in a little village is unsustainable. I think one destroyed more than what one got out of it, unconsciously."
>
> *Interviewer:* Do you know how the women reacted to this?
>
> "They weren't as offended, they felt that—yes, yes but in the forest project as we know there are only you men who are part of it. But I have talked mostly to my friends, the men in the village and they were damn offended, them too, but said, 'it is as usual'."

It was clear that there were deep interdependencies between the men and women in the village without which living in the rural areas would be difficult. The fact that these relationships could also be conflictual was highlighted by my research but even more so by my colleagues' reactions. Their part in 'village politics' became clearer to see. Axel and Niklas, needed to see themselves as and believed that they were neutral outsiders working for 'the people' and for the cause of local forest governance, not only in Drevdagen but in the whole Swedish countryside. The relationships that I wrote about were not new to the women and men in the village although they may not have conceptualized them in this particular way. My reports or papers became a source of discussion not when the people in the village had read them but when my colleagues at the university did so. As far as the paper was concerned, when I presented it to the women, several thought it was quite mild compared to what they thought and had said. It was our collective choice to continue meeting and mine to continue with my research, which also meant that it would be written about and the discussions in the forum would eventually become public.

Collaboration Revisited

There was an assumption that by my working together with the women, they would collaborate with the association and the forest project. Axel said to me when he read a draft chapter of my thesis,

> "I would have needed help to make the forest project more open . . . to find ways to make it more participatory . . ."

I too had begun my research with an idea of complementarity, in the sense that I believed that highlighting the problems that the women had might enable a dialogue towards development together, thus inscribing myself, as Frigga Haug (1999) would say, in dominant values. But during the researching process, by having the women rather than normative ideas of collaboration guide the process, I was questioning the idea of complementarity and collaboration, or at least the terms on which these were supposed to be carried out. And in their view I was making our work irrelevant for the men or rather I was taking our activities out of their familiar field. Collaboration on fairly equal terms would change the way local governance was envisaged today.

I was seen to be creating conflicts where on the surface there were none. Karl had said that nobody stopped women from joining the association. In a similar vein Niklas told me,

> "Nobody is complaining, so why are you bringing up all these conflicts."

Perhaps nobody was complaining publicly (as far as SLU knew) until I began to ask questions about local governance and village development.[16] The questions had not been open for discussion. People may have been complaining but that was also accepted. "Power is tolerable only on condition that it mask a substantial part of itself" (Foucault 1990, 86). The presence of a researcher from SLU asking questions created a space for people to be able to voice their feelings, thoughts and opinions. Local governance became a topic that could be discussed openly. In light of this, the women's wish for a forum may be understood as a place 'to talk about issues that one cannot do elsewhere.'

The critique that I presented was taken personally rather than as a challenge to open up the topic for discussion in its particular context. The topic, 'local management of the forests' was already seen as given and considered accepted by the people working with the forest project both in the village and at the university. Questioning the given was taken instead as an instance of some disgruntled women who wanted to be included (*you must have just spoken to Märta*) and of a researcher intent upon imposing ideas about gender from the South on a Swedish context. There was also an unease that arose in the face of a critique that may be seen to derive from the discourse on gender and equality (for better and for worse), as I discuss below.

'Gender' Trouble

Axel felt that in writing about activities spearheaded by the women and references to the men in the village association I gave the impression that all men had the potential to dominate. I seemed to group together all men in one category. He did not feel that way, believed in gender equality and considered himself a feminist. But at the same time he felt that it was not his task to interfere in how the villagers ran the association or the struggle for the forests from the village. In other words, he saw the SLU group as attempting to carry out a gender-neutral participatory approach that was non-intrusive. As Niklas pointed out, they had actually carried out a Participatory Rural Appraisal (PRA) in the village in which both men and women had been involved (see Chapter 5). And rightly so, in conversations, many women who had been part of the PRA, related that they had been happy with their involvement in the exercise and had looked forward to working with the issues that the PRA raised. But as Bill Cooke and Uma Kothari point out,

> "Although PRA seeks to reveal the realities of everyday life, paradoxically its public nature means that the more participatory it is, the more the power structure of the local community will be masked" (2001, 12).

Because of the PRA, for a while everyone felt able to participate as men and women in their own right. What many women and men believed was a shift in power enabled by the outsiders was a one-time event. Instead the PRA contributed to building up relationships between the outsiders and some of the men in the village that further confirmed the village men's authority.

The men in the association were not all alike and they mostly did not deliberately exclude women. Yet, they all had the potential to do so by the very fact of their unquestioning assumptions about what was normal. Not because of the persons they were but because they commanded that space for agency (in varying degrees) in the association at that time which the women did not. They guarded and reinforced the norms for work on the forests and for development work in general by accepting and acting out these norms. These norms became visible when the women exercised agency by organizing themselves. Even the space that the men had in the association did not become wholly available to the woman who became the chairperson of the association. It was not the arena that conferred that space to the men but their persons (their embodied selves). Thus, even involving women in such a case could mean including some women into associations and projects where the structures were already defined and the norms for gender relations already set.

A large amount of feminist literature theorizes differences among women. Obviously, differences among men are just as important in their shifting social/gender identities (e.g. Connell 2003). A parallel question then is how one can speak about 'men' or 'women' and still acknowledge differences among them. As I saw it, it was the agency that it was possible for men to exercise because they were 'men' in this particular rural community that made them different from the women or for the women the possibility of being sidelined without much opposition because they were (embodied) women. Men had access because their sex/gender was unquestioned. But for the women it was their sex/gender identity that was important. It may be seen as a positive effect of the women's organizing that some of the men in the association felt that there needed to be a woman as chairperson. This need was felt also after Sara stepped down because she was being outmaneuvered by some men. So, as I see it, the next woman who became the chairperson did so partly because of her sex, *i.e.* because she was a woman. But she was also very young and had moved back to the village (her childhood home) not long before she took that position and was not likely to question their leadership as would the older women. Did the visibility for 'women' (as a category) increase or decrease?

Everything that Niklas and Axel did was, of course, liable to be questioned. Whether they acknowledged it or not, their work did result in inclusions for some and exclusions for others. I understood that it was considered to be in the best interests of the work, the cause, not to stir it up at all, not to interfere, preferably not to acknowledge that there might be 'problems.' Talking about gender and power would mean admitting that these relationships existed in this particular context and that one had to deal with them. In fact I was told by Niklas,

> "This is not like the third world . . . this is different. Gender is not the same thing here."

Gender relations are indeed not the same here as in other places as is further highlighted by the following section on Nayagarh. Fraser writes,

> "status hierarchy is illegitimate in modern society. The most basic principle of legitimacy in this society is liberal equality, as expressed both

> in market ideals, such as equal exchange, the career open to talents, and meritocratic competition, and in democratic ideals such as equal citizenship and status equality. Status hierarchy violates all these ideals. Far from being socially legitimate, it contravenes fundamental norms of market and democratic legitimacy" (2003, 56).

The notion of gender equality made it difficult to talk about gender in Drevdagen. The question of 'marginalization' put the practitioners/activists in a difficult position, because at the university, we saw ourselves as working with the people in the *glesbygd*, in what is the periphery, the margins of Swedish society. This meant a strong notion of struggling from below and at the same time, it conferred on those of us working with these issues, the position of being the 'saviors of marginality' (Spivak 1990, 226). Niklas and Axel were operating within this discourse in our work with community forestry and in supporting 'local people.' When I began to speak about discrimination within this setting of the local, I took over that mantle. It could not be questioned so easily. I had virtue on my side. Women and men are supposed to be equal and everyone agreed on that. Speaking about the critique to me was potentially dangerous because it would acknowledge a 'gender' position. The inertia to deal with questions of gender may be likened to what has been termed 'white inertia' in feminist analysis in face of the problematic of race (c.f. Lewis and Mills 2003, 7). This was a sort of male inertia, a fear of getting it wrong in relation to gender; it was considered more prudent simply to try and ignore it. Or rather a gender critique could not be discussed because it had the potential to reveal one's own privilege (and bias). Gender may be a 'development problem' and yet it is also extremely personal. Implicit in Axel and Niklas' behavior was a frustration that by admitting that the world is gendered and unequal, did that mean that they should not do anything? (I take this up in 'the practitioner's dilemma').

As an earlier quote illustrates, the women believed that the men from SLU did not recognize that the process was not participatory. It reveals the contradictory nature of development work and activism, even when beginning from the bottom-up. Axel expected the village men to involve the rest of the village, to open up the space to make the forest process more participatory. Axel and Niklas spoke about it as the responsibility of the men in the village working with the forests. However, by being upset about my research and discussing it with the men in the village, they made the position of the women's forum and their activities in the village more difficult. They felt that acknowledging differences or unequal relations in the village could jeopardize the impact that the village association might achieve *vis-à-vis* external entities like the state or the forest company. These were problems they relegated to the realm of village politics. In doing so, they diminished the importance of the critique from the women about the village association and the forest project for the men in the village.

Gender relations between the men and the women within the village were thus as much the result of the village men's relations to the outsiders as they were of my relationship to the *kvinnoforum*. The vision of men and women working together in harmony with the forests came in the way of recognizing power relations that favored some and excluded others in the village. I now turn to look at Nayagarh and discuss how some of the relationships between development practitioners and researchers and the villagers were articulated there on the question of 'gender.'

OUTSIDERS IN NAYAGARH

One aim of the women's program, as some men in the BOJBP and the *Mahasangha* saw it, was to be able to 'integrate' women into the *Mahasangha* and thereby make it more gender sensitive. The women were never a part of designing their own program. According to Anita, the coordinator of the women's program, it was the BOJBP and Oxfam who decided on the programs and how the money was to be spent. When I spoke to the BOJBP president, he complained that the Oxfam officer did not like them and that Oxfam would like to decide themselves how to allocate the money. He criticized Oxfam for insisting on a women's bank and micro-credit schemes and for not realizing that there were several other issues important for the women in Nayagarh. Oxfam in turn believed that the BOJBP was becoming increasingly bureaucratized and losing its base among the people, "becoming an NGO, rather than a people's movement that it used to be." This caused unpleasantness between the BOJBP and Oxfam to add to the already strained atmosphere between the *Mahasangha* and the BOJBP. Partly because of this growing uneasiness between the *Mahasangha*, the BOJBP and Oxfam, the women's groups got drawn into the eye of the storm.

Once the *Mahasangha* took over the coordination of most forest related activities, the BOJBP's major responsibility was the implementation of the Oxfam funded Women's Development Program. The *Mahasangha*, that was trying to enlarge its base approached the *mahila samitis* in the hope that more women could be drawn into the movement. The BOJBP saw this as *Mahasangha*'s interference in their women's program. Members of the *Mahasangha* claimed that the BOJBP had told Anita to tell the women's groups not to attend *Mahasangha* meetings. Influence over the women's groups became important for both the male-dominated organizations in their conflicts with each other and narrowed the choices available for the women in following their own interests.

Women's activities, even where they worked for goals that specifically concerned 'women's development,' were linked to those of the men and at times supported by them. They had to interact with the men in their day-to-day life as well as when they went about these specific activities. However, in situations that could become conflictual, support from outside was important. The *Mahasangha* and the BOJBP networks in some measure provided a counterweight to committees in their own villages. According to one of the *Mahasangha* workers,

> "We held a program planning group this year (1998) where we invited many women. Some of the women talked about how the forest committees in their villages were becoming exclusive . . . their links to the villages were disappearing."

Several women claimed that it was easier for them to attend meetings or workshops outside of their own villages than in their own villages. It was easier to express their views if their male relatives, especially their fathers-in-law or older brothers-in-law, were not present at the meetings, where the more immediate relations of gender and power that constricted them were not so overbearing. For example, the women of Jagannathprasad reportedly told *Mahasangha* staff,

> "Why is our organization not a part of the *Mahasangha*? We are not ready to sit in the village meetings but can do so outside."

This may explain why the village of Kesharpur that was at the center of the forestry movement did not have an active *samiti*. The presence of strong, male organizations could be inhibiting for the women's groups. Women tried to gain legitimacy for their groups by being recognized for their work by outside NGOs as for example when women from Abhimanpur travelled to Macchipada to attend a meeting on the forests to tell the NGOs present there about their work. In this particular case however they were unable to do so (see incident in Chapter 8).

As far as the Oxfam officer was concerned, their objective with the program was to involve women in forest governance,

> "My other objective was . . . again . . . supporting women's good organization and then to culminate it with the *Mahasangha*. I mean integrate real gender strategies into the *Mahasangha*. Because . . . *Mahasangha* independently . . . I was not sure *Mahasangha* was in a position to take up two things at a time. One is organizing *Mahasangha* in itself . . . self-sustaining membership, structure . . . all those issues. And Nayagarh is not a very gender sensitive pocket for that matter."

Many *samitis* active in Nayagarh took up questions of women's rights, in the village and in the family, while some also demanded their right to be part of the *Mahasangha*. According to the Oxfam officer, this was an increasing source of discomfort for the BOJBP. But ever more uncomfortable was perhaps the activism of BOJBP's women staff who supported the idea of women's federation. The BOJBP members' remarks to me about Anita not being a volunteer and not following program procedures, during my visit there in 1999, seemed to foreshadow coming problems. Towards the end of 1999, funding to the BOJBP for the women's program was stopped by Oxfam. In 2004, I spoke to the Oxfam officer who had been responsible for the project,

> "I think, again BOJBP might have thought that the Savings & Credit program is more of pacifying Oxfam, as this was primarily pushed by Oxfam on the basis of an ODA review in 1992–93. So they never thought it would become such a big constituency where women would demand for rights. For that matter, any sister organization working with BOJBP might have been convinced the same way by BOJBP . . . like Chadhiapalli . . . as long as you are working with savings and credit, its fine . . . don't talk of rights . . . and they (the women's groups) took up violence against women quite seriously."

According to him, the staff of the women's program complained to them at Oxfam that BOJBP officials were making things very difficult for them. Some BOJBP members complained if they took their children with them to meetings or to work.[17] Oxfam tried to intervene but Oxfam's relationships with BOJBP were already strained. Oxfam felt that the BOJBP was mismanaging the program and mistreating the staff. Discussions between them led nowhere,

> "We were pursuing it hard but it came to a head on collision between Oxfam and BOJBP . . . It was an unfortunate decision but I said . . . . I can't support you otherwise."

The loss of funding meant that the coordinator and the organizers who were the lynchpins in the coordination among all the women's groups, and who gave the groups a certain amount of legitimacy, would disappear. But, according to the Oxfam officer,

> "With these contradictions how can you support the women's program? . . . I visited a lot of women's groups . . . I said you please carry on because we don't know how to support it . . . because we cannot have violence against women."

These were the structures through which the program was supported and now the channels had closed. I wondered why the groups could not be supported directly?

> "How can you channelize the funds? The other problem . . . they (the staff of the women's program) feared that BOJBP would not allow them to work properly."

Funding was stopped and with that, for the moment, plans for a women's federation were also halted. "Planning and implementation is a male-driven machine" (Agnihotri 2001, on Odisha's administration), a machine regimented by its programs, and one that has difficulties in taking or encompassing action outside its frame. The BOJBP's women's program and other programs such as the DWCRA had provided openings. Although the links of the women's groups to the BOJBP entailed a dependency on them, they also provided a standing for the women *vis-à-vis* the men in their communities and played a role in the women being able to take action. Their ties to an established organization gave them legitimacy. However, once that link was broken, there were no direct channels to them. The only other option according to the Oxfam officer, would have been to continue to provide support through the *Mahasangha*. He said,

> "I was literally feeling bad . . . I was trying to tell Biswal that can we build some kind of program . . . then Biswal said fine . . . but he can't decide, it has to come through the EC (Executive Committee) and the EC is again a male dominated area and already probably some of them might be facing the brunt in their own villages with these groups."

What happens when channels close down and women's links to the formal structure are broken? Does this mean that women's groups have no direct recourse other than going through intermediaries? Neither in Nayagarh or Drevdagen were the women's collectives seen as representatives of the community as opposed to the forest groups? In Nayagarh, the women continued to organize themselves in their own groups although they were scattered all over the district with few chances to build a larger network. Some of the staff members are still active in the areas where they live. How does one support their agency? And how does one link up with them? Despite wanting to work with them, the outsiders, Oxfam in this case were unable to do so. One reason for this is the view that many development agencies have on gender.

This is reflected in a draft report on Oxfam's work in Orissa. The report was based on fieldwork conducted at approximately the same time I was there. The chapter on women in the report starts by looking at structural inequalities in Orissa. This is emphasized in the beginning by the following story,

> "For instance, Orissa is the only state in the country which disallows a woman from boarding a bus, if she be the first passenger when it starts in the morning. She would have to wait for a male to board the bus first, irrespective of the age of the male. Even a small child would do. If there are no males around, she simply cannot get on" (Mitra 1997, 94).

The authors continue,

> "The above is just an instance of the silent, quiet suppression of women that takes place. It is a day-to-day phenomenon. What it points to is how extremely difficult it is to bring about gender equity in a social system where such inequities and attitudes are so deeply entrenched." (ibid.)

The report is aimed at development agents (Oxfam to be more specific) and hence discusses their role in this change. The authors look at the structural problems faced by women and not necessarily at their agency. They did not, as I did, see the women's efforts to organize on their own as gathering self-assurance to act. The patriarchal nature of society is emphasized and this lens is then used to examine the BOJBP. And true enough one does see the gender discrimination in the movement and in society, entrenched in day-to-day phenomena as the authors describe.

The other side of the picture, that is, to see what the women are doing from day to day in order to work around this discrimination and how such work may be supported, is not given equal attention.[18] The women's non-attendance at *Mahasangha* meetings is attributed to the rivalry between the BOJBP and the *Mahasangha*. They write that the women's groups were being told by Anita not to attend the meetings of the forest federation. The reason for women's absence could well have been due to BOJBP's admonition but it was equally likely it was because, as a woman expressed it dismissively,

> "they can't force us to come to their meetings just to sit and listen to them."

There is almost no mention of the work that the women's groups had been doing. In another book, a scholarly and meticulously researched history of the movement, acts of agency by women are hailed but are seen as one-time events. The reader is cautioned not to read too much into the fact that some of the women's groups had organized themselves, although the authors do write that such acts reflect the potential and an emerging trend of women's involvement in development activities in the area (Human and Pattanaik 2000, 108).

Comparing my report with the draft report on Oxfam's work with community forestry, I was struck by how research could see situations so differently. The optimism and the vision of the women and their confidence of having actually brought about changes in the forests and the community that, as I was reminded by more than one group in Nayagarh, 'the men had not been able to' was very tangible. For the other researchers, the women's efforts were seen as sporadic and informal and not necessarily as part of a long-term strategy. The dominant and recognizable norm of how to organize and bring about change did not fit in with women's organizing. Their organizing did not take the shape in which 'development' could be recognized. The fact that the women were questioning how the program was planned and how the money was being spent 'on them' without them having a say, was not taken up. They saw the women exercising some agency but the underlying assumption, expressed both in the report and in the book by Human and Pattanaik above is that the aim was for women was to be integrated into the *Mahasangha*. This assumption was based on a well-founded apprehension that with the establishment of women's groups, the women could be segregated and disregarded

(I discuss this to some extent in the following section). The women themselves offered no one answer to this. The solutions they proposed were diverse just as much as the women were diverse. Some wanted their own federation in order to be able to influence the *Mahasangha*, others believed that it was important to be a part of the *Mahasangha,* while others still felt that the *Mahasangha* was not their concern. The women's attempts to form their own federation, or wanting to do so, is not mentioned in either of the two texts. Measures for gender equity and social justice are highlighted, but they are done so in a frame that is already set.

As far as my role in Nayagarh is concerned there was little space for feedback since the research was carried out more conventionally. But there are some effects that can be pointed out. For one, by taking up the question of the *samitis* I contributed to highlighting the issue of gender as did the report that I cite earlier although both did so in very different ways. My visit to Nayagarh may have also played a part in heightening the contradictions between the BOJBP and Anita. The presence of a researcher studying the women in the movement may have created more space for her critique of those "who always tried to decide over the women's groups"—the BOJBP and Oxfam and even the *Mahasangha* who wanted the women as 'statues.'

When I sent the BOJBP my fieldwork report after I returned to my university, I received a reply from Anita about an error in the report. I had written that there was no active women's group in Kesharpur. I had gone on to speculate if that was because of the strong presence of the male-dominated associations in the village. Anita's letter said that there was indeed a *mahila samiti* in the village, contradicting her own words to me in Kesharpur. I had no doubt put her in an awkward situation and added to the strained relations with the BOJBP. According to the Oxfam officer, the BOJBP had also blamed the *Mahasangha* staffer who was helping me to organize my trips to the villages, for trying to create trouble by taking me to the *Dalit* hamlet where the women and men had complained (on video) about harassment by the other castes in Kesharpur.

DEFINING THE LOCAL

Even a comparatively short visit by an outside, apparently neutral researcher contributed in many small ways to the gender and power relations in the Nayagarh context. Outsiders also contributed to constructing identities in different discursive contexts. In Drevdagen, for example, whenver the older men in the association acted as representatives of the village, the school was always brought up. The people from SLU, who aimed to help them in their local resource management activities, needed to hear these accounts of independent work by the villagers and of a history of collective action around the school that would make future collective action feasible. In fact, the school strike was so much bound up as the identity of Drevdagen that people who read my papers at the university, eager to find pockets of resistance by marginalized communities, wondered why I did not delve into it more. I had not given it prime space because when I was there 'to speak to the women about their work,' it was not taken up as a central issue. On the contrary, many spoke of the burden of that identity in their daily interactions with local authorities. They spoke to me as 'women' in Drevdagen and this identity sometimes stood in conflict with the one presented to outsiders as a villager of Drevdagen. As researchers or practitioners we are complicit in articulations of local identities in what we present as 'the important questions.'

The group from SLU had an agenda. They wanted to help people to gain rights to their environments. They were faced by forces strongly aligned against such efforts. As they saw it, broader discussion of participation and gender equity had the potential to disturb the already fragile nature of their efforts and to feed the resistance that they faced from the authorities and forest companies. An emphasis on gender relations challenged those efforts and their ownership of the ideal of working for the people. I was also stepping into someone else's territory whose boundaries were already defined. As Kristina in the FTPP/SLU group said to me,

> "We did not know that researchers were going to be involved in our project. . . . Why don't you focus on looking at women's networks."

What I was doing was women's matters (with the women), what they were doing was working with the community (with the men). I was indulging in village politics and they were working with questions of environmental governance. Can these territories be separate? It was a question of the bigger question as opposed to the smaller one. What I learnt from this experience was a lesson applicable not merely to development out there but for 'here,' at the university: about how complicated a vision can be, the vested interests in the topics and areas already defined and in the theories already written. And about us, development practitioners and researchers who try and shape development.

THE PRACTITIONER'S DILEMMA

Speaking about the structural problems of gender, the Oxfam review cited earlier states,

> "The difficulty is compounded for agencies like Oxfam which has to work through the existing organizations like the CBO and NGOs,[19] meaning that beyond a point, it cannot really change the ways of the functioning or the thinking on a particular issue of the organization concerned. At best it can stop giving funds to it" (Mitra 1997, 94).

On the one hand, inequality is recognized and stressed and on the other, given Oxfam's mandate to work through CBOs/NGOs, these are recognized as the representative organizations of the community, albeit inequitable and chauvinistic. This problem recurs in Drevdagen. Does it mean that the outsiders stop working within such contexts or with such organizations? Or does it mean that gender inequality is recognized and that, there is greater reflexivity on the part of development workers to see how they might in fact be strengthening inequitable relationships.

Even within Oxfam and in the report that pointed to the discrimination of women and the 'patriarchal nature of society,' there was an acceptance of a framework that was given. The solution sought was to make existing structures equitable. This approach has its limitations as I go on to theorize in Chapter 8. Support to women's groups from the outside is considered important. Oxfam opened the space for exploring this option by insisting on a women's program. But both for Oxfam and FTPP/SLU support to or involvement in the community was mediated by the 'formal' organizations. It was not considered possible to support the women other than by insisting on their inclusion.

My colleagues from SLU were practitioners and activists who wanted to support local forest management in Drevdagen. What was the point, Niklas said to me, of talking about the critiques of the association when the forest company was going to start felling the following month and clear-cut another area around the village. Recognition of the exercise of power that was discriminatory did not mean that practitioners and activists stop work but that they are aware of how they work, of whose interests they support and their own positions in the matrices of power. By treating these issues as irrelevant to the larger and important question (the felling of the forest) or as personal village politics, power relations block the building of non-normative ways of thinking about the issue. This does not mean that all norms are bad. Norms are discursive practices and to study them is to investigate how they also may make room for domination, by looking at what may be said and what may not be said on a particular topic. The rhetoric of local governance thus set the rules for radical political practice in such a way as to delegitimize the claims of the women.

CONCLUSION

This chapter examines how gender is constructed in the initiatives taken by the men and women in Drevdagen and Nayagarh. By choosing to organize separately, the women were not withdrawing from public spaces as claimed by the associations in their complaints of passive or illiterate women. They were in fact affirming their interest and willingness to work with village development and the environment. When the women did articulate a way of working with these issues, the organizations trying to bring about democratic change in the villages, hastened to take action to maintain the gendered *status quo*. . .(for the bigger cause). By looking at their everyday experiences, it is possible to understand the constraints on women within village organizations. The differences between the village organizations and the women's collectives lay not in visions for local governance and development, but in how such visions were to be defined and carried out.

The ideal picture of gender harmony among the men in the organizations was that women would collaborate with the men for the good of the community. There was no doubt that it was by the women joining the right forums, that is, those that the men had proclaimed as community organizations. The inclusion of women in these organizations however did not automatically challenge gendered inequalities. The increasing bureaucratization of village development work and formal organizations meant that the women were required to accommodate themselves to existing norms and structures rather than that the structures would be changed to accommodate their subjective positions, needs and ideas.

In both Nayagarh and Drevdagen they had begun by taking up what they called social issues, or development, along with the question of the forests. With the involvement of the development practitioners, the focus shifted increasingly to the forests, as the 'bigger' and more important question. Both cases are examples of a failure of support from practitioners outside, who despite their best intentions especially in Nayagarh were unable to support marginalized groups in the villages. In fact, the outsiders inadvertently strengthened male interests and gendered inequalities by supporting the men. The concept of unequal collaboration was reinforced by them, while they were trying to promote democracy and greater equality within decision-making. SLU practitioners expected the village association to take care of differences in power while they did not recognize how their own relationships impacted on village relations. The discourse of local governance *versus* empirical inconveniences like gender relations and especially in Nayagarh, the inabilities of addressing them directly despite wanting to, bring up inconsistencies between the abstract and the concrete, the theory and the practicalities of development.

There was a tendency among the outside development practitioners to separate the work of the women's groups and environmental governance into two different activities. This could be seen, for example, in the suggestion that I focus on women's networking and that the forest project did not have anything to do with it. Questions of interconnection and power were transformed into questions of discrete and separate categories instead of recognizing the importance of power in organizing the community. Differences are in fact intertwined and hierarchically organized. Disregard of the connections contributes to hiding exclusions or people's choices to opt out of formal spaces, who by doing so, affect the working of the formal groups and associations. Discounting everyday life precludes an understanding of the agency exercised by those not included in the formal forums and of the dynamic power relations that shape development and the environment. By avoiding or circumventing 'village politics' SLU practitioners for example avoided the heart of local governance, the local realities and relationships that must enter decision-making—and ran the risk of undermining the very project they hoped to promote. Given the contradictions and complexities that characterize each context, what may be said about gender equality, environmental governance and development in the two places and what lessons may be drawn? Before I outline these in Chapter 8, I turn to look beyond the micropolitics of the two places in Chapter 7 to what ideas about development mean for substantive gender equality in our present 'global' times.

7 Discordant Connections

Discourses on Gender and Grassroots Activism

In 2004 Wangari Maathai was awarded the Nobel Peace Prize, and the issue of women's rights in environmental matters appeared briefly on the international agenda. In a joint article, Maathai and Lena Sommestad, both active in the network of female environmental ministers, emphasized that women's interests must be taken into account when environmental policies are formulated (Maathai and Sommestad 2005). They position equality between men and women as a crucial development question—necessary for effective and sustainable development, especially in poorer countries. The importance of gender equality and of the relationship between third-world women and the environment is evident. Development and a certain standard of welfare make these issues appear to be less urgent in a wealthier country such as Sweden. However, research with the women's groups in the forest communities in India and Sweden showed otherwise. First, questions of gender and power in environmental management are relevant not only in a poorer country such as India but also in a richer country such as Sweden. In the latter, they can take forms that make gender discrimination more difficult to contest. Second, development discourses about equality and empowerment of oppressed third-world women not only affect how gender equality is conceptualized and practiced in the global South but also shape the possibilities for gender equality in the North. Understanding how this takes place opens an opportunity for interruption in an order and in a space (a global/social order and a developed and gender-equal space) that appears to have become narrower under the umbrella of development, welfare, and growth. It brings into question the category of development not only in a Southern but also in a Northern context, where the North, especially Sweden, is taken as a referent for development and gender equality.

In this chapter, I trace some of the contradictions and connections in the ways in which gender equality and women's empowerment are conceptualized in women's struggles in Nayagarh, India, and in the village of Drevdagen in Sweden. Examples of the women's grassroots activism from the two case studies give material form to abstract discussions about

This chapter previously published in *Signs*.

the possibilities for women's agency in different cultural settings. In both study sites, women in villages in rural and peripheral areas (in relation to policy—and decision-making centers) formed organizations parallel to the male-dominated organizations in their villages. In absolute terms, the women in Sweden were far better off: in health care, wealth, availability of food, choice to work and marry, and geographical mobility. Yet their meetings as women were hedged with ambiguity and sparked resistance in the village. Power and discrimination were veiled and subtle in Sweden. Paradoxically, the rhetoric of gender equality that is pervasive in Sweden serves to mask forms of subordination and makes it difficult to question the purported neutrality of given structures. The Indian women were more vocal about discrimination against them. Outside intervention in gender issues was acceptable in the Indian development context but was regarded as interference in what were considered to be personal relations in the case in Sweden.

Gender and environmental relations were conceptualized in ways that were specific to each context but also carried the impress of outside forces. Strong normative assumptions about development, gender equality, and empowerment resonated with one another in both places. A complex movement of ideas at the global level—about what it means to be developed, rural or urban, empowered, and independent—found expression in the everyday practice of development in both places.

THE RELATIONAL ANALYSIS

Third-world feminists and others have challenged universal conceptions of gender. They emphasize that understanding the different ways in which meanings are produced and challenged reveals the complex and specific political choices that caution us against ahistorical and universalizing categories (see Mohanty 2003). Gender is a historically and culturally variable category. Yet, as the studies show, overlapping discursive contexts and recurring practices in the politics of everyday life also reveal links between distant places, links that in turn pose new questions for the study of gender and power in an interconnected world. Ideas about gender and gender equality are formed by various local material practices, but as the two cases indicate, they are also a hybrid of different influences. Despite shifting meanings and contextual relations, the practices of gender equality in particular places echo one another, are marked by the histories and relationships of power that structure the world, and are linked to ideas about modernity and development. According to Katz, situated knowledge assumes knowledge at a single point, the knowing subject. This, she argues, has tended to facilitate a collapse of dimensionality. She calls instead for a topography to elucidate the intersection of processes with others elsewhere and thereby inspire a different kind of politics, one in which crossing space and "jumping scale" are obligatory rather than overlooked (2001, 1230–1231).

Crossing space by reading stories from India and Sweden made it possible for me to develop a relational analysis that I have drawn upon in earlier chapters and elaborate further here. The methodology outlined earlier in Chapter 1 and that I employ in this chapter to study different analytic frameworks and different geographies includes three elements: freezing time, reversing the gaze from North to South, and embracing critical subjectivity. Drawing on the material presented in the preceding three chapters, I scrutinize language and actions as indications of underlying structures of meaning, indications that tell us not just about the person speaking and acting but about a wider discursive context that goes beyond the micropolitics of the villages. I study not only collective action but also how individual women define their subjective positions within a collective. I use the case study from India as a frame of reference rather than accepting conventional assumptions of gender equality where Northern principles are the reference points. As a researcher working in both the global North and the global South, I became aware of a global discourse on gender and the need for reflexivity in situations where I am both an academic and an active participant.

When one is discussing gender, equality, or empowerment, the challenge is to look beyond macrogeneralizations while also avoiding a fixation on difference between the places. By arguing that relationships of power can determine the flows of ideas on equality, I do not imply that the North or the South is symbolically and ideologically fixed or that there is a homogeneous body of ideas. However, there are dominant ways of thinking about development in which the West is a referent (see Mohanty 2003; Pieterse 1991; Ang 2001). Nor do the connections between the two places imply a one-way flow. Conversations between them have unexpected effects. The relational analysis calls into question prevailing metaphors and categorical divides while keeping in sight the relationships of power that organize the world. It has been possible to locate each case in its context yet carry out a dialogue between the two across what might be regarded as the development divide.

People in the two locations in India and Sweden were linked by the fact that both were affected by similar discussions on gender and development, although their experiences were not the same. This can be seen in Western influence in policy making on gender in India. But a colonial discourse on oppressed women is also palpable in how Sweden positions itself in terms of gender equality, as unique in its relations to others. Though Sweden was never a colonial power itself, the contemporary effects of colonization and of immigration to Sweden clearly reflect thinking about the other (de los Reyes, Molina, and Mulinari 2002). Women in Nayagarh gave substance to wider social debates about women and development in unanticipated ways as they took up issues of discrimination and argued for their cause.

In Drevdagen, the categories of development and gender equality were used to stall change and disregard inequalities. In the following sections, I move between different geographical levels as I analyze the two places. The first section is a discussion of public policy making and dominant discourses on gender equality and empowerment that framed the women's activism. I study how national discourses and policies on gender, equality, and empowerment played an important part in forming women's subjectivities and modes of identification. In the second section, I go on to examine how beliefs about gender, equality, and empowerment are given meaning in the material and discursive practices of the men and women in both study sites. In the third and in the last section, I analyze how these beliefs influenced dimensions of difference in conceptualizing collective and individual agency and in what counted as gender equality or empowerment in the two contexts, and I trace the connections between the two places.

JÄMSTÄLLDHET IN SWEDEN AND EMPOWERMENT IN INDIA

Striking in discussions about gender in Sweden is how male dominance and the different treatment of women and men have become illegitimate as a basic social principle, both in state policies and in wider discourses in society. Discourses of the new fatherhood and gender equality are culturally dominant today, regardless of actual practice (Plantin, Månsson, and Kearney 2000). "Contemporary mainstream researchers, decision makers and journalists often describe the transformation of Sweden following the introduction of general suffrage as having created a society which is both more egalitarian and more women-friendly than most others. Public policies aim at making it possible to achieve gender neutrality, defined as equal opportunities for women and men in the labor market, the family and political life" (Gustafsson 1997, 42). Sweden's path to gender equality has been through the labor market, and women's presence in the labor force has been an accomplishment. Gender-neutral policies were effectively promoted as the way to achieve gender equality so much so that gender equality has become conflated with neutrality. The state is seen as the main source of economic and moral support for gender equality through its welfare policies and through the public-sector labor market, which employs large numbers of women. A sense of uniqueness, of having come far in questions of gender equality, permeates Sweden. The subtle yet significant presence of the not quite-developed South is evident in how gender equality is defined in policy but also in the subjectivities of women in the Swedish village I worked with, as I demonstrate below. The following lines taken from the Swedish government memorandum on gender equality epitomize this thinking,

> "We in Sweden have come a long way compared with other nations, yes, in fact, we are far ahead of the rest of the world. We are glad to

> share our experiences; we are glad to export our Swedish model for gender equality. But this, our first place, should not lead us to think that we are done. As yet there is a lot to be done in many areas. . . .We all have a responsibility to ensure gender equality. All the ministers, all the parliamentarians, and Swedish citizens in general must feel like Sweden's gender equality ministers" (Skrivelse 1999/2000, 6).

The nationalistic tone in dominant policy and research discourses on Sweden's exceptional record on gender equality has led to a line of feminist argument that claims that the emphasis on gender equality has shifted attention from the real problem, that is, discrimination against women. The word for gender equality, *jämställdhet* that gained currency in the 1990s is considered problematic by several feminists. The basic reason, argues Rönnblom, is that a word symbolizing a vision is being used to name a problem (2002, 213). The term is infused with positive connotations and with a focus on goals and aspirations without naming the group that is disadvantaged. This consensus term (Tollin 2000) is used to discuss and explain power relations between women and men and is linked to democracy and justice. Since it refers to a vision, there is a great deal of variance in how the term is interpreted in practice. To speak of injustice in society by linking power and gender becomes difficult when the official word available is a description of a political ideal and one that emphasizes harmonious interdependence. Yet sexual difference is implicit in political discourse, not least in the framing of *jämställdhet*, which, in contrast to *jämlikhet* (equality), is a term used specifically for equality between men and women. Thus, a discourse is created where the rhetoric of equality and assumptions about political decision-making as a gender-neutral activity conceal the existence of a gendered political order and the continued subordination of women (see Gustafsson 1997).

Problematizing this further, postcolonial feminist writers in Sweden maintain that *jämställdhet* has been used to distinguish Swedes from immigrant populations and has been established as a basic part of the Swedish self-image, in relation to the rest of the world as well as to the immigrant populations (de los Reyes, Molina, and Mulinari 2002, 306).[1] According to Diana Mulinari and Anders Neergard, Sweden has long been characterized by a form of welfare state nationalism that is based on a "we pride" (2004, 210) in contrast to a world that is created as irrational, chaotic, and filled with conflict. They write that the image of the generous and tolerant Swedish identity has been weakened in the past twenty years in the context of the shrinking welfare state and through events such as the Palme murder, the Göteborg fire, and Nazi murders that have acquired symbolic significance.[2] Mulinari and Neergard (2004) write that against this background, *jämställdhet*, or gender equality between men and women, is the only successful 'cultural product' that can be used as an ethnic marker against those who are constructed as 'the other.'

A diffracted image of gender equality in Sweden appears in the Indian national context. Here gender is "an 'issue' in another sense of the word: a crisis, a problem, a scandal" (Sundar Rajan 1999, 2). Rajeswari Sundar Rajan traces this conceptualization to the milestone report on gender equality published in 1974 (*Towards Equality*, produced by the government of India) that pointed to the skewed demographics of the female/male population ratio, the decline in women's workforce participation levels and in levels of literacy and health, all of which showed how poorly women were faring in independent India. Gender gaps in development, employment, nutrition, land distribution and inheritance became impossible to overlook. Thus, across the board in government concerns, social movements, discourses, disciplines, and sites of action, gender began to figure as an issue as well as a category of analysis (1999).

Debates on gender have meshed directly with and have actively constituted prevailing conceptions of India's national identity, conceptions that include the reconfigured primacy accorded to development (John 1999, 110). The fate of women became linked to mainstream development agendas,

> "Development experts cite 'gender bias' as the cause of poverty in the 'Third World'; population planners declare their commitment to the empowerment of Indian women; economists speak of the feminization of the Indian labor force. . . . There is a sense, therefore, in which the new visibility is an index of the success of the women's movement. But clearly this success is also problematic" (Tharu and Niranjana 2001, 494).

Increasingly, women are represented as efficient workers and economic subjects, reflecting a national discourse and international influences. Nevertheless, policies and programs still treat women as needy, and images of victimhood and incapacity persist. The help provided to women, such as family planning programs or sanitation, is in keeping with stereotypical ideas about women's roles. However, there have been unexpected exceptions. Awareness-raising programs have led women to organize against oppressive state organs, resulting in "a peculiar situation of the state sponsoring women's struggles against itself" (Lingam 2002, 317).

Outside influences on how gender is construed can be felt more tangibly in India than in Sweden, reflecting an overt power difference between the North and South. International donor agencies and nongovernmental organizations are important in shaping policies and development activities. Women's marginalization from centers of power is widely discussed, not least because the large amount of development literature has helped to create a space for so-called women's issues. International feminist networks have been able to influence where and how various forms of development aid are channeled. Northern aid agencies often demand a gender perspective or gender component to their programs in the South. Although the validity and the effects vary, they often succeed in treating women as a special category. This has led to the co-option of such agendas by bureaucracies. Gender becomes a technocratic measure, resulting in its depoliticization as it is turned into a matter of monitoring and planning rather than struggle (Baden and Goetz 1998). Empowerment through self-help groups or support for women's groups has often been bureaucratized and interpreted by government and nongovernmental organizations or aid agencies in a simplistic manner. Underscoring these measures is an assumption of inequality and of an obvious male dominance that characterizes much of the discussion on gender. Formal structures such as administrative arms of the government, forest committees, or village organizations evidently lack women and are not necessarily seen to represent women as a group.

Images of the gender-neutral and gender-equal Sweden, as opposed to the patriarchal nature of the state and society in India, have played out in various ways in women's organizing in both Nayagarh and Drevdagen in their respective modes of self-identification as well as in the actions taken by women in both sites. When seen in relation to each other, the two cases make clear women's possibilities for action in different national and discursive settings.

MODES OF SELF-IDENTIFICATION

Meeting in the *kvinnoforum* in Sweden or in the *mahila samitis* in India was neither natural nor self-evident. Both were spaces that the women had consciously constructed. The making of these spaces was not only the result of the women's social location. Social boundaries between them—such as class, age, and their place in the labor force or caste—were not always erased as the women sought to organize together, but these boundaries were often acknowledged as the women found ways to relate to one another over them. The experience of collectivity proved to be their strength rather than a sign of their weakness as individuals who were unable to act individually and independently. However, a fear of being seen as weak and incapable as a result of choosing to organize in their own group troubled the women in different ways at both study sites.

Ideals about equality and about the gender neutrality of common spaces were present in Drevdagen in several ways in the women's own doubts about organizing separately and in the opposition to their organizing. It became apparent that the women saw themselves as autonomous, but they also talked about the male dominance ingrained in much of the *föreningsliv*, the associational life of Swedish villages. However, none of the women thought of themselves as being personally disadvantaged simply by being a woman. On personal and individual levels, they saw themselves as equal with men. In spite of this (or perhaps because of this), when it came to forming the women's group, there was a certain amount of tension. Taking on an identity as a member of a women's group was uncomfortable for some since officially there were already neutral committees in the village in which both men and women could be involved.

To complain in what was regarded as a gender-equal system could be seen as being hysterical. For the women in Drevdagen, the ideas on equality thus functioned as a form of self-restraint, preventing the women from openly voicing their discontent if they were excluded or discriminated against. The women themselves spoke of being strong women. For them, acknowledging discrimination and thereby assuming the role of a victim would be antithetical to that identity. In justifying their group, the women chose consciously to build on their strengths rather than emphasize disadvantage. They considered themselves equal with the men. This did not mean that they did not see disadvantage, but that it expressed itself differently for different women. Age and their life experiences (the kind of employment that they had or their level of education) made a difference in how they regarded and dealt with feelings of injustice. Some women who had lived in the city before felt that it was easier to deal with municipal authorities than others who felt that the authorities regarded them as backward, rural women. The women's relations to the men in the village were also varied. They felt it important to emphasize their differences.

There was thus a tension in acknowledging unequal power relations. It meant acknowledging discrimination, which could imply loss of self-worth and power in a system in which everyone was supposed to be equal. Tensions such as these sometimes made it difficult for the women to articulate a common identity (or rather the identity needed to be reaffirmed each time) or to make their activities and discussions more stable and continuous. Their need for informality stemmed partly from this. It put together women who were different and wanted to do things differently. For example, some felt that it was important to involve men in their forum whereas others did not. In comparison, the women's identity as members of women's groups in Nayagarh was not in question. The women claimed that it was through their group that they saw themselves as making a difference. They were working purposively for activities that needed organizing. They were doing more than just going about their daily chores, which they do at the individual or family level and which are often governed by tradition and custom (regulated by the men and, for the younger women, also by older women). While in the groups they communicated and acted together for something that concerned most of them or when individual women needed the support of the others. They seemed to have more of a sense of identity as a coherent group in comparison to the women in Drevdagen.

The Swedish women drew on a repository of meanings that existed outside them as they described their experiences. Initially, in get-togethers they sometimes explained women's lack of participation in village and forest committees as a result of low self-esteem. However, nobody spoke of herself as having low self-esteem. This image was always used to describe someone else:

the old-fashioned, shy, and traditional woman, an image that the women saw themselves working against. They did not see their own roles as mothers or wives as conservative, a label they applied when discussing the previous generation. I described my research in Nayagarh to members of the *kvinnoforum*, prompting a discussion on what it meant to be modern in India with respect to gender relations and equality. One woman remarked,

> "I have heard that in India women have become stronger . . . have developed quite a lot, ever since India has become modern. Perhaps that is why they have been able to do these things together."

Another woman was offended at being associated with the women in Nayagarh.

> "But we are different," she told me. "We are working women."[3]

The Swedish women's subjective positions as modern women were built very much in contrast to the earlier generation as well as to the not-so-modern women of the third world who were not working women in the same sense. Not surprisingly, this attitude was absent in the stories of the older women (in their sixties, seventies, and eighties) who spoke of the strong women of the past, women in their mothers' generation who had moved to these mountains and built up farming communities.

The importance of being working women recurred often in our conversations. The women's involvement in the workforce, mostly in service positions, was an important part of their identity as independent women, reflecting Sweden's efforts over the years to bring about gender equality through the labor market.[4] This was an important component of their status: being modern working women provided a sense of liberation from the drudgery of the past.

Yet, in the stories of the younger women (ages 30–60) in the forum, contradictory images abound. There were tensions in how the women regarded their working lives. They were proud of working outside the home, but many felt confined by not being able to do community work for the village and by having to travel long distances to work. Although many worked outside the home, they also spoke of not being able to do the work they wanted on their own terms and of being trapped in the jobs they had. Their involvement in the workforce—which in some respects provided them with economic freedom and an identity—also made them prisoners of a system over which they had little or no control. Several worked in the health sector and spoke of their difficult positions and the fact that they "were made to do all kinds of strange things" in the bouts of rationalization of health care services undertaken by the state during the 1990s. Many women insisted that motherhood, in comparison to work, was a relationship that was rewarding, in which they were appreciated (described in greater detail in Chapter 5).

This was not a glorification of motherhood but reflected the practicalities of their lives. It was "central to many women's ideas about themselves" for which many felt there was "little or no validation in dominant discourses" (O'Connor 1998, 131). A strong notion of mothers as primarily responsible for children in Sweden is juxtaposed with ideas about gender equality, employment, and dual responsibility (Elvin-Nowak and Thomsson 2001). Dual responsibility is a strong discourse in Sweden regardless of actual practice (Magnusson 2001). For some women, living and working in the village meant that negotiations over the use of their time and juggling responsibilities and work were for their own benefit rather than that of their employers, suggesting that to work in paid jobs was not always rewarding.

For the women in Nayagarh, discrimination was self-evident. They linked their disadvantage in the villages to wider orders beyond their immediate or local context. Mamta Tiwari, one of the field organizers for the women's program, expressed this in a report,

> "The government has reserved 33 percent of seats for women. It may rise to 50 percent in the future. But this reservation will not solve our problem unless we represent our problems effectively. Women should not only conduct environmental work, they should protect themselves, build up awareness in society. The purpose of the *mahila* program should not be only confined to discussions and meetings, rather it should be translated into action" (Tiwari n.d.).

DIMENSIONS OF DIFFERENCE

The women's modes of self-identification were reinforced by several dimensions that bring out the contextual differences between the two places: the formality or informality of the groups, the rhetoric they used, and the ways in which they took action. Being publicly women, that is, presenting themselves formally as women's groups, was possible for the women in Nayagarh in a way that was not for the Drevdagen women. Since the *mahila samitis* were part of the women's development program, they followed certain rules and regulations: they had officeholders, documented their activities, and carried out economic activity together. But what really made them formal was that they presented themselves as a women's group and were accepted as such by the rest of the village. The *samitis* also provided a separate space sanctioned by the forest organization and the village. The women's program accorded them a legitimacy that the women would not have had otherwise. It drew them together outside their households into a public space sanctioned by the community and the state. In acquiring even limited visibility as a formal group, the women had nondomestic reasons to meet, to establish linkages, and perhaps to build nascent ideas of solidarity (see Krishna 2004, 33).

The formality of the program gave the groups the opportunity to become stable entities within the village (for a while) and to link up with other groups. The *samitis* differed from one another to the varying extent to which they were active and in terms of the questions with which they chose to work. Their formality sometimes resulted in greater bargaining power for women *vis-à-vis* other groups such as landlords, forest committees, violent husbands, or in-laws.

In Drevdagen the women found it necessary to work informally. They had few prospects for influencing discussions in the formal structures on questions important to them. The issues they took up were often considered subordinate to what were regarded as more important questions. The men in the village associations worked hard to maintain existing power relations by asserting the gender neutrality of common spaces. "Nobody has stopped the women from attending the village associations," retorted one of the men in the association when he was told that many women felt apprehensive about attending meetings.[5] For the women, it was difficult to challenge a system that was suffused with notions of equality and welfare for everyone, that existed under constant threat from the urban center, and where there was a culture of self-imposed guilt at going against the order. Speaking of discrimination or gender made you someone who was looking for problems. It was against village harmony. This was reflected in the women's ambivalence about speaking (or limitations in being able to speak) from within or as an all-women group. It was not as if disadvantages for women were not recognized at all. But as the quotation above makes evident, the problem was individualized. Women who did not attend meetings or speak out were considered lacking in self-confidence, disinterested in village affairs, old-fashioned, or passive. It was made into the problem of individual women and not one of an order of gender and power. In this conception, there were other "normal" ways of dealing with problems that women in the village may have with certain men, through proper channels. Formal equality, however, precluded an analysis of substantive inequality. This was one reason for the need for informality. While in Nayagarh it was through the formal nature of the group that the women were able to wield greater bargaining power *vis-à-vis* other groups, in Sweden it was the group's informal nature—its not really being a group at all, nor being a women's project—that was important. The *kvinnoforum* came into being whenever the women met rather than being a stable entity. This strategic informality made the *kvinnoforum* more difficult to pin down and oppose. The informality enabled the group to be more inclusive of different women and to take up a range of issues.

The women in Nayagarh often got their demands met by confronting formal authorities such as male landlords or district officials, as in the stories described in Chapter 5. By taking action publicly, the women were demolishing the myth of being victims and beneficiaries as they demanded what they considered rightfully theirs. They communicated their message in a bodily way, exhibiting bodies that are otherwise meant to be confined to the home.

By taking part in the action, they affirmed their own identity. Although some of these demonstrations initially were started by one *samiti*, women from other castes and villages also joined in, making their identity as women (rather than as caste members or village residents) important for the moment. As Bauman writes, "In action one can be a victim without shame" (1995, 73). The women of Nayagarh were using and demolishing their victimhood in these terms.

Politics in Drevdagen did not have space for such action. Similar actions by women would be seen as embarrassing because women in Sweden were understood to be equal, definitely not victims, even though they were regarded as passive by both men and women. The importance of the women's bodies in Nayagarh and the way in which the women made use of them are significant. In Sweden, in an assumed neutrality of male and female, the implications of the body are to be denied. Here it was something far less dramatic, merely meeting as women, that became controversial. The collective brought to light unequal gender relations in Sweden in a way that was already obvious in India. Perhaps that also explains why it appeared more threatening. Difference was given a political meaning.

In keeping with this was a noticeable difference in the rhetoric used by the *samitis* in Nayagarh and by the *kvinnoforum* in Drevdagen. There was a certain self-restraint in the language in the *kvinnoforum*. Although their actions suggested that the reason for organizing was the need for this space as women, the women were quick to emphasize that they were working for the benefit of the village and its development. Except for one occasion, their reticence at the prospect of publicly challenging male domination and exclusion from decision-making in the village association was the result of an effort to not draw undue attention to themselves as women—a position that would make them vulnerable in a society built on notions of neutrality. This was a strategic move that may be seen as the opposite of strategic essentialism—a strategic neutrality. Nor did they speak out publicly as a women's collective, unlike the women in Nayagarh.

The women's modes of action in both places were conditioned by the role of external intervention and by the village men's varying responses to their organizing. Ideals and discourses about gender relations were reflected in the images the women had about the men. When I asked the women in a Nayagarh village what made them successful as a group, one answer was,

> "Our men are good. The men in other villages get jealous when their women get more advanced and try and stop them from acting together" (see Chapter 5).

This was contradictory to the views of women in the *kvinnoforum*. They often spoke of how old habits die hard, implying a backward-looking view on gender relations among many men in the rural areas. They compared the village men to my colleagues working with the forest project. The women believed that the city men did not know about the discrimination in the village, would not behave in this manner themselves, and would do something about it if they did know.[6] There was a belief that times had changed and that everyone was in fact equal. The unequal relations that kept recurring were regarded not as a reflection of present values but as remains of the past.

Although not quite indulging in gender wars, the married women in India were much more outspoken about expressing conflictual relations with the men in their households and villages. In Sweden, personal relationships with male partners were rarely the subject matter of group discussions. When they were, they were characterized as a 'love contract' (Magnusson 2001), where relations are negotiated through love, making the relationship personal and unique. This is not to say that there are no wars in Swedish households or no love in Indian ones. Rather, these images are descriptive of normative ways of talking about male-female relations. Marriage in India is more a social arrangement than only a private matter between the couple, as it is regarded in Sweden.

It is necessary to theorize not only the separate social interests that women's groups may have but also the deep interdependencies between men and women, which are vital for understanding gender relations. Differences in the men's responses were as important as the differences among the women and had a role in shaping women's activism. In Sweden, many projects spearheaded by the women could be carried out because of the support of men and women in the village. Both in Sweden and in India there were men who believed that the women needed their own groups. In the view of the Swedish women, there was a generational difference in this respect among the men in the village. It was considered easier to speak to the younger men. It was through younger men, who were often relatives, that the women sometimes tried to influence association meetings. The opposition expressed by some of these younger and "good" men (to use the terminology of the women in Naygarh), however, contributed to the uncertainty among the women. These men's hostility may have sharpened the sense of discrimination. It contradicted the commonplace assumption in Sweden that gender equality is being brought about via a generational shift.

Different men responded in different ways, although they cannot necessarily be placed in different categories (such as age) in their relation to the women's organizing. The male leadership of the forest organizations in Nayagarh, mainly the older generation, spoke of the need to make the women aware, to impart training. The younger generation (though far from all) spoke about needing to involve women in the forest federation for reasons of both efficiency and equity. The Oxfam officer responsible for the funding of the women's development program also held this view. Men's response to the need for the women to have their own group depended on the particular situation and the men's involvement in that situation, although a normative order was also being negotiated. For example, in Drevdagen, the younger men in the association spoke about the importance of women's networks and considered it important to work toward gender equality. Yet the presence of a *kvinnoforum* in their own village was deemed dangerous, especially if it interfered in forest matters, traditionally a male domain.

Women's activism in Nayagarh was sometimes aided by the men ("our men are good"), and at other times it was a response to violence against women. Forest committee members at the forestry offices often invited me to come and see how well the *mahila samitis* in their villages were working. This did not necessarily mean that they believed in them for the same reasons as the women, but it does indicate support for the women's organizing. As the coordinator for the women's program said to me,

> "As it is now, some men are supportive in some places while in others they do not want the women to get together or go for training camps or get-togethers. They feel that the women just go there to eat and get smart and then destroy the household. They are afraid that the women won't listen to the men after having organized. *Mahila samitis* can be strong if they are supported by the men."[7]

The development practitioners who worked with the men in the communities in Drevdagen and Nayagarh also happened to be men. In Drevdagen, the development practitioners insisted that women were included in the village associations. However, they regarded the women's critique as being a result of personal politics that the women needed to be able to solve with the men in their village. In Nayagarh, although the development practitioners wanted to support the women in the *mahila samitis*, they felt unable to relate to them directly instead of through village organizations. But for a brief period the women had support in their organizing from Oxfam-funded programs implemented through the forest organizations.

The women's relations with the men in their villages once again reflected larger discourses in their societies. Nayagarh was considered male-dominated, and individual men who were different were seen as progressive. In Sweden, regarded as a leader in gender equality internationally but also in its own image, men in rural areas who exercised power over others were seen as relics from the past. This power, however, is not a phenomenon of the past but is rooted very much in the present. References to the past to explain unequal relations make acceptable inequalities that are embedded in and have their own history in existing relations of power.

WOMEN ARE LIKE BOATS: THE CONUNDRUMS OF PERSONAL AND COLLECTIVE AGENCY

Studying the trajectories of the two groups in relation to each other directs attention to how the personal and the collective take shape in different ways. One of the men in the forest federation in Nayagarh said with a sigh that women refused to come to meetings and training workshops unless several were invited together,

> "Women are like boats," he concluded, referring to the convoys of catamarans that went out to fish in the sea. "They always want to go out together. When they will be able to go out alone, become educated and do things on their own, they will be independent . . . empowered."[8]

But was it this independence that constituted empowerment for the women in the two places? Kabeer (2001) writes that one facet of empowerment is the ability to choose. In this sense empowerment may be seen as a somewhat normative idea. The women in Sweden were able to choose (more or less) where they lived, whom to marry, and how many children to have, choices that were not available for many women in India. In that respect, the women of Sweden were already empowered. But their space for collective agency was circumscribed by the dominant discourse on equality and modernization. The ideal and discourse of gender equality, by making discrimination illegitimate, had the negative effect of creating barriers for what women may, or may not, do or question in their everyday lives.

In Nayagarh, women's agency was not always recognized. The notion of individual empowerment through modernization was not consistent with the idea of the women organizing in groups. True enough, the women's activism in Nayagarh did not always lead to a better life for them. On a personal level, once home from meetings, they were still expected to cover their heads and not to speak in the presence of older males. These were the same women who had fought for their cause with male moneylenders and forest officials. Their confidence in themselves and their success, in certain instances, did lead to changes in houschold gender relations, but there was no direct cause and effect. In a draft evaluation report on the community forestry groups commissioned by Oxfam (referred to in Chapter 6), the authors narrate the story of the president of one of the women's groups whose husband beat her for taking up the cause of a village woman who had been cast out by her own husband (Mitra 1997). The authors use this single case to dismiss what the women were saying or were doing in everyday village life: solving disputes, dealing with violent husbands and nasty mothers-in-law, and working with problems related to dowry. Espousing the idea of the individual empowered woman, they claimed that the women's groups were ineffective in changing gender domination in the home.

Cleaver puts it succinctly, "As 'empowerment' has become a buzzword in development, an essential objective of projects, its radical, challenging and transformatory edge has been lost. The concept of action has become individualized, empowerment depoliticized" (2001, 37). Third-world feminists have criticized the focus on "a singular women's consciousness" (Mohanty 2003, 81). Mohanty writes that the strategy is to speak from within a collective. Doris Sommer "identifies the 'plural' or 'collective' self of Latin American women's testimonials as 'the possibility to get beyond the gap between public and private spheres and beyond the often helpless solitude that has plagued Western women even more than men since the rise of capitalism'" (Mohanty 2003, 82, quoting Sommer). Collective organizing may seem to jeopardize gains made by individual women who are able to find a place for themselves in the system. But, both in India and in Sweden, acting together on their own terms constituted empowerment for the women at the collective and village levels, highlighting that there is not always a correlate between individual and collective empowerment or between the strategic and the practical.

On the one hand, by regarding women as incapable, the men in Nayagarh held attitudes that limited the women. On the other hand, the experience of discrimination due to poverty gave both men and women a lens through which to develop a structural analysis of certain inequalities and the need for collective action. The men and women here, by and large, were spared the kind of individualism that attributes every inequality to personal failures on the part of the less rewarded. Understanding caste and class discrimination perhaps helps one understand the fact of sex discrimination, and understanding the need for an independent community forestry movement might help one to understand the need for women's groups. This may be one reason (apart from the fact that the women's program was part of the community forestry movement) why several men active in the movement tended to support the women's groups although they had their own views on how the groups were to function in relation to themselves (c.f. Jane Mansbridge 1999, 300 whose reasoning explains the differential support for the women's movement among white and black men and women in the United States). The women's groups tended not to position themselves in opposition to individual men but in opposition to what they regarded as male behavior, especially in cases of violence and dowry, because their men or some men could be good. In their view, development was indeed incomplete without gender. But for them, development was a transformation not only in which women became independent or empowered but in which jealous men became good.

In an ideal world there would be more direct correlation between personal and collective agency that leads to empowerment. However, discrimination takes many different forms, and though it may be systematic, there is not necessarily a cause-and-effect relationship between the personal and the collective or the strategic and the practical. We need to be open in imagining what women's liberation will be like in the multiple spaces in which women may choose to act individually but also collectively.

Clearly, women in both places worked not only for themselves but also for an equitable society for women and men. But issues of power were highlighted more often in India. As one of the field organizers wrote in a report,

> "There is no point talking about the forests when women do not have power themselves" (Tiwari n.d.).

The Indian women described themselves as a women's group and took up questions that may be seen to be more challenging of gender relations and were more specifically related to discrimination against women in comparison with the women's group in Sweden. This does not imply that power and discrimination were not issues in the Swedish village. Rather, the space for taking up questions of power and discrimination was smaller. But the women were resisted all the same, not because of what they said but because of what their collectiveness suggested.

To organize as women in the village in Sweden felt illegitimate. A rhetoric of collaboration and gender harmony hid unequal power relations. This was reinforced by wider orders of meanings in policy and institutions. Women's organizing became a "forbidden action" (Eduards 2002). An important contextual distinction between the two places is that in India there was a marked perception and acknowledgement of difference whereas in Sweden that difference was expected to be minimized for reasons of equality. It is a contrast not so much in perception of difference but in the response to it.

Although their actions were by no means seamless or noncontradictory, by stressing the need to have their own space the women of the *kvinnoforum* produced what Patti Lather calls "new configurations of social relations rather than reproduc[ing] . . . the behaviors that instil dominant values in us" (Lather 1991, 96). The very act of forming the *kvinnoforum* was an act of interrupting dominant practice, although nothing was said overtly about challenging the status quo. The women's plans and everyday activities such as organizing village festivities or keeping the village clean as part of the *kvinnoforum* or the *samitis* were not very different from the work they may have done in the absence of these groups. It was, instead, the structure of the alternative spaces they created for themselves that made their organizing political and caused antagonism. By organizing as women, the women made men visible as men and not as neutral individuals.

The "surprise factor" (Smith and Smith 1983, 114) of experiencing their subordination as a result of a structure that went beyond their immediate relationships was not relevant in the case of the women in Nayagarh, as it was in Drevdagen. The Nayagarh women did not expect to have much direct influence over the committees as individual women or over state agencies. They had less to lose and much to gain by speaking from within a women's group.

For several activists and scholars in the Swedish context, violence against women is the perpetuation of male power over women. Eduards writes that in women's collective action related to the body, violence and power are particularly challenging for democracy because it is men who are singled out as responsible, and this in turn because they are men, "The gender power order is revealed in its nakedness" (1997, 21). In India, however, this connection is far from simple. In the perception of the women in Nayagarh, mothers-in-law (and other female relatives) were often instrumental in instigating, abetting, and sometimes taking part in violence against a daughter-in-law. The women's organizing in Nayagarh was directed as much against inhumane mothers-in-law as, for instance, against husbands and fathers-in-law.

Men from outside the villages played an important role in both places. Development projects, especially those with participatory approaches, have been criticized for reinforcing unequal relationships by prioritizing those who are most vocal at meetings or by constructing certain male members as 'the community' (see Guijt and Shah 1998). As compared to the case in Sweden, however, in India it was permissible for development practitioners to challenge unequal relationships. The reason is that these inequalities are more obvious in India but also, importantly, that it is more permissible to challenge inequalities in a rural, third-world society that is saturated with development discourses and in which inequality is a premise to begin with. Outside intervention did not cause the change, but, based on an understanding of gender inequalities, it provided a little extra space for the women, which some of them used to negotiate power relations. Intervention in gender relations from outside had more legitimacy.

The relational analysis in this article has uncovered new ground by dwelling on the connections between the Swedish and Indian contexts. The connections played out in ways that were contextual but also discordant. Development discourses about oppressed women and the need for women's empowerment in the global South shaped the spaces for conceptualizing gender equality in both sites: in India, a country where assertions for the need to empower its rural women are frequent, but also in developed Sweden, with its self-image of being far ahead in gender equality in relation to other countries. Statements about victimized and incapable women who need help circumscribed the actions of women in India. At the same time, the discussion of male dominance and victimized women gave the Indian women space to bring up discrimination and to press for change. In Sweden the debates centered on equality and participation. This vision of equality encouraged the idea that the system was good and that women just needed to be added to it to make it perfect. The appreciation of being developed was echoed in how women in Drevdagen formed their subject positions as modern working women in contrast to traditional women in the past and in third-world countries as well as in their ambivalence about whether and how much to challenge the system. It was also reflected in the ease with which my university colleagues regarded gendered inequality in environmental governance as a problem in the global South but not relevant in Sweden.

Crossing space and jumping scale reveal how discourses are reproduced at different levels, from the international and national policy levels to village politics in Sweden and India. The use of the term 'development' showed connections in dominating assumptions both in India and in Sweden about what development is and how gender relations ought to be organized in a developed society. My comparative analysis of the gender politics in both places challenges the linearity inherent in discussions of development and modernization, the notion that women's empowerment follows from economic development or that gender equality comes from a linear progression into modernity. The focus on individual equality in Sweden put the onus on women because it made exclusion and discrimination their responsibility. The notion of the individual, empowered modern woman was also held up as an example to follow in India, thus negating the gains made in collective action. The two instances present examples of the travel of ideas and their specific material forms. They reflect the "scattered hegemonies" (Grewal and Kaplan 1994) of ideas about gender equality and development, not only in the South but also in the North.

8 Development Practice and Environmental Governance

Flexible Spaces for Political Action

Decentralization of environmental decision-making and development is a richly debated subject. The threat of climate change and its close links to development have led national governments and international organizations to turn their attention to processes of decentralization as the path to sustainable development and environmental governance. Policy discourses in both India and Sweden are replete with references to the need for new organizational forms for development and environmental governance. While the focus in the 1990s was often on community groups and public participation, it now subsists along with and is overwritten by strong neoliberal prescriptions. Renewed discourses on participation emphasize behavior change and individual action while private interests and public-private partnerships play an important role. Nevertheless, arguments and solutions to environmental problems appear to turn in the last resort, to the need for good governance arrangements. Local organizations and institutions play an important part in this reasoning, reflected in the academic literature that has burgeoned around these issues.[1] They are positioned as the hope and a prerequisite for sustainable environmental governance. Discussions have centered on how institutions can be designed such that diverse stakeholders and conflicting interests are managed through a process of deliberation and a framework for accountability.[2] The inclusion of different social groups in the deliberative process is seen to bring about greater democratic practice. However, the singular focus on mainstream organizations and institutions (i.e. the rules, regulations and organizations dominant in the community) has been problematic. It has masked alternative, less visible but equally robust forms and practices in which the environment is managed and development carried out at the local level.

In both Nayagarh and Drevdagen, inclusive structures were needed for the management of the forests. However, village women's organizing within exclusively women's collectives in parallel and connected to mainstream organizations was the only way in which they felt able to gain a voice in the gendered politics of local forest governance. The women found it necessary to organize separately to make space for their claims within the mainstream organizations where their particular interests got lost in wider issues. The form in which the women in the two study sites chose to organize (in informal networks or formalized committees) was important but contextual. It provided insights about the space for women to exercise agency in the two contexts as is clear from the previous chapter. It was, however, the women's choice of alternative organizing, their appropriation of a space between the public and the private and the resistance they encountered from mainstream organizations that is significant. It draws attention to the need to redefine how we study spaces of environmental decision-making and the different ways in which social groups choose to organize. It also means redefining how we think about the boundaries of the political.

It has long been a dilemma in environmental governance and more so in sciences that seek to study them on how to reconcile the abstract and the specific, objectivity and subjectivities. At the heart of this dilemma is how we conceptualize the political and the complexity of social relations in environmental governance. I use the category of gender to bring this 'space off'[3] of environmental governance in greater relief, its blind spots and the micro-politics that are constitutive of the issues. The examples from Nayagarh and Drevdagen challenge us to find ways to, "articulate and enact individual and collective political identities, commitment, responsibility, and critique in nontraditional, non-normalizing, yet emancipatory ways" (Taylor and Vintges 2004, 9).

When power over resources is at stake or where power is being challenged, there will be resistance on the part of those wielding power to recognize the claims of the others. How are these claims to be heard? What structures may bring to the surface different claims, even those not yet made? The power of discursive frameworks such as deliberative democracy and local governance is important to note. But it is equally important to analyze the importance of agency in transforming them. Decisions are made in varied settings and an analysis of the multiple spaces where decisions are made is critical. The role of space in adjudicating power is thus indispensable in theorizing on structures of decision-making and citizenship as I elaborate further in the chapter.

In the following section I begin with an analysis of how the discourse of the center *versus* the periphery and the structuring of public space for local governance in Nayagarh and Drevdagen limited the women in both places. In the next section, I show how ideas of local governance also provided the language necessary for appropriating and 'opening up a space' in the politics of environment and development in the two places. The section on deliberative politics and the realm of freedom after that discusses the limitations of the public space and the discursive and argues for the need for structural change. The main argument in this chapter is that although inclusive and heterogeneous structures are essential for the sustainable and equitable governance of environmental resources such as forests, in order to be able to function effectively and justly, they need to be able to relate to other spaces that are exclusive and represent particular interests as for example the women's groups in this instance. The analysis calls into question the assumption that mainstream organizations provide a public space for unequal social groups to negotiate conflicting interests. It is not enough to make mainstream organizations responsive to different interests and heterogeneities but also to examine the alternative spaces and forms in which women and men choose to work and make claims. Thus, in the last two sections of the chapter I theorize on these alternative spaces *vis-à-vis* mainstream organizations and the need to rethink public space and decision-making. I end the chapter with a conceptualization of particular and wider interests in environmental governance and development and the need for an ongoing reframing of the public space that connections between them can engender.

I draw on different traditions in this chapter, some of which are often seen to be antithetical to each other: Foucaldian feminism is called upon in tandem with critical theory, political philosophers such as Iris Marion Young and post-Marxist political theorists like Ernesto Laclau dialogue with feminist geography. However diverse their thinking might be, insights from these fields are instructive in thinking through thorny issues in environmental governance and development. Together, they provide important guideposts in working towards a gender just world and freedom of thought.

DEMOCRATIC DEVELOPMENT AND PEOPLE'S PARTICIPATION IN ENVIRONMENTAL GOVERNANCE

The idea of local governance inspired hope for democratic development and environmental relations in both Nayagarh and Drevdagen. In some measure, it brought with it a sense of agency where through cooperation the villagers would be part of determining their own future. Theoretically, the idea that various social groups could deliberate upon issues and reach an understanding well grounded in the local context has been typical of several environmental studies. Many draw on the idea of participatory justice such as the work of Habermas who proposes a discourse model of legitimacy to enhance citizen's possibilities for the more effective exercise of political agency and control (c.f. Benhabib 1992, 81). In studying environmental and development practices in Nayagarh and Drevdagen, it becomes clear that it is not the provenance of ideas and categories associated with local governance but their use that is important, especially in the relationships imagined when these categories are mobilized. How do these generalized categories that represent democracy respond to differentiated claims in specific places? To understand this, I turn from overarching discourses and general categories to the specifics of Drevdagen and Nayagarh to investigate the not so obvious but critical gendered practices that point to the connections in the doing of institutions in the two places and in their hopes for environmental democracy.

'LOCAL GOVERNANCE' AND THE CENTER-PERIPHERY DIVIDE: A LIMITING DISCOURSE FOR THE WOMEN'S GROUPS?

As the rhetoric of local governance and community participation made itself felt in Nayagarh and Drevdagen, citizens needed to present themselves as 'the local community' just as authorities and development practitioners needed 'local communities' to take over development responsibilities. In doing so, they redefined their claims to the environment and their relationships to each other. To different extents in both places, discourses of marginalization by state authorities (see Chapter 4) laid the ground for political mobilization and claim making from the state. The discussions on marginalization reproduced a discourse of the center *versus* the periphery, deepening the polarization between the villages and authorities. While the men working with the forest question in both Nayagarh and Drevdagen needed to generate political representations of the 'local' in order to cohere, the making of the category of the 'local' also became its Achilles heel, especially so in Drevdagen.

In Drevdagen, the hardening of the divide between the authorities and the village created what some women and men in the village believed were unnecessary tensions in village relations with the municipality. It also put the women, reliant on the state for employment and public services, in a double bind. They rued that the older men had managed to aggravate the municipality, making it difficult for the women to work with municipal bureaucrats on their projects. Voicing a general disgruntlement, Karin pointed out at a get-together that by circumventing local authorities and trying to negotiate directly with the center in Stockholm on the question of local forest governance, the village association had made it difficult for the village in the long run. According to her,

> "local governance should also be discussed locally—within the village, the municipality and the county."

For the women and many men, justifications of the threat from outside denied the circulation of ideas and interactions with people from outside the villages, increasing feelings of isolation.

In Nayagarh, initially, women's marginality *vis-à-vis* state bodies or their distance from the center tended to function as an empowering force. They were supported by men in the forest committees to access funds and other programs from the authorities. The men's own sense of discrimination led them to support the women in relation to those they felt wielded power over them. However, tensions occasioned by the women's organizing were seen to come in the way of the larger struggle of the periphery and the center. The men in the forest organizations had defined what was 'local' and this was accepted (in fact needed) by outsiders such as Oxfam to be able to work with them. The privileging of the 'local' or 'community' presented a problem for the women in both places because it rendered their concerns, political collectivities and resistance invisible or pushed them to the margins. This made it difficult to think in new ways not only for the women but also for the mainstream associations in the villages.

Due to the radical potential of the idea of 'local governance,' the men in the forest organizations in both places did not have to defend or explain their position to the rest of the villages. Drawing attention to gendered differences on forest governance was something that could be seen as standing in the way of the changes for greater autonomy for the 'local.' Questioning 'local' governance had the potential to be considered conservative in light of the strong narratives of the marginalized periphery *versus* the center. The perceived threat from outside forces was thus used to stall any change in unequal relations within the villages. Outsiders on the other hand found it difficult to collaborate with groups if not through the dominant organizations that they legitimized with their support. In such instances, local governance became a limiting discourse for the women's groups who saw the need to work differently.

MIRRORING BUREAUCRATIC NORMS: THE TROJAN HORSE ENTERS THE IMAGINATION

The men working with local forest governance in Nayagarh and Drevdagen proposed new ways to work with environmental management. Their ideas about local governance differed from the official system of forest governance and organization of development, and it also acquired many characteristics (at the level of organization and method) of the system that it hoped to change. The men's understanding differed from the official in the belief that local explanations are superior to more general ones (although local management in general was considered good), that people are capable of managing their own environments and that dynamism for local development comes from the people in the communities concerned.

At the same time, they shared some of the values of the prevailing official system. These included a belief in the structural division of the center and periphery, a concept of universal (masculine) subjectivity; the importance of policy and planning and, the primacy of economic returns and insertion into current market norms, as for example in Drevdagen when the solution to local management was to form a company to work with the forests. In other words, the theories and objectives differed but the methods and form became similar. Based on this framework, the key issues or the bigger questions were defined. There were dimensions of life and development that could not be talked about within this framework of rules (c.f. Foucault 1990, 12)—what was excluded in this case was the social, spiritual, emotional, the everyday and the non-economic spaces.[4]

The women in Drevdagen who chose not to insert themselves into this framework were seen as passive ("with low self-esteem") and many of those who criticized it were seen as complainers ("it is as usual") and some of those who tried to involve themselves or chose to organise outside of this framework were seen as aggressive or power hungry ("took too much place on the stage and not so organized"). For many men and women in Drevdagen, who wanted to bring environmental governance to the local level, the association's work with the forest project began to mirror the bureaucratic norms that they sought to replace. The meetings about the forests (those that were in fact announced) were considered tedious, the social aspects and other village connections were excluded and the discussion became grounded in increasingly complicated references to the practices of the forest sector.

In Nayagarh, the inclusion of the everyday and the spiritual had been the basis of BOJBP's success in its early days. Although gender was not taken up specifically, the environmental movement had linked itself explicitly to social development. Eradication of caste differences and discrimination of women were important aspects. With the increasing formalization of the movement, women tended to disappear even from the rank and file. The BOJBP registered itself as an NGO partly to be able to get support from foreign funders such as Oxfam for its various programs. Several people complained of what they called the NGOization of the movement. Over the years, the leaders remained the same and membership became static. Eventually, the organization began to be identified with a handful of older men in the executive committee.

The bureaucratization of the village association in Drevdagen and of the BOJBP closed the door to the emergence and valuation of the different meanings that people ascribed to development, community and local governance. Development and environmental relations became situated in a discourse of 'governance' or 'management' rather than one that responded to the experiences of women and men in the villages. The outsiders helping the villagers were complicit in this shift. The villagers in Drevdagen for instance, wanted to create a living countryside; SLU wanted to support them in this by working with local governance. Among other things, they wanted to open up a space in policy for local initiatives in relation to forest governance. Although the villagers were concerned with problems that affected their particular village, they were at the same time enthused by the thought of initiating change in the Swedish countryside. As one person interviewed during the SLU evaluation said,

> "I think SLU wants to see the pilot project on management above all, while we in the village want to see concrete things—a living *fäbod*, camping spot, you know, the practical things. What Axel means will surely take ten years. That which is most important must happen sooner, although everything anyway goes hand in hand. If you talk to the people in the village, then you can get asked: if we do get local management, who is going to be responsible? Who will do it? Those questions are hard to answer, because I don't know either."

The person continued,

> "At the same time one doesn't want to let go of the management question because it is so exciting. It concerns the whole of the Swedish countryside, that is why it is important to work with it."

The question that arose from the village had the potential of bringing a change in policy. But in order for that to happen it needed to be grounded in the village. By ignoring the women's critique and focusing on negotiations outside the village, SLU practitioners had contributed to distancing the issue from the place and weakening the move for local governance. The differences at stake in the villages were often not over the issue itself, that is, local governance of their environments especially the forests, but the power relations involved—whose opinion (and definitions) were considered to be relevant. The attempts by the women to strengthen community cohesion, their concern for childcare, old age homes and community spirit, lay outside the concern of the market and were not regarded as political measures or as important as the 'larger questions.' The women's organizations brought to light the need to talk and work with the forests in ways that are grounded in gendered subjectivities of both men and women and the importance of affect and emotion in the ways men and women relate to or 'govern' the environment.

The forestry groups in both places became enmeshed in state practices and the market. Especially in Drevdagen, the forests group felt the need to organize themselves into a company and as the economic sphere became the reference for negotiations on decentralization, it was certain men who came to represent the 'local.' The result, as Dianne Rocheleau citing the work of Raymond Bryant in the Phillipines shows, was how apparently progressive efforts by non-government or other semi-private and community actors,

> "can become part of state practice, internalize agendas in ways they themselves, their members or their constituencies may not predict or intend. Under this approach, the Trojan horse does not breach the gates but enters the imagination, restructures the self and redirects the practices of willing subjects" (2007, 235).

But as she also points out, this is not a one-way process. Counter assimilation is part of an under-theorized and overlooked environmentality.[5] There is a need to understand not only how people absorb but also make use of these openings in current discourses. It is to these openings that I turn in the following section.

OPENING UP A SPACE

As I show above, 'local governance' became a limiting discourse for the women in the practices of the village organizations that began to be identified with a particular group of men. But, ideas on local governance too were an ideology that like other hegemonic ideologies, "must by definition, represent an idealization, which therefore inevitably creates the contradictions that permit it to be criticized *in its own terms*." (Scott 1985, 317). The idea of local governance and people's participation in their own development enlarged the idea of politics in Nayagarh and Drevdagen. Local governance was a politics in which everyone could take part. It brought with it a language of democracy that was legitimate in new ways.

The Self-Governing Village

The women in both places argued for a more holistic approach to forest governance by linking it to everyday village life.[6] They reasoned that activities needed to be viewed in relation to each other rather than in isolation. Voicing her frustration at the *Drevdagen Village Association*'s attempt to institute a private company in the village to work with local forest governance, Cecilia put it eloquently,

> "For the village to survive, if one succeeds with something, it needs to find resonance in the village . . . village development cannot be done merely as private companies . . . The bigger thought, the self-governing village is where day care, youth activities, old age homes and so on are all part of a vision for the village."

According to her, the men in the association in the village had focused only on the forests to the detriment of everything else. A locally governed forest would be incongruous without a self-governed village where the villagers felt involved. In the same way, village activities could not be viewed without the forests, the material environment. As the women envisioned it, community forestry needed to be embedded in community life and all those rural development efforts that may seem unrelated at first sight.

In Nayagarh, the women's groups spoke of the importance of being able to discuss their activities and work in relation to the decisions about the forests at the meetings of the forest federation.[7] They, as in Drevdagen disturbed the hierarchy of work (the big and the small questions) even in the more gender differentiated activities in Nayagarh. As the history of the BOJBP had shown in the past, it was reaching out to all the villagers, both women and men that enabled them take up the cause of forest protection successfully (although even there, the women were not formally involved). In both places, local governance could not be separated from cohesive decision-making in the villages. And for that the terms and the agenda of the institutions for management needed to be negotiable and different ways of relating to the forests needed to be recognized.

The Social Forest

There were many people who had moved to Drevdagen for a special kind of life. The women in the inquiry who had done so, spoke about being able to be close to nature and to be able to bring up their children far from urban environments, which they felt were unhealthy. Many of those who had moved back had roots and relatives in the village. Others had moved in search of or to take up work opportunities in tourism. But whatever the reason, in most cases, it was often combined with a yearning to live in a special way, to be 'close to nature.' I was told by Cecilia,

> "Several families with children have moved back to the village because of the environment, the nature, the good environment for the children . . . and to be part of a *gemenskap*."

To be part of a community was important. As Linda, a single mother who was originally from the village said,

> "There is security in smaller villages . . . you know everyone . . . if anything were to go wrong."

Several researchers theorizing the rural (e.g. Forsberg 1994; Myrdal 2001) as well as policy documents (e.g. Skrivelse 2001/02:173) discuss a change in the ways that people relate to the Swedish countryside. They show for example that migration within the country has been prompted by other values beyond only the economic. These have to do with an intimacy to nature and a way of living. Some women felt that the men in the association looked at the forests with an 'economic gaze.' As is clear from the title of the article they wrote on our research together, *För oss är naturen en lisa för själen*[8] the women spoke of other ways of relating to the forests which found no place in the routines and practices of the project's work with the forests. They spoke of the forests as a social place, and an integral part of everyday community life.

The women's wish to make space for these perspectives even within the straitjacket of 'projects' was not a wish to romanticize the place, but to draw attention to the relational nature of the forests and that ties to the forests were not only economic. With *gemenskap* as the point of departure, constantly renewing community relationships was fundamental to this endeavor. The everyday social, spiritual, emotional and political dimensions of the forests were important for them. The nesting of the forests in other concerns was central to how the people chose to live their lives and one important reason for living there. As Cleaver writes, ". . . both individual and collective action are likely to be shaped by both economically 'rational' incentives and socially embedded motivations" (1998, 358). Feeling isolated from the way in which the issue was handled led to the estrangement of the villagers from the association. Taking account of people's experiences and of relations to the forests and the village opens up the space for working not merely with structures and agencies, but from people's subjectivities.

Conceptualizing the self-governing village in Drevdagen, *gemenskap* and of what I term the social forest were discursive shifts: from what was perceived as the distant governance of the forest and of the village association, from the emphasis on forests as an economic resource and only as a provider of employment and from its bureaucratic structures. In their groups, the women raised issues that called into question these definitions of the forests and village institutions and tried to open up the space for articulating community life as well as environmental governance and development differently. A perspective that looks upon the forests only as an economic resource obscures the social relations among the villagers and between the villagers and the forests that generated the value of the forests for them. Local governance, although still diffuse and uncertain for men and women in Naygarh and Drevdagen at that time, meant being able to make their dreams come true. It meant power to the people—both the women and the men. In contesting the meaning of local governance, the women were in effect negotiating the frame in which the discourse on the forests was situated.

The *kvinnoforum*'s insistence on *gemenskap* as the basis for village activities and their insistence on open, informal forums within their own organizing was a reaction to what they felt was lacking in the common forums in the village. It was an effort to bring up issues together which were otherwise hierarchically organized in terms of importance and closely connected with certain groups in the village. For the women, the question was not only one of moving decision-making from one place to another (from the center to the periphery),[9] but also for different ways of working. This differentiation became all the more apparent in the way that the women chose to organize and the opposition to it. The events in these places makes it important to shift and widen the development debate: (1) from the need to include women and marginalized groups in existing organizations to also taking seriously alternative organizing as a valid and equal partner in development, and crucially (2) in theorizing the tensions and the connections between the spaces from which they choose to act. It is to this that I now shift the discussion and begin by analyzing deliberative politics and the spaces available for doing politics within environmental governance and development.

DELIBERATIVE POLITICS AND THE REALM OF FREEDOM?

Political theorists such as Frank Fischer (2006) argue for civil society as the appropriate location for deliberative politics. Benhabib advocates a pluralistic model that acknowledges the variety of institutions, associations, and movements in civil society through the interaction of which an anonymous public conversation results. The decentered public sphere consists of mutually overlapping networks and associations of opinion forming as well as decisional bodies (2002, 138–139). Examples from Nayagarh and Drevdagen present two challenges to conceptualizations of what might constitute the realm of freedom. The first has to do with the changing roles of the state and civil society: how is one to conceptualize the increasingly sliding differences between what might be the civil society and state practices. This confluence of the 'local' and the 'official' is for example especially apparent in Sweden, not least because of a concerted effort by the state to promote 'development from below,' endorsed to a large extent by grants from the European Union. This development from below however also needs to conform to an elaborate infrastructure of rules to access grants for local development. In India, a similar devolution of development activities can be seen operating in a vast array of programs including micro-credit and savings and credit programs for the women. The second challenge for freedom concerns the idea of deliberative democracy itself and its limitations for democratic politics.

In local efforts for rural development or local environmental governance, public spaces created by local organizations are often seen to represent civil society, as distinct from governmental structures and commercial institutions of the market. Scholars have regarded them as spaces for participation and deliberative democracy that hold the potential promise of broad participation in collective decision-making, where heterogeneity is prized and where different claims may be negotiated. The absence of women in these spaces has been criticized and scholars have argued for their inclusion (Chapter 2). However, as events in Drevdagen showed, the entry of women in the public space of the village association, although important in many ways for the women, did not necessarily change the gender *status-quo*. The space for local governance as it had been defined was guarded and there was a constant effort to maintain and protect that space (Chapter 6). The so-called public spaces were rigorously defined although epistemologically they were in the public. When women did enter public spaces, (as the women who spoke out at meetings in Nayagarh or when a woman became the chairperson of the *Drevdagen Village Association*) unequal gender relations were assiduously maintained (see Chapter 6).

Feminists have argued for the presence of a critical mass of women in such public spaces (e.g. Agarwal 1997). But would a critical mass solve the problems of a political space cast as neutral and unjustly framed? (c.f. Fraser 1993, 147). As Young writes,

> "The concepts of exclusion and inclusion lose meaning if they are used to label all problems of social conflict and injustice" (2000, 13).

In these particular cases, the problem was also that of sexism. Questions of gender discrimination and unequal social relationships needed to be brought into the political. As Fraser puts it cogently, gender is neither simply a class nor a status group. It is a hybrid category rooted simultaneously in the economic structure and the status order of society. Gendered divisions involve injustices that are traceable to both. Thus understanding and redressing gender injustice requires attending to both recognition and redistribution (Fraser and Honneth 2003, 19).

The idea of inserting women in existing organizations or public space does not only fall short of its democratic aspirations, as the case of the village forest organizations made clear, it is also epistemologically problematic. Benhabib writes,

> "a theory of universalist morality or of the public sphere cannot simply 'ignore' women and be subsequently 'corrected' by their reinsertion into the picture from which they were missing. Women's absence points to some categorical distortions within these theories; that is to say, because they exclude women these theories are systematically skewed. The exclusion of women and their point of view is not just a political omission and a moral blind spot but constitutes an epistemological deficit as well" (1992, 13).

Drawing on Habermas' ideas on deliberative democracy and principle of discourse ethics, Benhabib pleads for a radically proceduralist model of the public sphere,[10] "neither the scope nor the agenda of which can be limited a priori, and whose lines can be drawn by the participants in the conversation" (ibid., 12). This reasoning calls for a 'discursive' democracy that offers the scope for circumventing the problems of the hierarchization into the 'larger' and the 'smaller' questions (see Chapter 6) as contenders are able to debate their issues. According to her, the seemingly non-political nature of certain topics would not be foreclosed in the discussions. She proposes that because the deliberative model does not restrict the agenda of public conversation: in the sense that all questions are valid and as long as different groups uphold the autonomy of persons publicly, it encourages discourse about the lines separating the public from the private and the public-private dichotomy is erased (1992, 110).

In practical terms for the women in Nayagarh and Drevdagen, this would imply that they would be able to take up their questions which would be given equal weight in the public space of the joint forums—such as the village and forest organizations. And for brief flashes, we do see this thought working. At a district level meeting organized at Macchipada in Nayagarh by *Vasundhara* and *Sanhati* (an NGO alliance based in Bhubaneswar) to discuss a possible comprehensive policy on community forestry in the spring of 1999, several forest committees and *Mahasangha* members took part. Among approximately forty-five participants, only two were women. They sat through the entire meeting and listened but did not say anything. I met them the next day in their village and asked them why they had come there. They said that they knew there were going to be people from outside (the NGOs) and wanted to tell them that even women have been doing 'good work' in their villages. But they were not given a chance to speak.

Biswal, the young *Mahasangha* staff member who was there with me told them that all they had needed to do was to put their hand up and they would have been asked to speak. But the women pointed out that it was almost impossible to do that in between the long speeches made by the men.

> "It isn't that easy for women to speak out. Nobody asked me to speak, I was waiting to be asked. Its only when we become more than half in numbers at such meetings then we will be able to speak out."

On the other hand, she told us about another *Mahasangha* meeting at Katrajhari where they actually did speak, facilitated by the form of the meeting. Since there were so many participants at that particular meeting, the organizers had reserved slots for those who wanted to speak and participants could go and give in their names beforehand. She was then assigned a slot and could speak uninterrupted about what she wanted to say.

Most men did ignore her but it was also a sign of change. The fact that women now had an opportunity (though slight and not always guaranteed) to speak up for themselves was a widening of the public 'discursive' sphere. At the same time, as is clear from both Nayagarh and Drevdagen, inclusion did not make it a conversation. The women in Drevdagen were not stopped from attending meetings but the men waited patiently for women to finish their interventions so that they could proceed with their discussion (though this changed in periods especially when the women had backing from a space outside).[11] Inconsistencies between prescribed ideas about participation and inclusion and the reality of village politics and social relations became a cause for tensions.

The idea of dialogue in deliberative democracy is not uncomplicated. On the one hand, the notion of dialogue shifts the discussion to a terrain where standpoints can be argued about, rather than treated as givens (Stoetzler and Yuval-Davis 2002). On the other, putting these ideas into practice raises other issues. Eva Wollenberg, Jon Anderson and David Edmunds point out,

> ". . . creating a common language for communication poses many challenges. . . . Even if a common language could be agreed upon, however, its meaning to different groups might still vary. . . . It seems likely to us that for most issues concerning forest management among numerous and very diverse interest groups, the rational debate of the meaning of specific terms would never reach a final conclusion. The common language of accommodation is probably a temporary fiction rather than an enduring fact in these cases. It is a way to explore differences among interest groups and understand them better, but does not eliminate problems associated with communication" (2001, 209).

Recalling the Drevdagen women's statements on how men and women speak different languages, Kohn's argument is all the more compelling,

> "... language competence is not shared equally. Any consensus that brackets rather than engages this fact is likely to reproduce existing social and political inequalities. By appealing to the standards of rationality and reason, discursive democracy masks an irrational core at the heart of its project" (2000, 147).

Much like Chantal Mouffe (1999), Margaret Kohn argues for another definition of politics, rooted in contestation, struggle and resistance. She believes that a purely discursive vision of politics has a tendency to reproduce the status quo. Empirical evidence indicates that political struggles that take place on the basis of deliberation are heavily weighted in favor of the élites. What is needed, she argues, are structural or institutional changes in the basis of power, and may even require strategically separate spaces (2000). I direct attention to what such spaces might be and how we can think about them.

WHAT ARE THE SPACES IN WHICH WE THINK OF POLITICS? AND WHAT DOES THE WOMEN'S PRACTICE TELL US?

Public and Private Space

As I write in Chapter 2, feminist theorists maintain that the drawing of the public-private dichotomy has been part of a discourse of domination that legitimizes women's oppression and exploitation in the private realm. All that is deemed incompatible with citizenship is relegated to the private, female sphere characterized by the 'ethic of care' while the public sphere associated with the male public citizen and an 'ethic of justice' is related to the market and the state (Lister 1997). Women's work with village activities in Nayagarh and Drevdagen transcended the boundaries of the public and the private. The women made clear that the public sphere characterized by an 'ethic of justice' is in practice indivisible from an 'ethic of care.' Local development and forest governance could not be separated from the care work of women and men in the community. Their work was integral to making local development and environmental governance work.

Benhabib (citing Fraser 1992, 110) presumes that the discourse model, precisely because it proceeds from a fundamental norm of egalitarian reciprocity and precisely because it projects the democratization of all social norms, cannot preclude the democratization of familial norms and of norms governing the gender division of labor in the family. The two cases of Nayagarh and Drevdagen when seen in conjunction—i.e. in their particular contexts and at the same time in relation and in connection to each other—question this view. Power relations in the public and the private are connected yet those connections do not follow logical paths. The Swedish women's private independence and rights did not correspond to public status. Similarly, the Indian women's success in public space made a difference but did not preclude violence in the private (see Chapter 7). Affect rather than logic is important in this case. The public and the private might be regulated by similar relationships but they are organized by principles that serve different purposes. It is clear from the previous chapters how the organizations worked hard to separate the political with the social, the bigger question from the smaller, the wider from the particular.

Herein lies what I believe to be a contradiction inherent in deliberative democracy. Although the erasure of boundaries might bring into discourse issues from the private sphere, the relationships that operate in these spaces are different. This is all the more so in the case of gender than it might be for other social groups based for example on culture or religion. Different principles operate and although the same men and women might be contemporaries in public spaces with equal moral and political rights, they might also be tied to each other in relationships of affect as husband and wife or daughter-in-law and mother-in-law at home, in other words, by relationships that are organized by a different logic or principles (for example to put it somewhat simplistically love or loyalty and not remuneration).[12] While feminists point out (e.g. Hekman 2004) that subjectivities need to enter the public realm, I contend that these different organizing principles also have to be recognized and theorized further.

The public discourse model originally premised on the distinction between the private and public would need structural change to be relevant. While Benhabib advocates the need for feminists to complement the Habermas model of the public sphere by a critical theory of the public sphere (1992, 112), others (e.g. Laclau and Mouffe 2001) advocate an agonistic politics based on contestation and struggle. However as Benhabib writes, it is not only discourse theory that needs to be confronted with feminist claims; feminist theory itself sorely needs a model of public space and public speech which returns it to the politics of empowerment. It is here that I turn to the two cases to analyze what the women's practices may offer us in the way of understanding how space, somewhere between the public and the private, can be an arbitrator in practices of empowerment.

APPROPRIATING IN-BETWEEN SPACES

The co-ordinator and fieldworkers of the women's development program in Nayagarh helped to create a space within the official program that responded to what the women thought was important. In Drevdagen the women came together to discuss their lives and hopes for the village, their projects and to socialize. The women's intentions in their collectives were not very different from what they may have wanted to do otherwise. It was instead the structure of the political space they created that made it different. It had the potential to change existing relationships between the women and their relationships to their villages. The groups were different from other conventional women's spaces because they were inclusive in new ways. Although they built on prior networks (such as caste in Nayagarh), in the actions that they took, for example, in demanding land for a road from landowners, women from different castes joined together. Women's groups in villages that had not taken part in these incidents identified with them. The idea of forming a women's federation was disturbing in part because it would have cut across lines of caste and other social boundaries like age that ordered relations in Nayagarh.

In both Nayagarh and Drevdagen, it was their experience of being 'women of the village' that brought the women together. But this did not come merely from their social location of being women. Through their organizing and their discussions, they positioned themselves as a women's group. It was a political position that was brought into play for brief periods and in response to particular situations, reflecting questions of power rather than a question of having a different view based on their gender.

Creating alternative structures was far from easy and the exception rather than the norm. The situation in Nayagarh suggests that the presence of strong male committees in villages was not always conducive to strong women's groups. Kesharpur was the hub of the community forestry movement for several years and was responsible for setting up *mahila samitis* in several villages. But Kesharpur's *mahila samitis* did not last very long. Nor were women from Kesharpur very active in forest activities. BOJBP officials blamed the coordinator of the women's program for being lazy, while she spoke of infighting among the wives of the BOJBP officials as the cause. In Manapur, the BOJBP secretary who lived in the village had helped the women organize themselves into a government program for women (DWACRA). He had registered the *samiti*, helped in setting it up and continued to play an important role. The presence of strong male committees or strong male leaders may not always inhibit the formation of strong women's groups, but in Kesharpur and Manapur this appeared to be the case. The help of the men from the villages made it more difficult to circumvent established relationships of power and for the women to create a separate space for themselves. On the other hand, different men played different roles that were also supportive in other ways as I discuss in the previous chapter.

A contradiction of creating an alternative space and at the same time remaining outside the conventional organizational framework is illustrated by the example from a *Dalit* village in Jakalla. The women here made bamboo goods and sold them to other women in neighboring villages. The women told me,

> "We go far and sell our goods . . . rice huskers, baskets, nets . . . to other women . . . Only the women buy these things since they know the quality. That is why we have to go from village to village instead of going to the market. . . . Even the men would like to purchase because they don't want to spend the money for these things . . . We exchange the goods for rice, wheat, potatoes, onions . . . everything. We do not go to the weekly haat in Gania, Daspalla . . . Because rice is better to get . . . . We can't manage all the bargaining, manipulation . . . Other villagers sell such things in the market . . . those close to the market."

The women selling the bamboo goods and those buying them in exchange for rice, wheat and potatoes had established an informal market for themselves, beneficial to both sides. For the women in Jakalla, this relationship had its costs as they had to leave the village in the daytime and their small children in the care of older siblings, not much older than them. Much has been written about the importance of providing marketing channels for women and how the opening up of local *haats* (markets) where women could sell their non-timber forest products (NTFPs) gives them an important leverage. But also, as the women pointed out, as soon as they enter the markets they come under conditions set by others and over which they have little control. Instead, by maintaining the women-to-women channels described above, by retaining the rights to be the best judge of quality, and by exchanging in kind, the women of Jakalla and their customers had for this brief period managed to maintain some measure of control over their exchange.[13]

And yet, the informal channels and spaces that the women in Nayagarh had created were tenuous. They would have little power compared with the formal market. Informal exchange did not provide them with cash, which is also a source of power. How then may women be supported, other than by opening up a male-determined marketplace or only by going through male-dominated organizations that are often defined by development practitioners but also in research as local people's institutions (illustrated by Oxfam's inability to support the women directly)? David Edmunds and Eva Wollenberg write about the need to put in place processes that enable disadvantaged groups to mobilize and negotiate directly (2003, 9). But how is this negotiation to be achieved in practice where women's groups are not seen as representatives of the community, as are, for example, the forest groups? These examples suggest that bringing women into existing structures is not always beneficial for them. It is in fact a step backwards if the conditions in which women come into these organizations are not simultaneously subjected to scrutiny. Forming a group outside the mainstream can be marginalizing. So why did the women actively choose to do so?

In creating alternative spaces, the women in Naygarh and Drevdagen disturbed the power of public spaces. They appropriated an in-between space that challenged how politics was done. Within their groups they constructed new forms of subjectivity that opened up the possibility of critique. The women's collectives questioned the normalizing of norms for development and environmental governance. This power was emancipatory. Reiterating the argument against the division of the strategic and practical that I discuss earlier (see Chapters 2 and 5), strategic change is not something to be achieved by escaping norms as they exist. Its' basis lies in new subjectivities and ways of being in practice (in the practical and the everyday). To paraphrase the feminist slogan, the 'practical is the political' and strategic.

It was the freedom of being able to take up a range of issues and to take action on them from within their collectivities that proved to be crucial for the women in advancing their interests. Studying the absence of women in forestry user groups in Nepal, Anupama Lama and Marlène Buchy (2004) write that some of the women interviewed reported that they were not interested in meetings of the forestry user groups. The authors attribute this lack of interest partly to women's lack of self-esteem, and partly to the women's difficulties in forming women-only committees because of their illiteracy and inability to implement the rules according to the operational plan. They write further that in a process where the women had no influence themselves, they would be unlikely to be motivated to take part. The case of Drevdagen indicates that even though they were literate, it was the feeling of being unable to influence the process that worked against women taking part in village and forestry plans.

The requirement to follow the rules and regulations drawn up by all-male committees is not ideal from the women's points of view. Women have little incentive in taking part in forest governance if they have no power over their own lives. The *samitis* in some Nayagarh villages thus provided one possible space where the women could take account of the everyday in their own lives, and work to change that reality, hand in hand with their involvement in forest activities. The expectation that women will be motivated to form groups only with the aim of forest protection (as defined by the men in their villages and by government bodies) is questionable in light of the obvious discrimination they experience in their everyday lives.

The groups grew out of the women's dissatisfaction with being represented by a structure that did not respect their stake or give them voice about the issue. Attempts by village and forest organizations to include women within their spaces was, in the long run, not an acknowledgement of them as actors. Rather it bestowed on them the role of spectators. Not attending formal village meetings was one way to evade being bound by rules that did not favor them. The groups raised issues that differed from those prioritized by the forest organizations. They chose instead to create their own spaces from where they could take action and obtain validation for their perspectives. The *kvinnoforum* in Drevdagen and the *samitis* in Nayagarh became places to talk about or articulate constructions of the forests and the village which did not find place in the village associations. In taking action publicly, the women in Nayagarh took responsibility for much of what they always did.

The usefulness of these spaces was most in creating non-normalizing practices as the women created new selves for themselves in their relationships to each other. Like Amy Allen I want to emphasize the role that mutuality, reciprocity and recognition played in the creation of subjectivities in the groups (or a sense of self as she calls it), something that Allen indicates is lacking in Foucault's emphasis on the strategic relations of power. Building on feminist arguments for a symmetrical or egalitarian form of reciprocity she argues for a broader view of social relations, as not just strategic but also as (potentially) reciprocal, communicative, and/or mutual-enabling the formation of agency and autonomy (2004, 248).[14] In creating these spaces the women may be seen as appropriating what Fraser calls 'subaltern counter publics' (1993), from which to mobilize and assert their claims.

IDENTITIES IN PRACTICE

While some may look upon this as identity politics, like Young I disagree with the claim that group based public expressions are solely the assertion of a group identity or self-regarding interest. Following her I take them to be socially situated interests, proposals, claims and expressions of experience that are often an important resource for democratic discussion and decision-making. Such situated knowledges can both pluralize and relativize hegemonic discourses and offer otherwise unspoken knowledge to contribute to wise decisions (Young 2010, 7). The women's organizing that I analyze in Chapter 5 shows how they needed a separate space to situate their knowledge. These spaces thus cannot be seen in isolation with other decision-making spaces and arenas.

And while this did involve the forging of an identity, this process was embedded in webs of relationships that changed with changing subjectivities. Situated knowledges are contextual and the spaces the women created were contextual and hence contingent. Space as Doreen Massey reminds us, is a product of interrelations, as constituted through interactions. It is never finished; never closed. Perhaps we could imagine space as a simultaneity of stories-so-far. The spatial is political (2005). This can be seen empirically (as the women in Nayagarh regrouped in different ways and the women in Drevdagen came together in different periods with different women (and men) and took up new issues). This was so not only because the women emphasized differences amongst themselves, but also because their difference *vis-à-vis* the association and other structures could not be frozen. Since identities were practiced or 'performed' in everyday repetitive acts (Butler 1990), making people what they were, they were also open to change. This does not however exclude the possibility of a normative vision or an ideology.

The important question missing from questions of local environmental politics is thus how it could be possible to have justice and deliberative democracy without the fixing of identities for all times? The question of identity is also linked to that of representation. Whom did the few women that were included in the forest organizations represent? Feminist scholars have shown over the years how women's identities are crosscut by differences such as age, class, caste, occupation and much else, that they are socially mediated and contingent. While the women in Nayagarh were more socially differentiated, crosscutting axes were equally obvious in Drevdagen. The fact that the *kvinnoforum* in Drevdagen was made up of different women who often thought differently was a vital aspect and corresponded to their need to not formalize the group. By keeping themselves informal, the women resisted the freezing of their group difference or that some of them would or could represent them all. Pertinent to thinking on environmental governance is Susan Hekman's caution about identity politics,

> "There is a pervasive assumption in contemporary liberal polity that fixing identities is the necessary complement of the move to a multicultural polity. This assumption is pernicious. It is also ironic" (2004, 209).

Hekman goes on to show the while the emergence of identity politics has served to reveal the constructed nature of identity, it has also served to essentialize identities. In climate discourses for instance (Arora-Jonsson 2011), while the importance of gender and discrimination of women is recognized, women are almost always cast only as vulnerable or pro-environmental necessitating certain standard responses. How then could we think about environmental interests that affect everyone and may be seen as a common interest *vis-à-vis* particular interests of specific social groups that are prone to change from time to time?

PARTICULAR AND WIDER INTERESTS IN DEVELOPMENT AND ENVIRONMENTAL GOVERNANCE: ORGANIZING TOGETHER AND/BUT IN SEPARATE SPACES

Conflicting interests and competing claims to truth are not always reconcilable within structures that begin on an unequal footing. Social groups with particular interests need to organize separately and in relation to mainstream organizations in order to influence decision-making. However, these cannot be solidified in particular interests with unchanging identities. Hence, going back to Benhabib, the discursive is important. At the same time, as I cite Kohn and others, structural change is needed in the ways in which we conceptualize public space.

First, we need to rethink the ways in which we imagine decision-making spaces and frame disputes within them. Young writes that "Under circumstance of pluralism, appeals to supposedly shared understandings may be completely fair; on the other hand, they exclude or marginalize certain people or groups. This assumption of commonality constructs the political public as enclosed, implicitly saying that we can co-operate with each other only if we distinguish ourselves together from outsiders whom we define as different." She argues for a theory that gives account of the practice and function of openness and difference and room for particular interests (2010, 41). The idea that their peripheral geography and the wider and common interest in the forest would unite various social groups was widespread in Nayagarh and Drevdagen among both women and men. Local governance was in fact a common interest. It was not the idea of local governance that was being debated, rather *how* local governance was to be done, about where the political stopped and the social began. Particular interests that the women's groups represented were thus linked in a very specific way to the wider notion of local forest governance. From within their own spaces, the women claimed that they were carrying out development and environmental management but that they were not recognized as doing so.

For democratic decision-making, the women needed alternative and exclusive spaces that needed to be acknowledged as representing their particular interests. Analyzing a dispute over public space in Australia, Kurt Iveson (2010, 216) argues that spaces of withdrawal in existing conditions of inequality can serve as protected spaces where people can take the risk of exploring who they might 'become' with relative safety from attack and abuse. Like him, I argue that the 'us' recognized in spaces of withdrawal is not totally open, but it is not totally closed either. These forms of exclusions actually work to deepen democracy. My argument for structural change in decision-making is thus not merely for a widening of the public space as it exists but also an acknowledgement of multiple spaces where decision-making takes place.

Second, we need to acknowledge the possibility of citizens to take part in different ways in these multiple spaces. The women in both places desired to be able to participate through a variety of different forms, in concert with each other, from within their own spaces, but also as individuals from within formal institutions. These different ways of working and positions taken by women, however, did not fit with the existing organization of power relations, or in the emerging new institutions for local forest management, that all too soon began to mirror the bureaucratic norms they sought to replace. While the women's groups did represent particular interests, they did not want to be 'forced to speak in a single representative voice.' Gender could not be separated from class, caste, education or other potential differences. Nor were their identities static. As Lister argues, citizenship needs to be understood as a process, not just an outcome. The struggle to gain new rights and to give substance to existing ones is as important as the substance of those rights (1997, 5).

Environment and development politics are central to claims over citizenship in rural areas. Women's work in communities, the organization of their livelihoods and the social relations these generate are an important site for experience of citizenship. Viewing citizenship as process gives due accord to women's agency and to other groups that organize in time-bound and flexible ways to forward their struggles. In this sense I lean towards Laclau and Mouffe for whom a final consensus in democratic politics is the result of a hegemonic articulation. This consensus always has an 'outside' that impedes its full realization. Laclau and Mouffe do not see this as undermining the democratic project but as the very condition of its possibility (2001, xix). There always will be the particular and the outside that needs to be brought into focus. In a similar vein, Fraser notes, "politics always involves a frame in the sense of closure, in that there is always an inside and an outside—hence that exclusions arise as a matter of necessity . . . But the question arises as to whether these exclusions are unjust, and if so, whether there is a way to remedy them . . . in the best case scenario we should envision an ongoing process of critique, reframing, critique, reframing and so on" (2008, 149–150). And like Young, I prefer to view such politics with its basis not necessarily in antagonism but in struggle (2010), as new groupings find new forms of relating to each other.

Public space in environmental governance and development needs to be sustained by its connections to spaces representing particular interests and to be able to reframe agendas and disputes as a result of these connections and struggles. The crux of the matter is not only to bring the particular into politics but to acknowledge other contingent spaces where politics is done and power negotiated. Wider interests cannot be seen but in relation to the particular. What I hope for here is a theory to acknowledge multiple, temporary spaces and spheres of decision-making, while all the time heeding the *connections* between them and their possibility to reframe mainstream agendas and hold them accountable. Justice or liberation that reframing makes possible, would imply the end of domination though not the end of power. Using Margaret McLaren's words, "Liberation from domination does, however, result in expanded possibilities for freedom. Freedom is not a final state to be realized but occurs only through its exercise as reversal, resistance and other practices" (2004, 224). In this book I have argued for conceptualizing spaces that make visible disorder and the space-off of the politics of the environment and development, spaces that are flexible, always protean, open to changing relations and subjectivities and for spaces that need to be reframed in order to be responsive to injustice. Turning upside down Sharon Traweek's description of what scientists yearn for (1988, 162), I call instead for making spaces for development politics in a world *with* passion, loose ends, with temperament, gender, nationalism or other sources of disorders and for an environment embedded in human space and time.

9 Conclusion

Up-Close in a Jigsaw World: Guideposts from the Present

Studying environmental governance and development can be daunting if one is serious about taking into account the messy realities that surround these processes. Rural contexts are crosscut with plural values and fractured identities. Theorists are faced with a situation where claims no longer converge on a singular form of institutional change; and the solutions to the problems of gender inequality do not only lie in finding ways of including all men and women in the new institutions. Critical, activist scholarship wanting to work towards positive change in rural areas may meet a situation where 'rural development' and 'local governance' itself are in doubt. Claims for development, local governance and 'gender equality' put forward by different groups can have diametrically different meanings and are in need of deconstruction in an increasingly global world where accepted ideas about development and progress are put to test in everyday practice.

Such conditions framed my research. They challenge the assumptions underlying the three constraining discourses that I refer to in the introductory chapters: that equitable environmental citizenship involves managing resources through open and public deliberation, that greater individual equality presupposes greater space for collective agency and that the correct way to go about scientific inquiry is to maintain a neutral distance from the field and start with the right questions. Fragments of these constraints existed concurrently in everyday practice as well as in theories about environmental governance, rural development, and gender. In the present world, while there is a conviction that good governance would lead to better environments, that economic growth will take care of development, and that gender equality comes with greater welfare, we have others (e.g. Jasanoff 2007) who draw our attention to the ethical dimensions of environmental problems, to the disintegrative effects of development, to the partiality of science and the great deal of humility with which we need to act in face of irredeemable uncertainty. We stand, as Hannah Arendt writes, between the past and the future. Like her, I believe that what we have, and what I offer here is not a debunking of the past or prescriptions for an utopian future, but an experience in thinking; thought itself that arises out of incidents of living experience and must remain bound to them as the only guideposts by which to take its bearings (c.f. Arendt 1954, 14).

Thus, I turn first to look at incidents from Nayagarh and Drevdagen that belied the assumption that environmental citizenship involves open and public deliberation on managing resources. The women's search for alternative spaces brings into focus that one is never outside of gender and power relations and that change comes from many different spaces. In Chapter 8, I question whether in environmental governance and development, we could then think of political space differently? And how might that provide the space for people to engage as citizens rather than be managed as subjects in environmental governance and development. The point is not only to bring the particular into politics but to acknowledge other contingent spaces where politics is done and power negotiated. Wider interests cannot be seen but in relation to the particular and the social, that need to be able to reframe mainstream agendas and hold them accountable.

A great deal of scholarship, especially feminist, shows how politics is realized in the social. I show in Chapter 4 how both in Nayagarh and Drevdagen, the strength of the forest movements and possibilities of moving forward with local forest governance were possible when it was part of a wider agenda of social change and when a large part of the community was supportive. The basis of this support was built on relations of affect and in Nayagarh, spirituality and social reform were central to it. This was a strength that was disregarded as village and forest organizations were enmeshed in market and state practices, became complicit in them and estranged from the social contexts from where the issues—of local governance and development, arose. Chapter 6 focuses on how the organizing principles of environmental governance and development that the village and forest organizations sought to establish drew not only on unequal gendered relations and norms but also from ideas on democracy and outside interventions that rather than challenge inequalities tended to reproduce them.

Local forest governance began to be framed increasingly in terms of possible material gains from the forests. However, in both places, wider support for ideas of local governance went far beyond expectations of material gains. Dreams for a democratic and living countryside encompassed much more. While there was a professed desire to include women in the local governance of forest and village activities, when the women in the two communities did try and take action, mainstream organizations hastened to take action to maintain the gender *status quo*. Local governance and development beg to be understood in their details. The women sought to create an alternative space for themselves as one arena from where they could take action. This contradicted the norms of local governance and development in the villages but also outside. Paying attention to the micropolitics in both places illustrates how the women tried to work with environmental governance, development and gender equality as interconnected aspects of village life. In their efforts to reroute politics of environmental governance through the social and the everyday, they force us to widen how we think and theorize on environmental governance and development (Chapter 8). These studies also show that environmental action and governance is development, or more appropriately that these practices are inseparable and need to be viewed together. In theories of environmental governance, gender is not an empirical inconveniency. It shapes the very object of study. Decision-making on the environment needs to be able to relate to multiple issues and spaces especially on the ground. The relationships that are engendered in these processes are a key part of the production of citizenship in rural areas.

Confronting the second constraining discourse, in Chapter 7 I elaborate upon the relational analysis to study how local, national and international discourses about equality, local environmental governance and development shape women's space for agency but also how they are given concrete form by the women. I add to what several others before me have shown convincingly, that development and wealth do not necessarily lead to greater gender equality. Existing relations and language that recur in development contexts, such that women are interested mainly in the 'social,' are passive at meetings or illiterate in general, circumscribed women's space for agency. That the women were circumscribed by current discourses is perhaps most noticeable in Drevdagen. Personal empowerment and rights did not necessarily lead to greater possibilities or space for collective agency. Paradoxically, discourses on equality and modernization, in delineating certain forms of freedom constrained women's actions. In their very articulation, practices of gender equality or *jämställdhet* contained the seeds of domination. And while collective action in Nayagarh brought about new social relations, this did not automatically imply greater personal freedom for individual women and in some cases produced a backlash. In fact, the notion of the independent and empowered modern woman was held up by some of the men in Nayagarh as an ideal to emulate, overriding the tangible changes that collective action by groups of women, rather than individually independent women, were bringing about. The notion of empowerment was individualized and managed. In other words, there is no direct cause and effect between the personal and the collective.

Outside connections were tangible in how life was organized in the villages. An attention to these connections reveals the multidimentionality of power across different scales, for example in how interventions intended for empowerment or democracy can simultaneously serve to reinforce gender hierarchies. In both places, development practitioners contributed to making 'gender' an issue by insisting on women's participation in forest governance. However, in their actions they reinforced gendered inequalities, especially in Drevdagen, by ignoring the women's critique and their organizing.

The ways in which another relationship and connection, that of North and South is integral to how we think about 'gender' becomes evident in how development practitioners approached the problem of gender inequalities in the two places. In India, development discourses and the language of gender inequality legitimated development practitioners to challenge unequal gender relations in this rural, third world context and support the women to some extent. In Sweden however, that was a question that did not arise. Equality was a premise to start with. Gendered inequalities were regarded as a case of village politics, as aberrations to be sorted out by the very men who were seen by the women to be exercising power unjustly. In such thinking, 'gender' in environment and development discourses is a problem to be dealt with mainly in the South.

Such micropolitics in Chapters 6 and 7 show how existing relations of power and language could be oppressive for women, both in the North and the South. Analyzing Foucault's later work, McLaren writes that freedom has to do with the possibility of new forms of subjectivity that are historically and socially constituted, not in escaping the social and historical altogether (2004, 218). This is evident in an analysis of women's stories from both case study sites. Analyzing connections between the cases also gives rise to a further paradox. "Freedom," as Karen Vintges writes citing Foucault, "is a situated thing. It exists within the social discourses and vocabularies . . . freedom . . . is neither absolute nor pure but the effect of discursive self-technologies" (2004, 281). On the one hand, the ubiquitous talk of gender equality in Sweden actually held back substantive equality by quashing women's attempts at organizing themselves and making claims. On the other hand, pervasive talk of the importance of women's participation and the normative standpoint and ethos of needing to be gender equal was also the ground for their success (more obvious in India but palpable also in Sweden). With ideas of people's participation or governance and gender equality entering mainstream discourse, 'gender' or 'the local' became issues, worthy of being discussed, in development and environmental discourse. For the men and women in the villages, it provided a language that helped make sense and render legible their experiences that had so far not been a part of discourses on the environment or development, subject instead to what Miranda Fricker calls, 'hermeneutic injustice' stemming from a gap in collective hermeneutic resources—a gap, that is, in our shared tools of social interpretations (2007, 7).

Although the trajectories of community struggles both in Nayagarh and Drevdagen were not new, the language of participation and local governance was unfamiliar. While it caused a great deal of confusion, it was appropriated for different purposes and contested. An associated contradiction that I point to in Chapter 3, is between the rhetoric of participation and governance and more recently that of 'global governance' organized increasingly by experts. And it is here that the paradox becomes most apparent. On the one hand, it provides a language to conceptualize injustice. On the other, it is always in tension with how the discourse is appropriated. As for example, when local forest governance or caring for the environment becomes transformed into bureaucratic images and practices of those whom the forest communities originally organized against or as in Sweden, when discourses on gender-equality become the straitjacket for further change.

The women organized themselves, using the language at hand to form an intersubjective space among them. In doing so, they created new subjectivities, put new sociabilities in motion and created new political engagements. In learning from their talk and action, I recognize, "one searches not for a new language but for a discourse at the margins of language" (Benhabib 1992, 243). As de Lauretis states, it is in the interstices of institutions and in the chinks and cracks of the power-knowledge apparati that the terms of a different construction of gender can be posed (1989b, 25). Power is realized in social relations but locating power does not mean that it is determinant or that a particular discourse is not appropriable for other purposes. This is clear in the ways in which the women's collectives chose to work with ideas about development and local governance in both Nayagarh and Drevdagen. In contesting the meanings of these terms, the women redefined the terrain of development and governance and in doing so, their own subjectivities. In contrast to power mainly as subordinating, Chapter 5 demonstrates how women's changing subjectivities were also productive of a power that was generative and emancipatory and engendered new possibilities of being. Crosscutting categories are important to understand in these contexts. The women and men had different loyalties, especially in terms of caste and age in Nayagarh and their position as urban, rural or employed in Drevdagen. These cut across how they perceived themselves but also others. However these were not unchanging and were something that could be worked on. Just as women could become 'independent,' men could become 'good.' Further scholarship is needed to understand how these manifold contradictions play out in particular contexts and how we can move forward in our thinking and action.

Third, and last, I come to the question of my action—the methodological and analytical approach that offers a way to identify and analyze these processes in action, and to interrupt discriminatory practices. The question is how one moves between conceptual categories and actual change. How may theoretical or academic knowledge be invigorated by those outside its frameworks so that it is accountable to the world it studies? In thinking this through I now consider ideas about framing the right questions, of letting categories of analysis emerge from the research process and research accountability and responsibility.

Approaching forest governance and local development from the women's collectives provided a vantage point that allowed me to go beyond conventional frames—of critiquing women's customary absence from local organizations and how women might be able to gain a foothold within them. It shifted the focus instead to understanding how the women framed their needs and issues and how they envisaged working in relation to village organizations. My involvement in the collaborative inquiry in Sweden also led me to ask these questions of the case in India. I came to understand how the women in the villages offered a potential challenge to the framing of village issues but also to the thinking about what the 'important and the right questions' were, both in the village and the university. The collaborative inquiry shifted the research focus by bringing to light the struggles over meanings of the categories that were being taken for granted in the village and the university: local forest governance and rural development. Getting to the 'right question' engaged us in a journey that we undertook together.

By leaving the framework of the research open for negotiation, the language and the categories that were relevant to the women in that context, at that time, defined the research, such as the making of the *kvinnoforum*, the importance of *gemenskap*, an analysis of 'collaboration.' In this process I also found aspects that were difficult to conceptualize. I realized as others before me, "the gulf between what is possible to be communicated in making public one's in-process efforts to do research more democratically and the finitude of what is actually spoken or written" (Lather 1991, 98). As I was mulling over how I could explain the discussions and what was spoken, my colleague Diane who had visited us at one get-together pointed out with insight, "It was not what was said but what was felt, the energy that was important in that process." Liz Stanley and Sue Wise comment,

> "That much human behavior and emotion cannot be described, let alone understood in unexplicated categorical terms is largely ignored or rather resolved by treating people's experiences as faulty versions of the theoretician's categories" (1990, 24).

By trying to describe the process of building the women's collectives and paying attention to the everyday, I have tried to highlight some of the dynamic processes, the emotions and the spirit that are integral to what relationships to the environment and development are about, but normally do not find place in its conceptualizations.

All methods have a political moment that at a fundamental level express a relationship between people (Gitlin et al. 1988, cited in Lather 1991, 91). The inquiry with the women in Sweden was one way of making the research relationship visible, for us to be able to question it, and for my position to be questioned in turn. However, the question of my accountability became far more complicated as the research unfolded. Was I accountable only to the women in the villages or also to the others that I write about? For instance, I had not decided with my colleagues, as they pointed out, that I would write about and critically analyze their work. I write not only about what was said and done within the inquiry, but I also look at how the inquiry and my research affected, and was affected by, others. But that was something I could not have negotiated in advance. There is also the question of being accountable to myself—that I write what I believe is important. This brings up ethical issues.

I criticize colleagues from the university for reproducing the *status quo* that favored men and disadvantaged women and in doing so reproduced the notion of the forests as a masculine domain. But as a researcher I had drawn on the same institution to justify stepping into people's lives in the name of research. It was a privilege that was accepted in the village without much questioning. My research is in many ways unconventional. I took the legitimacy accorded to me as a researcher to choose how to carry it out. There is perhaps the issue of me using or, some may feel, of misusing that position. Here I think of Spivak, who says,

> "If you are from within, your position constituted from within the academy . . . that is what gives you your power . . . (in this particular context) . . . you have to negotiate to see what positive role you can play from within its constraints . . . for breaking it open . . . you must intervene even as you inhabit those structures . . . one tries to change something that one is obliged to inhabit, since one is not working from the outside. In order to keep one's effectiveness, one must also preserve those structures- not cut them down completely. And that as far as I understand is negotiation" (in Gunew 1990, 72).

The desire to do participatory research and the mutual confidence that it creates drew me into a circle of trust that made me aware of the need to be cautious. A participatory process might be manipulated for the researcher's benefit. The collaborative inquiry in Drevdagen and the writing about the processes in the village are not one and the same thing. The idea behind the choice of the inquiry process was for us to work and analyze our process together. The tension between lived and felt experience and the interpretation and formalization of that experience that the writing entailed worried me a great deal initially. However, I came to realize that as an academic, the requirements for me to relate to literature and conceptualize the process (especially in relation to India) were beyond those that were of interest to my co-researchers. One of the women exclaimed when we discussed how I was going to write about our process, ". . . oh, that is Seema's secret." They were more than happy to let me do it on my own. At the time, her statement was troubling for me. But as I realized later, every inquiry is not an academic book and a book is something other than the research experience itself. The women theorized the inquiry and moved it forward by their practice and by taking action while my practice and action is writing and theorizing or as de Lauretis put it, "putting political practice into words is theory" (1989a, 14). Since then, the women in Drevdagen have also written about our process together from their point of view in an unusual book edited by Louise Fortmann, where 'civil scientists' speak directly (Bergelin, Emretsson, Halvarsson Lundgren and Ryen 2008). By putting words into practice, we were also practicing theory.[1] Thus in both our ways, we make this constructed division between theory and practice redundant. In retrospect it has meant, as Smith writes, to explicate the social organization of our experienced world that passed beyond what was immediately and directly known (1987, 89) at the time of our discussions together.

Nevertheless, when I turned to writing, I found that I had to assume the role of the person with the power to define (c.f. Acker, Barry, and Esseveld 1991, 142). Smith (1987) writes: 'how does one create a sociology for women and not about women?' I began my research believing that the answer lay in that it was to be 'with the women.' But then, I believe that my position as an outsider provided me not only with privileges but also with a different kind of responsibility from theirs as we looked to work in different ways with similar problems. It was at times useful for the women that I as a researcher interpreted events and told them how I looked upon things. As Kajsa put it, it was useful for them "to be able to see how others look upon us." In the end, as Robert Chambers would say, I am left holding the stick (a symbol for having knowledge and the right to speak), but I argue that it is a different stick than the one with which I started. I had begun with participatory research to bridge what I saw as the distance between the university and the field. I learned that the question was not merely one of bridging a distance. The research showed how forms of working are normalized and social relations of gender and power are reproduced and realized also across structural distances: in villages as well as universities, in policies, government offices as well as in the in-between spaces where these meet. These meetings are continually reconstituting environment, development and gender on the ground and we need to theorize these experiences to be able to think and act in new (and better) ways.

All this brings me finally to emphasize the need for theorizing connections. The relational analysis made it possible to analyze the gendered consequences of how discourses on the environment, development and gender take form in specific contexts. The relational analysis helped call into question prevailing metaphors and categorical divides, and to bear in mind the relationships of power that organize the world. It also offered me a 'double vision,' not only in seeing difference where previously there was only sameness (as Gadol 1975) but also seeing difference and connection *simultaneously* in a jigsaw world. This kind of double vision also made it clear that "a theorization of change cannot be separated from how subjects and selves are formed" (c.f. Couze 2002, 65) or that the collective and personal or the strategic and practical cannot help but be examined in connection. There is a need to think about broader interconnections across sites, places and power dynamics. Going back to the metaphor of the jigsaw world, like Freya Mathews, we could see it as a strategy rather than theory (Gibson-Graham, 2011, 4), as a piecing it together approach, of learning to know our own piece of the jigsaw but also to be aware of how it connects to the rest of our world.

Glossary

INDIA

BOJBP *Bruksha O' Jeevar Bandhu Parishad*: *Friends of Trees and Living Beings*: the forest organization/movement that started in Kesharpur village

Mahasangha: The forest federation spanning Nayagarh district

Mahila Samiti: Women's group

Odia: Language spoken in Orissa

DWACRA: Government program for Development of Women and Children in Rural Areas

Dalit: Designation for groups of people formerly regarded as the 'untouchables' by mainstream caste society. The term scheduled castes is also used due to a schedule in the Indian constitution that recognizes the historical disadvantage of these groups.

JFM: Joint Forest Management

Purdah: The practice of veiling/the veil.

SWEDEN

Bygd: Settled area

Fäbodar: Pasture areas in the forests

Fäboväsendet: The system of summer pasturage

FTPP: *Forests Trees and People Program*

Gemenskap: Community spirit, togetherness.

Glesbygd: Sparsely populated areas

Gubbe: Old man

Kvinnoforum: Women's forum

SLU (Sveriges Lantbruksuniversitet): Swedish University of Agricultural Sciences

Socken: Parish

Länsstyrelse: County administrative board

Norrland: Northern part of Sweden consisting of 9 provinces.

Notes

NOTES TO CHAPTER 1

1. The English spelling of the name was changed to Odisha from the previous Orissa on November 30, 2009.
2. All names except for those of a few well known leaders have been changed in the book for reasons of anonymity.
3. Red powder worn in hair parting.
4. Geezers/old men.
5. Swedish Rural Economy and Agricultural Societies.
6. These shifts and the history in the two countries are discussed in Chapter 3.
7. A recent issue of the journal *Environmental Conservation* shows how CBRNM in its many varied forms is still 'alive and kicking.' A great deal of the Common Property Resource literature draws on New Institutional Economics and an approach of 'crafting' institutions (e.g. Ostrom 1990).

NOTES TO CHAPTER 2

1. These are extensive and nuanced debates of which I only provide brief highlights, mainly to draw attention to the whole field of research generally ignored by mainstream environmental literature.
2. This is taken up further in chapters five and six. They also reveal different conceptions of exercising agency that I discuss further in this chapter.
3. "The power to deem particular spaces 'official' runs concomitant to the power to exclude certain groups from such sites on the basis of this very ascription. When might we be certain that any particular space is 'official' except when told so by those holding. . .power?" (Springer 2011, 537–538).
4. Springer writes that because public space cannot be established in the abstract, newspapers, radio, television, and the Internet are part of the public sphere and not public space (2011, 538). This might be seen in the initial 'Facebook revolution' in Egypt that started in the public sphere but needed the physical and material space of Tahrir Square to make it possible.
5. In response to Springer who writes, "While visibility is central to public space, theatricality is also required because whenever people gather, the space of appearance is not just there but actively (re)produced through recurring performances (Valentine 1996)" (2010, 537).
6. A corollary to this in the philosophy of science, "while women are not actively excluded from the operations of reason, neither can they be included as women. It is only in so far as women have neutral, sexually indifferent minds that they have access to reason" (Grosz 1991, 163).

7. The fact that this is often the case is testified to by many empirical studies.
8. Interview with Annapurna Maharana, Cuttack, Odisha, November 1993 cited in Arora-Jonsson (1995).
9. *Bhakti* poet and saint from the sixteenth century, known for her music and rejection of traditional divisions based on sex, class, caste and creed.
10. Just as from not being seen as farmers, ubiquitous slogans especially within development aid nowadays profess that most farmers in the world are indeed women. A parallel discourse in Sweden is about the entrepreneurial rural women who have been invisibilized in mainstream debates.
11. In relation to postmodernism postmodernism/structuralism (Foucault/Butler) and critical theory (Habermas/Benhabib), Nancy Fraser stresses this point in her commentaries on debates between four feminist theorists (1995).
12. This has become increasingly clear even outside academia especially in the wake of current climate debates (e.g. Berkhout 2010).
13. All translations here and from following Swedish texts are my own.
14. To me this had connotations of an outsider coming in and knowing that the world needed to be changed just there. I did not know yet what the women wanted.
15. As described by proponents of research circles in Sweden. A research circle is above all a meeting place. Whether you want to do academic research on what takes place (or write about it) is a different thing (Gunilla Härnsten, personal communication, 2001).
16. From my point of view it was a way of bridging the divide between 'practice' and 'theory,' i.e. my research at the university and the lives of the women in the glesbygd. Although I speak of theory and practice, theorizing about experiences and discussing our lives during the inquiry also may be seen as our practice or rather as taking place within our practice. They are not always two separate activities. The writing of this text is, however, a different kind of theorizing though that may also be seen as my practice. On the whole I consider theory to be that which has helped me to think about the world, not explain the world (c.f. Smith 1987, 54).
17. Neither Odia (Nayagarh) or Swedish (Drevdagen) are my first languages.

NOTES TO CHAPTER 3

1. The chapter is based mainly on secondary material. It is complemented by primary texts and interviews as well as participant observation in the villages and academic/policy settings.
2. Although Rajan points out that the colonial state seemed to be fighting a losing battle in the face of private interests in forests at this time especially in the forests of Burma.
3. Despite the presence of shifting cultivators and the large number of people using the forests, the area has been written about as forested and full of wild animals (see references by Pati 1993 for Odisha).
4. The term tribal denotes ethnically heterogeneous indigenous groups in India, several of whom inhabit forest areas. These are minority populations officially recognized by the Indian government as scheduled tribes in the fifth schedule of the constitution.
5. Travelers from the 1700s and 1800s describe instances of an extensively used landscape. Burned forests and naked ground are described as common. On the other hand, large areas are also described as untouched forests with large trees, snags, and dead wood. The forests of the 1800s were differently aged, multi-storied, open, marked by burned and pasture forest landscape. Contrary to this are the forests of the 1900s, especially since the changes in

forestry from the 1950 where the practice of clear cuts, clearing, planting etc. have led to forests with more uniform and younger, even aged stands and a loss of old forest stands. The quantity of dead wood has also radically declined (Ericsson 1997).

6. *Bygd* is a category that is used variously in literature but also colloquially. Johansson explains *bygd* as the context—the space, time and the social relations within agricultural and/or inhabited land. *Skog* is forest in Swedish. In this interpretation, the forest, *skog*, is the opposite of *bygd*, a place that people do not inhabit in the same way (Johansson 1994). In interviews and discussions with the people in Drevdagen, I had the impression that their references to the *bygd* included the forests in a concrete way, in the relationships they shared with each other and the forests.
7. The *slog* (*slogar* pl.), also called *slåttermark*, were the meadows (*ängar*) in the forests where winter fodder for the cattle was gathered. Montelius (1973) writes that the slåttermark were 'cultural meadows' (*kulturäng*), created with the classical weapons, fire, the axe and scythe, and then maintained mainly by the scythe.
8. Montelius cites a royal ordinance of 1686 that suggested that 'as far as possible' farmers engage women instead of boys to herd the cattle. Those who had the possibility and did not do so were to be fined. The reason for this was given as *den vederstyggliga tidelagssynden*, 'the abominable sin of sodomy.' He points out other reasons that led to the proclamation of the ordinance, an important one being a systematic effort by the state to involve more women in order to free men for waging war (1977, 19). According to the historian Jonas Liliequist, the trials that followed in the wake of the ordinance were a way of establishing hegemonic masculinity. The crossing of boundaries between man and animal was closely interwoven with gender transgressions in a society where unlike later it was not the threat from effeminacy that was regarded as threatening for manhood (1992).
9. There were however exceptions to this especially where the woman was a widow (Sjöberg, 2001).
10. Now the National Board of Forestry.
11. Outside influence was apparent in its makeup. Gadgil and Guha cite one of the early and most influential proponents of production forestry in India, "a visiting expert from the Food and Agriculture Organization, who observed, an expanding economy on the eve of modern industrialization requires the highest tonnage of production of organic raw material within the shortest possible period, and at the lowest possible cost" (Von Monroy 1960 cited in Gadgil and Guha 2004, 187).
12. Gadgil and Guha drive a convincing argument about the unscientific nature of scientific forestry. According to them, the basis of modern science is its careful grounding in empirical fact, systematic observation, modeling, verification in an ongoing process. None of these criteria were fulfilled in scientific forestry. Temperate forests such as single species stands of pine were the template for scientific forestry in India. Singularities such as the different nutrient cycles, the exceedingly diverse species-rich system, complex community-ecosystem interactions were ignored in scientific forestry introduced in India (2004, 212). This assertion has been challenged for the colonial period by other historians (Arnold 2006) according to whom, rather than the colonies meekly following or imperfectly replicating metropolitan science the colony was the experimental laboratory or the empirical field agent in the periphery for theory building in the core.
13. Present-day Maoist guerillas organized as the communist party of India (Maoist), rely on armed struggle for resisting state policies and are in effective

control of vast areas in central India. Claiming to represent tribal groups and also known as Naxalites, they have increasingly found a foothold in the southern and north-west districts of Odisha.

14. Although policies on regional equalization have been replaced by a competition politics, the aspiration still lives on in rhetoric and slogans such as 'All of Sweden will live.'
15. Present day efforts to mine in forest areas have resulted in flashpoints in several parts of Odisha. While the efforts to mine the sacred mountain of Niyamgiri by a UK based company have been stopped, conflicts have escalated around the permission given by the environment ministry to Posco, a South Korean enterprise for mining in iron ore, despite expert committees' advice to the contrary.
16. Forest certification (eco-labeling) was introduced in the early 1990s to address concerns of deforestation and forest degradation and to promote the maintenance of biological diversity as well as to promote strong environmental and social performance standards in forestry.
17. Following on Hobsbawm's concept of a moral economy.
18. This changed in later years to include other kinds of forests, though what is considered degraded by different social groups also differs.
19. However the act has been used by villagers in the Niyamgiri hills in Odisha to stop acquisition of village and forest land in their struggle against the mining company *Vedanta*. This has not worked in Jagatsinghpur district against the steel giant Posco where the environment ministry has disregarded the expert committee's findings of violations of the FRA.
20. Interviews from a current project, *Gender and Power in the Swedish Countryside* as well as the basis of this study.
21. Further in the book I reflect on the roles such experts including myself and my colleagues played in the events in Nayagarh and Drevdagen.
22. www.skogsindustrierna.org/web/skog_och_klimat.aspx.
23. http://skogsnätverket.se/2009/11/skydda-mer-svensk-skog-for-klimatets-skull/.
24. At the same time a dense interaction of global and local subjectivities, through the formation of new regional affiliations and identities is superimposed on existing territorial divisions (Jasanoff 2010, 247).
25. The economic rationale behind it being that it would be cheaper to do so in countries in the South. However this has been questioned from within neo-classical economics (e.g. Scocco and Alfredsson 2008).
26. The Clean Development Mechanism (CDM), defined in Article 12 of the Kyoto Protocol, allows a country with an emission-reduction or emission-limitation commitment (Annex B Party) to implement an emission-reduction project in developing countries. Such projects can earn saleable certified emission reduction (CER) credits.
27. For example see, http://www.cifor.cgiar.org/mediamultimedia/newsroom/press-releases/press-releases-detail-view/article/238/climate-change-highlights-need-for-women-to-take-greater-role-in-forest-management-experts-say-ahea.html.
28. Several scholars have written about this phenomenon as the 'feminization of responsibility.' Given this background, the current slogan within Swedish development aid, 'Invest in Women,' would suggest cause for alarm (presentation by Swedish minister for development cooperation at SLU, March 2011).
29. Ecological modernization is a school of thought in the social sciences that argues that the economy benefits from moves towards environmentalism and that economy and ecology can favorably be combined. For some of its proponents, better use of green technologies are seen as the solution to environmental problems.

NOTES TO CHAPTER 4

1. In Nayagarh (first in 1993–94 and then in 1998–99), I carried out group discussions and individual interviews (that I filmed) with women and men in the villages, attended meetings, and interacted informally during my stay there. All quotations in this and the following two chapters are taken from my research in Nayagarh, and especially in chapter five from group discussions with *mahila samiti* members between 1998 and 1999 unless specified otherwise. I also make use of interviews carried out by a colleague, Manoj Pattanaik who was working on a history of the movement during the same period. His interviews are marked with an asterisk * in the text. All names have been changed for reasons of anonymity. All translations from Hindi and Odia are my own. For help with translating the Odia especially the group discussions, I would especially like to thank Barna Bhai Panda.
2. Between 1998 and 2008, our process together went through a number of cycles that I outline in this and the following two chapters. The initial interviews were carried out with 23 women and 10 men in Drevdagen. This was followed by a collaborative inquiry with the women (1999–2000). We met every 6 weeks over a period of 2 years. After 2000 we met less frequently in the group and mainly to discuss what I was writing, though we had one large joint meeting in 2002. The most recent phase of our process (2007–8) was the analyses of our different experiences of the research in two articles, one by the *kvinnoforum* (Bergelin et al. 2008) and one by me (Arora-Jonsson 2008). The material used in this and the following chapters is from my field journals, interviews with other women and men in Drevdagen, anecdotes of actions taken, and reports of our get-togethers and discussions in the group. All quotations from Drevdagen are from the interviews, group discussions and other conversations during our get-togethers. All other quotes from individual interviews and conversations are specified in separate footnotes. In 2004, Maleleine Granvik, a researcher from SLU did an evaluation of forest activities in Drevdagen, excerpts of which have been specified with an asterisk*. All names have been changed for reasons of anonymity. All translations from the Swedish original are mine.
3. The recent conflagrations between local people and the state government's attempt to acquire land for bauxite mining in Niyamgiri and for Posco, a Korean steel company are two of the many flashpoints in a larger conflict over what growth and development imply for different groups in the state.
4. *Bruksha O' Jeevar Bandhu Parishad* will henceforth be referred to as the BOJBP.
5. The numbers have been put together by Manoj K. Rathi, a staff member at the BOJBP office in 1999.
6. He was professor in political science at Utkal University in Bhubaneswar, the state capital, when I interviewed him in Bhubaneswar, 1994.
7. Literally, a 'journey on foot,' a campaigning march.
8. A block is a district subdivision.
9. In India, especially in Hindu culture, by touching someone's feet, or prostrating yourself before them you are showing them that you respect them.
10. He was one of the few in Kesharpur who was a Brahmin (upper caste) in the movement.
11. ODA preceded the existing DFID—Department for International Development in the UK.
12. In more recent terminology, reflecting perhaps neoliberal influences, such groups all over India are called 'self-help groups' and are usually formed around micro-credit programs.

13. *Norrland* is a term for the northern parts of Sweden consisting of nine provinces.
14. Municipality.
15. This is reminiscent of my interview (1993) with Annapurna Maharana in Cuttack who comparing the present with the independence struggle mourned how people now thought the state to be their *mai-bap* (mother-father, givers of welfare), instead of relying on *lok-shakti* (people's power) as they did previously.
16. A detailed story of the school strike and the political intrigues can be found in Halvarsson (1999) and Ersson (1985).
17. I have discussed this at some length in Chapter 3.
18. More recently, strides have been made in certain areas especially in the case of fisheries.
19. The claim that the company was logging more than what is considered to be sustainable is also made by a former head of the forest board in a consultancy report. He writes that in response to pressure from shareholders the company had taxed the forests in Särna-Idre much more than is sustainable (Nilsson 1998).
20. I write about the film further in the chapter.
21. A participatory exercise popular in the development context where development agents and villagers (or others) participate in putting together information, analyzing the context, and developing plans. PRAs apply specific methods and processes that typically build on visualization techniques.
22. See next chapter on some of the disjunctures experienced by women who work outside and yet expected to perform in set ways in the village.

NOTES TO CHAPTER 5

1. Experience has been an important element for understanding subjectivity but has also been the subject of considerable debate. I shall not go into that here except to note that while Foucauldian poststructuralism brought with it a mistrust of experience and forced subjectivity to retreat to the production of the subject through power relations, experiences also form the grounds for critique and formation of new subjectivities (see chapter two for a discussion of subjectivity).
2. The DWACRA advanced a rotating sum of Rs. 15,000 to the *mahila samitis* which they could use to set up small enterprises.
3. More detailed accounts of the entire process as well as participatory methods adopted by the group can be found in Arora-Jonsson 2005 and 2008.
4. We often met in a cottage by a pond, in Swedish, a *damm*. Hence *dammiga* (which also means dusty) and *damer* is ladies.
5. Having grown up outside the village during a part of her life, she did not speak *Idremålet*, the local dialect.
6. The meaning the women gave to this phrase was to have employment outside the home and earn a salary, to have a profession. Though still the overriding positive image, it is being supplanted by current policy discourses exhorting women (and men) to start small-scale enterprises.
7. Although we are thought to be in a postmodern age, references to being modern in both places, illustrate the many ways in which we live within ideas of modernity.
8. For example see the text written by the women, Berglin et al. 2008.
9. The forum.

10. Binary oppositions have functioned in the social sciences as self-evident principles for categorizing and describing a rich multiplicity of phenomena-sacred/profane, nature/culture, formal/informal, active/passive and as I show in chapter 2 they are hierarchical and have gendered implications.
11. Described in the previous chapter.
12. The field organizer for the village appointed by BOJBP.
13. Bingolotto was a lottery on T.V. and it provided a whole evening entertainment with music etc. During the 1990s it was extremely popular in Sweden and was an institution in many ways.
14. Especially as the forum began to be questioned by others outside of its membership.
15. Whether or not the women's refusal to talk about discrimination might stand in the way of action is a discussion that I shall take up in Chapter 7.
16. As in villages like Manapur where gathering outside as women without any specific purpose was just not done.
17. The rural parliaments are convened by a social movement's campaign, *Hela Sverige Ska Leva*, All Sweden shall live. It was founded in the late 1980s and is composed of rural voluntary associations, governmental bodies and so on.
18. See Blackman et al. (2008, 16), who bring attention to these aspects of subjectivity.

NOTES TO CHAPTER 6

1. In most cases and on most issues, the people were not indifferent (or cannot be?) in a small village like this.
2. Although my writing about it was perceived as a problem by my colleagues working in the village. In the village itself both men and women had read the report that I had sent to the women I had interviewed.
3. As I discuss later in Chapter 7, these differences also were reflected in the women's organizing.
4. I am thankful to Erik Westholm for making this point.
5. Until I insisted on speaking to them.
6. This included the authorities.
7. This social role did not have the meaning conferred on it by the women as I show in the previous chapter.
8. Referring to Eisenstein (1988), Cooper writes about gender as an organizing principle interacting with other organizing principles, for example ethnicity, class that "although will be condensed differently according to the form or site in question, they are not recreated from scratch at each instance" (1995, 25).
9. In terms of party politics, she writes, "One can easily conclude that men dominate politics, at the same time as the message that is conveyed is that they are there not because they are men. They stand for a combination of self-evident presence and total absence. Thus the question: men, do they exist?" (2002, 106).
10. Reasons ranged from the irrelevance of questions addressed, the alien and intimidating forum, to the spokesmen being over committed (see Chapter 4).
11. Many of the older women had also lived and worked in other places.
12. Partly reflected in a skilled carpenters disdain for abstract deskwork.
13. Exceptions do exist. When I was in a village in Kashipur in Rayagada district to visit Sumoni Jhuria who led a tribal women's group in Odisha and whom I interviewed in 1993 (Arora-Jonsson 1995), the young men in the village said

they would be happy to join the group if the women let them, since it was the women's group that was dynamic in the village. But then these were younger men and Sumoni was older, making it less problematic.

14. Maud Eduards (2002, 154) cites Mary Spongberg (1997, 26) and writes that despite the role that men play in politics, it is important to erase all allusions to them as sexed or gendered beings. Men's privileges should not be visible. One of the fundamental contradictions is thus "that while the body politic may be male, in order for it to function, all vestiges of its maleness must be rendered invisible. The body politic must be both masculine and sexless at the same time."
15. While, Axel and Niklas had also placed the women's chances in jeopardy by strengthening the position of the men in the association.
16. Magnusson (2001, 11) cites Marla Steinberg (1996) who writes about fairness accounting by default, that is, if nobody is complaining, then that is taken as a sign that the situation is fair. In Steinberg's study of Canadian couples, it was striking to see that it was only the men who used this argument and not the women.
17. This had not been a problem when I was there. Anita the coordinator often took her infant baby with her to the villages when she was out on field trips all day.
18. The authors do mention however, that they spoke mainly to the coordinator of the women's program and some field organizers and it was difficult for them as two males to come in contact with the women. Yet they make rather far-reaching assumptions about the women's program. It was not considered the women's program but rather the BOJBP's since it was started by the BOJBP. In the words of Jackson, "It is a serious objection that in our attempts to recover women as subjects in social change we can, perversely, deny them subjectivity by representing them as passive recipients rather than active instigators of social change" (1998, 316).
19. Community-based organization and non-governmental organization.

NOTES TO CHAPTER 7

1. Some researchers in Sweden believe that a postcolonial perspective (where race and ethnicity play an important part in the conceptualization) is important to understanding Swedish society. For example, in their book *Sverige och de andra* (Sweden and the others), McEachrane and Faye (2001) write that although Sweden has never been a colonial power, the Swedish self-image has been formed by being inscribed into the cultural history of the West. This self-image has inevitably been colored by colonialism in Sweden's relations to other non-Western countries and in its relation to its nonwhite others (such as immigrants to the country).
2. The killing of Prime Minister Olof Palme in 1986 gave rise to a number of conspiracy theories and the brief arrest of a right-wing extremist and a Kurdish dissident living in Sweden. In 1999, the picture of Swedish neo-Nazis as working-class youths upset over immigration and often provoked by violent immigrant youths was shattered as a result of neo-Nazi attacks against journalists, trade union activists, and homosexuals, most of them native Swedes. The Göteborg fire in October 1998 took place in a disco; several young people died, most of whom were immigrants. There was tension because many believed that Swedish youths had set the fire. Eventually four Iranian men were found guilty.
3. Interview with a woman in Drevdagen at her home in April 1999.

4. Almost 90 percent of Swedish women work in the labor force. Despite this involvement in the labor force, Sweden has one of the most gender-segregated labor forces in Europe, with women in lower-paid and part-time professions.
5. See discussion between Karl, Jan and Sara referred to in Chapter 5 about the women's dissatisfaction with the village association at Sara's home in Drevdagen, June 1999.
6. Unfortunately, not only did the men from the university know about these discriminatory practices, but they participated in making women's efforts to resist them irrelevant by referring to them as personal and as village politics.
7. Interview with Anita, the women's groups' coordinator at the Office of the Forest Network in Kesharpur village, Odisha, February 1999.
8. Interview with an officeholder of the Nayagarh Forest Federation at the Forest Federation office, Nayagarh town, Nayagarh district, Odisha, February 1999.

NOTES TO CHAPTER 8

1. For a more detailed account of some of these trends, see Chapter 3.
2. See Chapter 2.
3. See Chapter 2 for an explanation. Here, it is important to remember that gender is always a relation, not a possession that one has.
4. In Foucault's words, it was not a power that they possessed or that possessed them, not something in them, but a feature of power itself, exercised in the form of a "strategy." A strategy is not to be understood as a unilateral imposition of power, but precisely an operation of power that is at once productive, diffuse, various in its forms (cited in Butler 2004, 183, translation from French). This power of normalization is diffused throughout society. Foucault argues that what is required is "a political philosophy that isn't erected around the problem of sovereignty, nor therefore around the problem of law and prohibition. We need to cut off the king's head: in political theory that has still to be done" (Foucault 1980, 121).
5. Rocheleau borrows the term environmentality from Arun Agrawal (2005) who analyzes the relationship between changing governmental environmental management and the spread of environmental awareness in citizens and subjects, the production of environmental subjectivity that occurs when people are involved in various ways in the management of the environment.
6. Researchers in Sweden and in India have stressed the holistic approach taken by women in their groups in the rural areas. What I also try to see in my cases is the circumstances that often prompt women to take such a stance.
7. It was also a practical issue. For example, Sarin et al. (2003), writing about another part of Odisha, describe how women who patrolled the forests also used their time to collect various forest products, i.e. to do other chores. For the men, in several cases it was found that when they took up protection responsibilities they looked upon these as separate tasks.
8. Translated in the English version as, "The forests for us: where peace comes dropping slow."
9. For e.g. Sarin et al. (2003, 18) write that in India, for many poor women, community forest management only meant a shift in the *danda* (stick) from the hands of the forest guard to the local youth.

10. With proceduralist qualities such as participation dialogue, transparency and accountability.
11. See some of the women's accounts of how they began to 'take place' in village meetings (Bergelin et al. 2008).
12. This does not mean that motivations from love/loyalty do not occur in the public sphere or from hope of remuneration in the private, but that these are examples of ascriptions that are meant to guide ideal behaviour. Further, this comparmentalization of the private/home and work/public and political prevented ideas about gender equality to collide with everyday practices that might be perceived as unequal.
13. Nancy Fraser writes that the participatory democracy we seek today is one that uses politics to tame markets and to steer society in the interests of justice (2009).
14. As Allen (2004, 251) clarifies, "What Fouacaldian feminists are struggling to get clear on: how can selves who have been constituted by disciplinary and normalizing relations of power start from where they are and yet still take up a self-constituting relation to themselves that is empowering and transformative?"

NOTES TO CHAPTER 9

1. The nature of this theorizing is accepted in action research and within much feminism. However as Eduards (2002, 130) writes, to claim that women's political practices may be seen as part of theorizing is to invite distancing taking by the traditional research society.

References

Acker, Joan, Kate Barry, and Johanna Esseveld. 1991. Objectivity and Truth. In *Beyond Methodology: Feminist Scholarship as Lived Research*, edited by M.M. Fonow and J.A. Cook. Bloomington and Indianapolis. Indiana University Press.

Agarwal, Anil, and Sunita Narain. 1991. Global Warming in an Unequal World: A Case of Environmental Colonialism. New Delhi: Centre for Science and Environment.

Agarwal, Bina. 1994. Gender and Command over Property: A Critical Gap in Economic Analysis and Policy in South Asia. *World Development* 22 (10):1455–1478.

Agarwal, Bina. 1997. Environmental Action, Gender Equity and Women's Participation. *Development and Change* 28 (1): 1–44.

Agarwal, Bina. 2003. Gender Inequality, Cooperation and Environmental Sustainability. In *Inequality, Collective Action and Environmental Sustainability*, edited by J.-M. Baland, S. Bowles, and P. Bardhan. New York: Russell Sage.

Agarwal, Bina. 2010. *Gender and Green Governance: The Political Economy of Women's Presence Within and Beyond Community Forestry*. Oxford: Oxford University Press.

Agnihotri, Anita. 2001. *Forest Interludes A Collection of Journals and Fiction.* New Delhi: Kali for Women.

Agrawal, Arun, Ashwini Chhatre, and Rebecca Hardin. 2008. Changing Governance of World's Forests. *Science* 320 (1460): 1460.

Agrawal, Arun, and Clark C. Gibson. 1999. Enchantment and Disenchantment: The Role of Community in Natural Resource Conservation. *World Development* 27 (4): 629–649.

Agrawal, Arun, and Jesse C. Ribot. 2000. Analyzing Decentralization: A Framework with South Asian and West African Environmental Cases. In *Environmental Governance in Africa (Working Paper)*. Washington D.C.: World Resource Institute.

Alcoff, Linda, and Elizabeth Potter, eds. 1993. *Feminist Epistemologies.* New York: Routledge.

Alinder, Kurt. 1945. Särna- och Idreskogarnas Historia under Svensk Tid: Ett Bidrag till Deras Rättshistoriska Utveckling. In *Särna-Idre 300 år*, edited by E. Björk, G. Hilde and P. O. Söderlund. Falun: Särna-Idre socknar.

Allardt, Erik. 1975. *Att ha, Att Älska, Att Vara : Om Välfärd i Norden.* Lund: Argos Förlag AB.

Allen, Amy. 2004. Foucault, Feminism and the Self: The Politics of Personal Transformation. In *Feminism and the Final Foucault*, edited by D. Taylor and K. Vintges. Urbana: University of Illinois.

Ang, Ien. 2001. I'm a Feminist but . . . 'Other' Women and Postnational Feminism. In *Feminism and Race*, edited by K. Bhavnani. Oxford: Oxford University Press.

Angelsen, Arild, ed. 2008. *Moving Ahead with REDD: Issues, Options and Implications*. Bogor Barat, Indonesia: CIFOR.

Arendt, Hannah. 1954. *Between Past and Future*. New York: Penguin.

Arnold, David. 2006. *The Tropics and the Travelling Gaze: India, Landscape, and Science, 1800–1856*. Seattle: University of Washington Press.

Arora-Jonsson, Seema. 1995. Constructive Politics In Orissa, Gandhian Organisations and Their Legacy. M.Phil. Dissertation, Department of History, Delhi University, Delhi.

Arora-Jonsson, Seema. 2005. Unsettling the Order: Gendered Subjects and Grassroots Activism in Two Forest Communities. Ph.D. dissertation, Department of Rural Development and Agroecology, Swedish University of Agricultural Sciences, Uppsala.

Arora-Jonsson, Seema. 2008. "Research Sounds So Big": Collaborative Inquiry with Women in Drevdagen. In *Participatory Research in Conservation and Rural Livelihoods: Doing Science Together*, edited by L. Fortmann. Oxford: Wiley-Blackwell.

Arora-Jonsson, Seema. 2011. Virtue and Vulnerability: Discourses on Women, Gender and Climate Change *Global Environmental Change* 21: 744–751.

Assi Domän. 1997. Projekt Nyskog, Förprospekt. Assi Domän.

Bacchi, Carol Lee. 1996. *The Politics of Affirmative Action: 'Women', Equality and Category Politics*. London: Sage.

Bacchi, Carol Lee. 1999. *Women, Policy and Politics: The Construction of Policy Problems*. London: Sage.

Baden, Sally, and Anne Marie Goetz. 1998. Who Needs [Sex] when You Can Have [Gender]? Conflicting Discourses on Gender at Beijing. In *Feminist Visions of Development: Gender Analysis and Policy*, edited by C. Jackson and R. Pearson. London: Routledge.

Baland, Jean-Marie, and Jean-Phillipe Platteau. 1996. *Halting Degradation of Natural Resources: Is There a Role for Rural Communities?* Oxford: FAO/ Clarendon Press.

Bauman, Zygmunt. 1995. *Life in Fragments: Essays in Postmodern Morality*. Oxford: Blackwell.

Baviskar, Amita. 2001. Written on the Body, Written on the Land: Violence and Environmental Struggles in Central India. In *Violent Environments*, edited by N.L. Peluso and M. Watts. Ithaca: Cornell University Press.

Benhabib, Seyla. 1992. *Situating the Self: Gender, Community and Postmodernism in Contemporary Ethics*. New York: Routledge.

Benhabib, Seyla. 2002. *The Claims of Culture: Equality and Diversity in the Global Era*. Princeton, NJ: Princeton University Press.

Bergelin, Åsa, Margareta Emretsson, Anne Lundgren Halvarsson, and Anna Ryen. 2008. "För Oss är Naturen en Lisa för Själen" (Where peace comes dropping slow: the forests and nature for oss). In *Participatory Research in Conservation and Rural Livelihoods: Doing Science Together*, edited by L. Fortmann. Oxford: Wiley-Blackwell.

Berkhout, Frans. 2010. Reconstructing Boundaries and Reason in the Climate Debate. *Global Environmental Change* 20: 565–569.

Berlant, Lauren, and Michael Warner. 2000. Sex in Public. In *Intimacy*, edited by L. Berlant. Chicago: Chicago University Press.

Bhavnani, Kumkum, John Foran, and Priya A. Kurian, eds. 2003. *Feminist Futures Reimagining Women, Cultures and Development*. London: Zed Books.

Blackman, Lisa, John Cromby, Derek Hook, Dimitris Papadopoulos, and Valerie Walkerdine. 2008. Creating Subjectivities. *Subjectivity* 22: 1–27.

Brandth, Berit, and Marit Haugen. 2000. From Lumberjack to Business Manager: Masculinity in the Norwegian Forestry Press. *Journal of Rural Studies* 16 (July): 343–355.

Buckingham, Susan. 2010. Call in the Women. *Nature* 468: 502.

Butler, Judith. 1990. *Gender Trouble: Feminism and the Subversion of Identity*. New York: Routledge.

Butler, Judith. 2004. Bodies and Power Revisited. In *Feminism and the Final Foucault*, edited by D. Taylor and K. Vintges. Urbana: University of Illinois Press.

Butler, Judith. 2005. *Giving an Account of Oneself*. New York: Fordham University Press.

Byskog. 1998. Byskog: Lokal Förvaltning i Särna-Idre.

Bäckstrand, Karin, Jamil Khan, Annica Kronsell, and Eva Lövbrand, eds. 2010. *Environmental Politics and Deliberative Democracy: Examing the Promise of New Modes of Governance*. Cheltenham: Edward Elgar.

Campioni, Mia, and Elizabeth Grosz. 1991. Love's Labours Lost: Marxism and Feminism. In *A Reader in Feminist Knowledge*, edited by S. Gunew. London/New York: Routledge.

Carlsson, Lars. 2001. Keeping Away from the Leviathan: The Case of the Swedish Common Forests. Management of Social Transformations (MOST) Discussion Paper 51. Working Paper. Paris. UNESCO.

Carruyo, Light. 2003. Dreams and Process in Development: Theory and Practice. In *Feminist Futures: Reimagining Women, Culture and Development*, edited by K. Bhavnani, J. Foran and P.A. Kurian. London: Zed Books.

Chaudhari, B. 1982. The State of the Economy in Eastern India at the Time the British Took Over: Signs of Decline Particularly in Orissa and Assam. In *The Cambridge Economic History of India, Vol. 2: c 1757–c. 1970*, edited by D. Kumar and M. Desai. Hyderabad: Orient Longman in association with Cambridge University Press.

Cleaver, Frances. 1998. Incentives and Informal Institutions: Gender and the Management of Water. *Agriculture and Human Values* 15 (4): 347–360.

Cleaver, Frances. 2001. Institutions, Agency and the Limitations of Participatory Approaches to Development. In *Participation: The New Tyranny ?* edited by B. Cooke and U. Kothari. London: Zed Books.

Cline-Cole, Reginald. 2007. Woodfuel Discourses and the Re-framing of Wood Energy. *Forum for Development Studies* 1: 121–153.

Connell, Robert W. 2003. Masculinities, Change, and Conflict in Global Society: Thinking about the Future of Men's Studies. *The Journal of Men's Studies* 11 (3): 249–266.

Cooke, Bill and Uma Kothari. 2001. The Case for Participation as Tyranny. In *Participation: The New Tyranny?*, edited by B. Cooke and U. Kothari. London: Zed Books.

Cooper, Davina. 1995. *Power in Struggle Feminism, Sexuality and the State*. Buckingham: Open University Press.

Cooper, Fredrick, and Randall Packard, eds. 1997. *International Development and the Social Sciences*. Berkeley: University of California Press.

Couze, Venn. 2002. Refiguring Subjectivity after Modernity. In *Challenging Subjects: Critical Psychology for a New Millenium*, edited by V. Walkerdine. Hampshire: Palgrave.

Cuomo, Chris J. 1998. *Feminism and Ecological Communities: An Ethic of Flourishing*. London: Routledge.

Dahlström, Margareta. 1996. Young Women in a Male Periphery: Experiences from the Scandinavian North. *Journal of Rural Studies* 12 (3): 259–271.

de Lauretis, Teresa. 1984. *Alice Doesn't: Feminism, Semiotics, Cinema*. Bloomington: Indiana University Press.

de Lauretis, Teresa. 1989a. The Essence of the Triangle or, Taking the Risk of Essentialism Seriously: Feminist Theory in Italy, the U.S., and Britain. *Differences: A Journal of Feminist Cultural Studies* 1(2): 33–37.

de Lauretis, Teresa. 1989b. *Technologies of Gender: Essays on Theory, Film, and Fiction.* Basingstoke: Macmillan.

de los Reyes, Paulina, Irene Molina, and Diana Mulinari, eds. 2002. *Maktens (o) lika förklädnader: Kön, Klass och Etnicitet i Det Postkoloniala Sverige.* Stockholm: Bokförlaget Atlas.

Denzin, Norman K. and Yvonna S. Lincoln, eds. 2000. *Handbook of Qualitative Research.* Thousand Oaks: Sage.

Ds. 2004. *Det Går Långsamt Fram.* Stockholm: Jordbruksdepartmentet.

Edmunds, David, and Eva Wollenberg. 2003. Whose Devolution is it Anyway? Divergent Constructs, Interests and Capacities between the Poorest Forest Users and States. In *Local Forest Management: The Impact of Devolution Policies*, edited by D. Edmunds and E. Wollenberg. London: Earthscan.

Eduards, Maud. 1992. Against the Rules of the Game: On the Importance of Women's Collective Actions. In *Rethinking Change Current Swedish Feminist Research*, edited by Edwards, M. L., I. Elgqvist-Saltzman, E. Lundgren, C. Sjöblad, E. Sundin and U. Wikander. Uppsala: Humanistisk-samhällsvetenskapliga forsknignsråd (HSFR).

Eduards, Maud. 1997. Interpreting Women's Organizing. In *Towards a New Democratic Order? Women's Organizing in Sweden in the 1990s*, edited by G. Gustafsson. Stockholm: Publica.

Eduards, Maud. 2002. *Förbjuden Handling: Om Kvinnors Organisering och Feministisk Teori, Demokrati i Förändring.* Malmö: Liber.

Elliot, Anthony. 2002. Identity Politics and Privatisation: Modern Fantasies, Postmodern Aftereffects. In *Challenging Subjects: Critical Psychology for a New Millenium*, edited by V. Walderdine. Hampshire: Palgrave.

Elvin-Nowak, Ylva, and Heléne Thomsson. 2001. Motherhood As an Idea and Practice: A Discursive Understanding of Employed Mothers in Sweden. *Gender and Society* 15 (3): 407–428.

Ericsson, Staffan. 1997. Alla Vill Beta Men Ingen Vill Bränna, Skogshistoria inom Särna-Idre Besparingsskog i Nordvästra Dalarna. Vol. Nr. 8, *Rapporter och Uppsatser.* Umeå: Institutionen för Skoglig Vegetationsekologi, Sveriges Lantbruksuniversitet.

Ersson, Boris. 1985. *Skogen i Våra Hjärtan: En bok Om Kärlek.* Polstjärnan och Skrivarförlaget-Norrbottens Bildningsförbund. Luleå.

Everingham, Jo-Anne. 2002. Mahila Sanghas as Feminist Groups: The Empowerment of Women in Coastal Orissa. *Indian Journal of Gender Studies* 9 (1): 43–60.

Fischer, Frank. 2006. Participatory Governance as Deliberative Empowerment: The Cultural Politics of Discursive Space. *The American Review of Public Administration* 36 (19): 19–40.

Flygare, A. Iréne. 2001. Länkar, Agenter och Alternativ. Kvinnogenerationer i 1900-talets Jordbruk. In *Kvinnor och Jord, Arbete och Ägande från Medeltid till Nutid*, edited by B. Liljewall, K. Niskanen and M. Sjöberg. Stockholm: Kungl. Skogs-och lantbruksakademien, Nordiska Museet och Sveriges Lantbruksuniversitet.

Flygare, A.Iréne. 1999. Generation och Kontinuitet: Familjjordbruket i Två Svenska Slättbygder under 1900-talet, Institutionen för Landskapsplanering, Sveriges Lantbruksuniversitet.

Fonow, Mary M., and Judith A. Cook, eds. 1991. *Beyond Methodology: Feminist Scholarship as Lived Research.* Bloomington: Indiana University Press.

Forsberg, Annette. 2001. Lokalt Utvecklingsarbete på Landsbygden. In *Social Ekonomi i Sverige*, edited by H. Westlund. Stockholm: Fritzes.

Forsberg, Gunnel. 1994. Befolkningsomflyttningar på Landsbygden: Kunskapsöversikt och Statistisk Analys. Uppsala: Kulturgeografiska Institutionen.
Forsberg, Gunnel. 1996. Landsbygdens Nykolonisation—En Brokig Bild Växer Fram. In *Med Periferin i Centrum: Om Landsbygden Som Motor i En Långsiktigt Hållbar Utveckling*, edited by H. Månsson. Östersund: Glesbygdsverket.
Forsberg, Gunnel. 1997. Rulltrapperregioner och Social Infrastruktur. In Om Makt och Kön: i Spåren av Offentliga Organisationers Omvandlig: Rapport till Utredningen om Fördelningen av Ekonomisk Makt och Ekonomiska Resurser Mellan Kvinnor och Män 1997: 83, edited by E. Sundin. Stockholm: Fritzes offentliga publikationer.
Forsberg, Gunnel. 1999. Könskvotering i regionalpolitiken—Förslag Till Framtida Åtgärder. Uppsala: IM-Gruppen i Uppsala AB.
Fortmann, Louise, ed. 2008. *Participatory Research in Conservation and Rural Livelihoods: Doing Science Together*. London: Wiley-Blackwell.
Foucault, Michel. 1979. *Discipline and Punish: The Birth of the Prison*. New York: Vintage Books.
Foucault, Michel (interview with Alessandro Fontana, Pasquale Pasquino). 1980. Truth and Power. In *Power/Knowledge: Selected Interviews and Other Writings* 1972–1977, edited by C. Gordon. Brighton: Harverster Press.
Foucault, Michel. 1990. *The History of Sexuality Vol. 1: An Introduction*. London: Penguin Books.
Foucault, Michel. 1991. Governmentality. In *The Foucault Effect: Studies in Governmentality*, edited by G. Burchell, C. Gordon and P. Miller. London: Harvester Wheatsheaf.
Frånberg, Gun-Marie. 1994. Kvinnliga Eldsjälar i Glesbygd: Lokal Mobilisering, Förändring och Anpassning. Östersund: Glesbygdsmyndigheten.
Fraser, Nancy. 1993. Rethinking the Public Sphere: A Contribution to the Critique of Actually Existing Democracy. In *Habermas and the Public Sphere*, edited by C. Calhoun. Cambridge: Massachusetts Institute of Technology.
Fraser, Nancy. 1995. False Antithesis: A Response to Seyla Benhabib and Judith Butler. In *Feminist Contentions: A Philosophical Exchange*. New York: Routledge.
Fraser, Nancy. 2008. *Scales of Justice: Reimagining Political Space in a Globalizing World*. Cambridge: Polity Press.
Fraser, Nancy. 2009. Feminism, Capitalism and the Cunning of History. *New Left Review* 56: 97–117.
Fraser, Nancy, and Axel Honneth. 2003. *Redistribution or Recognition? A Political-Philosophical Exchange*. Translated by J. Golb, J. Ingram and C. Wilke. London: Verso.
Freire, Paolo. 1972. *Pedagogy of the Oppressed*. Harmondsworth. Penguin.
Friberg, Tora. 2004. *Persontransporternas "Vita Fläckar": Om Arbetspendling Med Kollektiv Trafik ur Ett Jämställdhetsperspektiv*. Linköping: Centrum för Kommunstrategiska studier, Linköpings Universitet.
Fricker, Miranda. 2007. *Epistemic Injustice: Power and Ethics of Knowing*. Oxford: Oxford University Press.
Funtowicz, Silvio O, and Jerome R. Ravetz. 1993. Science for the Post-Normal Age. *Futures* 25 (7): 739–755.
Gadgil, Madhav, and Ramachandra Guha. 2004. *The Use and Abuse of Nature (Incorporating this Fissured Land, an Ecological History of India and Ecology and Equity)*. New Delhi: Oxford University Press.
Gadol, Joan Kelly. 1976. The Social Relation of the Sexes: Methodological Implications of Women's History. *Signs* 1 (4):809–823.
Gandhi, Nandita, and Nandita Shah. 1992. *The Issues at Stake: Theory and Practice in the Contemporary Women's Movement in India*. New Delhi: Kali for Women.
Gatens, Moira. 1991. A Critique of the Sex/Gender Distinction. In *A Reader in Feminist Knowledge*, edited by S. Gunew. London: Routledge. pp.143–160.

Gibson-Graham, J.K. 2011. A Feminist Project of Belonging for the Anthropocene. *Gender, Place and Culture* 18 (1): 1–21.

Government of India. 1952. *National Forest Policy*. 1952. 12th May, Ministry of Food and Agriculture. New Delhi: Government of India.

Government of India. 2006. *National Environment Policy*. Ministry of Environment and Forests. New Delhi. Government of India.

Government of India. 2006. *The Scheduled Tribes and Other Forest Dwellers* (Recognition of Forest Rights Act), 2006. Department of Law and Justice. New Delhi: The Gazette of India.

Grewal, Inderpal, and Caren Kaplan, eds. 1994. *Scattered Hegemonies: Postmodernity and Transnational Feminist Practices*. Minneapolis: University of Minnesota Press.

Grosz, Elizabeth. 1990. Criticism, Feminism, and the Institution. In *The Post-colonial Critic: Interviews, Strategies, Dialogues Gayatri Chakravorty Spivak*, edited by S. Harasym. New York: Routledge.

Grosz, Elizabeth. 1991. Philosophy, Introduction. In *A Reader in Feminist Knowledge*, edited by S. Gunew. London/New York: Routledge.

Grosz, Elizabeth. 1993. Bodies and Knowledges: Feminism and the Crisis of Reason. In *Feminist Epistemologies*, edited by L. Alcoff and E. Potter. New York: Routledge.

Grove, Richard H. 1995. *Green Imperialism: Colonial Expansion, Tropical Island Edens and the Origins of Environmentalism, 1600–1860*. Cambridge: Cambridge University Press.

Guha, Ramachandra, and Madhav Gadgil. 1989. State Forestry and Social Conflict in British India. *Past and Present* 123: 144–177.

Guha, Ramachandra, and Juan Martinez-Alier. 1998. *Varities of Environmentalism: Essays North and South*. New Delhi: Oxford University Press.

Guijt, Irene, and Meera Kaul Shah, eds. 1998. *The Myth of Community: Gender Issues in Participatory Development*. London: Intermediate Technology Publications.

Gunew, Sneja. 1990. Questions of Multi-culturalism. In *The Post-colonial Critic: Interviews, Strategies, Dialogues Gayatri Chakravorty Spivak*, edited by S. Harasym. New York: Routledge.

Gustafsson, Gunnel, ed. 1997. *Towards a New Democratic Order? Women's Organizing in Sweden in the 1990s*. Stockholm: Publica.

Halvarsson, Hans. 1999. *I Demokratisk Ordning Beslutat*. Stockholm: Författares Bokmaskin.

Hannam, Kevin. 2000a. Educating an Environmental Elite: The Training of the Indian Forest Service. *International Research in Geographical and Environmental Education* 9 (4): 285–295.

Hannam, Kevin. 2000b. Utilitarianism and the Identity of the Indian Forest Service. *Environment and History* 6: 205–228.

Hansen, Kjell. 2000. Mellan Inordning och Motstånd: Om Formering av Lokala Identiteter i Nordsvenska Skogsbygder. In *Skogsliv: Kulturella processer i nordiska skogsbygder*, edited by I. Kaldar, E. Johansson, B. Fritzböger and H. Snellman. Lund: Historiska Media.

Haraway, Donna J. 1991. *Simians, Cyborgs, and Women: The Reinvention of Nature*. First ed. London: Free Association Books.

Harcourt, Wendy, ed. 1994. *Feminist Perspectives on Sustainable Development*. London: Zed Books.

Harding, Sandra. 1998. *Is Science Multicultural? Postcolonialisms, Feminisms, and Epistemologies*. Bloomington: Indiana University Press.

Harding, Sandra, and Kathryn Norberg. 2005. New Feminist Approaches to Social Science Methodologies: An Introduction. *Signs* 30 (4): 2009–2015.

Haug, Frigga. 1999. *Female Sexualization: A Collective Work of Memory* (E. Carter, Trans. 3rd ed. Vol. 25). London: Verso.

Hawkins, Roberta, Diana Ojeda (Editors), Kiran Asher, Brigitte Baptiste, Leila Harris, Sharelen Mollet, Andrea Nightingale, Dianne Rocheleau, Joni Seager, and Farhana Sultana (Contributers). 2011. Gender and Environment: Critical Tradition and New Challenges. *Environment and Planning D: Society and Space* 29: 237–253.

Hay, Colin. 2002. *Political Analysis: A Critical Introduction*. Edited by B. G. Peters, J. Pierre and G. Stoker, *Political Analysis*. London: Palgrave.

Hazari, Narayan and Subas Chandra Hazari. 1987. *Community Action in Environmental Conservation: An experiment in Orissa*. New Delhi: Ashish Publishing House.

Hazari, Narayan and Subas Chandra Hazari. 1990. *Environmental Revolution in Orissa: The Buddhagram Experiment*. New Delhi: Ashish Publishing House.

Hekman, Susan. 2004. Feminist Identity Politics: Transforming the Political. In *Feminism and the Final Foucalt*, edited by D. Taylor and K. Vintges. Urbana: University of Illinois Press.

Henriques, Julian, Wendy Hollway, Cathy Urwin, Couze Venn, and Valerie Walkerdine, eds. 1998. *Changing the Subject: Psychology, Social Regulation and Subjectivity*. London: Routledge.

Herlitz, Ulla. 1989. Kvinnor och Glesbygdsstöd. Paper presented at the seminar Kvinnor på Landsbygden. Stockholm: Expertgruppen om Regional Utreckling (ERU).

Heynen, Nik, James McCarthy, Scott Prudham, and Paul Robbins. 2007. Introduction: False Promises. In *Neoliberal Environments: False Promises, Unnatural Consequences*, edited by N. Heynen, J. McCarthy, S. Prudham and P. Robbins. London: Routledge.

Hirdman, Yvonne. 1990. *The Gender System: Theoretical Reflections on the Social Subordination of Women*. Uppsala: Maktutredningen.

Hobson, Barbara. 2000. *Gender and Citizenship in Transition*. New York: Routledge.

Holmbäck, Åke. 1920. *Studier Över de Svenska Allmänningarnas Historia I. Rättsreglerna för Intaga av Jord vid den Fasta Bosättningen Uppkomsten av Särskilda Slag av Allmänningar, Uppsala Universitets Årsskrift 1920, Juridik. I.* Uppsala: A.-B Akademiska Bokhandel, Almqvist och Wiksells Boktryckeri-A.-B.

Holmbäck, Åke. 1934. *Uppkomsten av Kronans Anspråk på Skog Inom Älvdalens Socken: En Utredning på Uppdrag av älvdalens Sockens Jordägande Socknemän*. Uppsala och Stockholm: Almqvist & Wiksells Boktryckeri-A-B.

Holmgren, Eva, Gun Lidestav, and Göran Kempe. 2004. Forest Condition and Management in Swedish Forest Commons. *Small-scale Forest Economics, Management and Policy* 3 (3): 453–468.

hooks, bell. 1991. Sisterhood: Political Solidarity between Women. In *A Reader in Feminist Knowledge*, edited by S. Gunew. London: Routledge.

Hulme, Mike. 2010. Problems with Making and Governing Global Kinds of Knowledge. *Global Environmental Change* 20: 558–564.

Human, Joe, and Manoj Pattanaik. 2000. *Community Forest Management: A Casebook from India*. Oxford: Oxfam Publication.

Hysing, Erik. 2009. From Government to Governance? A Comparison of Environmental Governing in Swedish Forestry and Transport. *Governance: An International Journal of Policy, Administration, and Institutions* 22 (4): 647–672.

Irigaray, Luce. 2002. *To Speak is Never Neutral*. Translated by G. Shwab. New York: Routledge.

Isaksson, Svante. 1999. *Ingen Frid i Fjällen*. Skellefteå: Ord och Visor förlag.

Iveson, Kurt. 2010. Justifying Exclusion: The Politics of Public Space and the Dispute over Access to McIvers Ladies' Baths, Sydney. *Gender, Place & Culture* 10(3): 215–228.

Jackson, Cecile. 1998. Gender, Irrigation, and Environment: Arguing for Agency. *Agriculture and Human Values* 15 (4): 313–324.

Jasanoff, Sheila. 2007. Technologies of Humility. *Nature* 450 (1): 33.

Jasanoff, Sheila. 2010. A New Climate for Society. *Theory, Culture and Society* 27 (233): 233–253.

Javefors Grauers, Eva , and Anna Eskilsson. 2003. Kvinnor Inom Jord—och Skogsbruk i Fem Regioner i Sverige—En Studie av Lantbrukarkvinnors Försörjningsstrategier. Linköping: Linköpings Universitet.

Jaworski, Adam, and Nikolas Coupland. 1999. Introduction: Perspectives on Discourse Analysis. In *The Discourse Reader*, edited by A. Jaworski and N. Coupland. London: Routledge.

Jefferey, Roger, and Nandini Sundar, eds. 1999. *A New Moral Economy for India's Forests? Discourses of Community and Participation.* New Delhi: Sage.

Jensen, Ebba Lisberg. 2002. Som Man Ropar i Skogen: Modernitet, Makt och Mångfald i Kampen om Njakafjäll och i Den Svenska Skogsbruksdebatten 1970–2000. Lund Studies in Human Ecology 3, Lund University, Lund.

Johanisson, Bengt, Lars Olof Persson, and Ulf Wiberg. 1989. Urbaniserad Glesbygd. Stockholm: ERU, Arbetsmarknadsdepartementet.

Johansson, Ella. 1994. *Skogarnas Fria Söner, Maskulinitet och Modernitet i Norrländskt Skogsarbete.* Vol. 118, *Nordiska Museets Handlingar.* Stockholm: Nordiska Museet.

Johansson, Ella. 2000. Skogslöpare och Vedbodstökare. In *Skogsliv: Kulturella Processer i Nordiska Skogsbygder* edited by Ingar Kaldar, Ella Johansson, Bo Fritzböger & Hanna Snellman, (pp. 37–62). Lund: Historiska Media.

John, Mary E. 1999. Gender, Development and the Women's Movement: Problems for a History of the Present. In *Signposts*, edited by R. Sundar Rajan. New Delhi: Kali for Women.

Kabeer, Naila. 1999. From Feminist Insights to an Analytical Framework: An Institutional Perspective on Gender Inequality. In *Institutions, Relations and Outcomes: A Framework and Case Studies for Gender-aware Planning*, edited by N. Kabeer and R. Subramanian. New Delhi: Kali for Women.

Kabeer, Naila. 2001. Resources, Agency, Achievements: Reflections on the Measurement of Women's Empowerment. In *Discussing Women's Empowerment: Theory and Practice.* Stockholm: Sida.

Kaldal, Ingar. 2000. Skog, Arbeid og Dagligliv i Kvinners og Mens Fortellninger fra Trysil og Nord-Värmland Etter 1930. In *Skogsliv: Kulturella processer i skogsbygden*, edited by I. Kaldar, E. Johansson, B. Fritzböger and H. Snellman. Lund: Historiska Media.

Kant, Shashi, Neera M. Singh, and Kundan K. Singh. 1991. Community-Based Forest Management Systems (Case studies from Orissa). New Delhi: Indian Institute of Forest Management, Bhopal/SIDA/ISO, Swedforest.

Katz, Cindi. 2001. On the Grounds of Globalization: A Topography for Feminist Political Engagement. *Signs: Journal of Women in Culture and Society* 26 (4):1213–1234.

Katz, Cindi. 2004. *Growing up Global: Economic Restructuring and Children's Everyday Lives.* Minneapolis: University of Minnesota Press.

Kobayashi, Audrey. 2001. Negotiating the Personal and the Political in Critical Qualitative Research. In *Qualitative Methodologies for Geographers: Issues and Debates*, edited by M. Limb and C. Dwyer. London: Arnold.

Kohn, Margaret. 2000. Language, Power, and Persuasion: Towards a Critique of Deliberative Democracy. *Constellations* 7 (3): 408–429.

Krishna, Sumi, ed. 2004. *Livelihood and Gender: Equity in Community Resource Management.* New Delhi: Sage.

Kumar, Dharma, ed. 1982. *The Cambridge Economic History of India Vol II c. 1757–c. 1970*. Edited by D. Kumar and T. Raychaudhari. Hyderabad: Orient Longman in association with Cambridge University Press.

Laclau, Ernesto, and Chantal Mouffe. 2001. *Hegemony and Socialist Strategy: Towards a Radical Democratic Politics*. Second Edition. London: Verso.

Lama, Anupama and Marlène Buchy. 2004. Gender, Class, Caste and Participation: Community Forestry in Central Nepal. In *Livelihoods and Gender: Equity in Community Resource Management*, edited by S. Krishna. New Delhi/Thousand Oaks/London: Sage Publications.

Larner, Wendy. 1998. Post-Welfare State Governance: Towards a Code of Social and Family Responsibility. Paper presented at Refashioning Sociology: Responses to a New World Order at Brisbane: Queensland, University of Technology.

Larner, Wendy. 2007. Neoliberal Governmentalities. In *Neoliberal Environments: False Promises and Unnatural Consequences*, edited by N. Heynen, J. McCarthy, S. Prudham and P. Robbins. London: Routledge.

Lather, Patti. 1991. Getting Smart: Feminist Research and Pedagogy with/in the Postmodern. New York: Routledge.

Leach, Melissa. 2007. Earth Mother Myths and Other Ecofeminist Fables: How a Strategic Notion Rose and Fell. *Development and Change* 38 (1): 67–85.

Lewis, Reina, and Sara Mills. 2003. Introduction. In *Feminist Postcolonial Theory: A Reader*, edited by R. Lewis and S. Mills. Edinburgh: Edinburgh University Press.

Li, Tania Murray. 2007. *The Will to Improve: Governmentality, Development, and the Practices of Politics*. Durham/London: Duke University Press.

Lidestav, Gun. 2003. Fakta Skog—Vad gör kön i skogen? Report 10. Institutionen för skogsskötsel. Umeå. Umeå University.

Liliequist, Jonas. 1992. Peasants against Nature: Crossing the Boundaries between Man and Animal in Seventeenth- and Eighteenth-Century Sweden. In *Forbidden History: The State, Society and the Regulation of Sexuality in Modern Europe*, edited by J.C. Fout. Chicago/London: The University of Chicago Press.

Lingam, Lakshmi. 2002. Taking Stock: Women's Movement and the State. In *Social Movements and the State*, edited by G. Shah. New Delhi: Sage.

Lister, Ruth. 1997. *Citizenship: Feminist Perspectives*. Basingstoke: Macmillan.

Little, Jo. 2002. *Gender and Rural Geography: Identity, Sexuality and Power in the Countryside*. Essex: Pearson Education.

Little, Jo. 2003. 'Riding the Rural Love Train': Heterosexuality and the Rural Community. *Sociologia Ruralis* 43 (4): 401–417.

Loomba, Ania, Suvir Kaul, Matti Bunzl, Antoinette Burton, and Jed Esty. 2007. *Postcolonial Studies and Beyond*. Ranikhet: Permanent Black.

Maathai, Waangari, and Lena Sommestad. 2005. Fredspristagare: Genombrott för kvinnors betydelse i miljöarbetet. *Göteborgs-Posten,* 26 februari 2005.

Magnusson, Eva. 1997. Att Vara En Riktigt Kvinna På Kontoret: När Kvinnor Skapar Trivsel, Skapar Trivseln Samtidigt Kvinnor. In *Makt och Kön Tretton Bidrag till Feministisk Kunskap*, edited by G. Norborg. Stockholm: Brutus Östlings Bokförlag Symposion.

Magnusson, Eva. 2001. Politics, Psychology, and Gender in Heterosexual Couples: Welfare States as Laboratories for the Future? Paper presented at 109th APA Convention, August 25, 2001, San Francisco.

Maguire, Patricia. 1996. Proposing a more feminist participatory research: knowing and being embraced openly. In *Participatory research in health: Issues and Experiences*, edited by K. de Koning and M. Martin. Johannesburg/London/New Jersey: National Progressive Primary Health Care Network (NPPHCN), Zed Books Ltd.

Mansbridge, Jane J. 1999. "You're too Independent": How Gender, Race and Class Make Many Feminisms. In *The Cultural Territories of Race: Black and White Boundaries*, edited by M. Lamont. Chicago: University of Chicago Press.

Massey, Doreen. 1994. *Space, Place and Gender.* Cambridge: Polity Press.

Massey, Doreen. 2005. *For Space.* London: Sage.

McEachrane, Michael, and L. Faye, eds. 2001. *Sverige och de Andra: Postkoloniala Perspektiv.* Falun. Natur och Kultur.

McLaren, Margaret A. 2004. Foucault and Feminism: Power, Resistance and Freedom. In *Feminism and the Final Foucault*, edited by D. Taylor and K. Vintges. Urbana: University of Illinois Press.

McNay, Lois. 2000. *Gender and Agency: Reconfiguring the Subject in Feminist and Social Theory.* Malden, MA: Polity Press.

McPhillips, Kathleen. 2002. Refiguring the Sacred: Re-enchantment and the Postmodern World. In *Challenging Subjects: Critical Psychology for a New Millenium*, edited by V. Walkerdine. Hampshire: Palgrave.

Mies, Maria. 1991. Women's Research or Feminist Research? The Debate Surrounding Feminist Science and Methodology. In *Beyond Methodology: Feminist Scholarship as Lived Research*, edited by M.M. Fonow and J.A. Cook. Bloomington: Indiana University Press.

Mill, John Stuart. (1869)1997. *The Subjection of Women.* Edited by S. Appelbaum, *Dover Thrift Editions.* Mineola, New York: Dover Publications.

Mills, Sara. 1997. *Discourse.* Edited by J. Drakakis, *The New Critical Idiom.* London: Routledge.

Mills, Sara. 2002. Post-Feminist Text Anaysis. In *Critical Discourse Analysis: Critical Concepts in Linguistics*, edited by M. J. Toolan. London: Routledge.

Mitchell, Timothy. 2002. *Rule of Experts: Egypt, Techno-Politics, Modernity.* Berkeley: University of California Press.

Mitra, Amit and Sanjoy Patnaik. 1997. Community Forest Management in Orissa and the Role of Oxfam: A Review (unpublished draft report for discussion and comments). Oxfam. New Delhi.

Mohanty, Chandra Talpade. 2003. *Feminism without Borders: Decolonizing Theory, Practicing Solidarity.* New Delhi: Zubaan, an associate of Kali for Women.

Molyneux, Maxine. 1985. Mobilization without Emancipation? Women's Interests, the State and Revolution in Nicaragua. *Feminist Studies* 11 (2): 227–254.

Montelius, Sigvard. 1973. *Kultur Landskap i Omvandling, Dalarnas Museums Serie av Småskrifter.* Falun: Dalarnas Museum.

Montelius, Sigvard. 1977a. Dalarnas Skogar: En Ekonomisk-Historisk Rapsodi. In *Dalarnas Hembygdsbok.* Falun: Dalarnas fornminnes- och hembygdsförbund, 1931–1993.

Montelius, Sigvard. 1977b. *Fäbodväsendet i Övre Dalarna.* Stockholm: Akademilitteratur, Gotab Stockholm.

Mouffe, Chantal. 1999. Deliberative Democracy or Agonistic Pluralism. *Social Research* 66 (3):745–758.

Mulinari, Diana, and Anders Neergard. 2004. Syster, Du är Ju Annorlunda: Migration, Institutionell Förändring och Kön. In *Framtiden i samtiden: Könsrelationer i Förändring i Sverige och Omvärlden*, edited by C. Florin and C. Bergqvist. Stockholm: Institutet för Framtidsstudier.

Myrdal, Janken. 2001. Den Nya Produktionen—Det Nya Uppdraget: Jordbrukets Framtid i Ett Historiskt Perspektiv. Stockholm: Jordbruksdepartmentet.

Naturvårdsverket. 2003. Lokal förankring genom deltagande och dialog. Stockholm: Naturvårdsverket.

Nilsson, N. E. 1998. Skogssituationen i Särna-Idre. Unpublished report. Bäsinge.

Niskanen, Kirsti. 2001. Husbondeväldets Röst: Äktenskap, Egendom och Kön Under Första Delen av 1900-talet. In *Kvinnor och Jord: Arbete och Ägande Från Medeltid Till Nutid*, edited by B. Liljewall, K. Niskanen and M. Sjöberg. Stockholm: Nordiska museet.

O'Connor, Pat. 1998. Women's Friendships in a Post-modern World. In *Placing Friendship in Context*, edited by R.G. Adams and G. Allan. Cambridge: Cambridge University Press.

Ostrom, Elinor. 1990. *Governing the Commons: The Evolution of Institutions for Collective Action*. New York: Cambridge University Press.

Outhwaite, William, ed. 1996. *The Habermas Reader*. Cambridge: Polity Press.

Paldanius, Sam. 2000. *Kunskapslyftet—Till Vilken Nytta Då? Berättelser om Olika Skäl Till Att Avstå Från Kunskapslyftet*. Linköping: Linköpings Universitet.

Pateman, Carole. 1988. *The Sexual Contract*. Stanford, CA: Stanford University Press.

Pati, Biswamoy. 1993. *Resisting Domination: Peasants, Tribals and the National Movement in Orissa 1920–50*. New Delhi: Manohar.

Peters, Guy B., and John Pierre. 1998. Governance without Government? Rethinking Public Administration. *Journal of Public Administration Research and Theory* 8 (2): 223–243.

Pettersson, Katarina, and Seema Arora-Jonsson. 2009. Den Osynliga Entreprenören: Genus och Företagande i De Gröna Näringarna. Stockholm: LRF's Jämställdhetsakademi.

Pettersson, Ronny. 1995. Äganderätten, Laga Skiftet och Skogarnas Avtagande. In *Äganderätten i Lantbrukets Historia*, edited by M. Widgren. Stockholm: Nordiska museet.

Phelps, Jacob, Edward L. Webb, and Arun Agrawal. 2010. Does REDD+ Threaten to Recentralize Forest Governance? *Science* 328: 312–313.

Pieterse, Jan Nederveen. 1991. Dilemmas of Development Discourse: The Crisis of Developmentalism and the Comparative Method. *Development and Change* 22: 5–29.

Pigg, Stacy Leigh. 1996. The Credible and the Credulous: The Question of "Villger's Beliefs" in Nepal. *Cultural Anthropology* 11 (2): 160–201.

Plantin, Lars, Sven-Axel Månsson, and Jeremy Kearney. 2000. Mäns Föräldrarskap: Om Faderskap och Manlighet i Sverige och England" *Socialvetenskaplig Tidskrift* (1–2): 24–42.

Plummer, Ken. 1995. *Telling Sexual Stories: Power, Change and Social Worlds*. London: Routledge.

Povinelli, Elizabeth A. 2007. A Flight from Freedom. In *Postcolonial Studies and Beyond*, edited by A. Loomba, S. Kaul, M. Bunzl, A. Burton and J. Esty. Ranikhet: Permanent Black.

Predd, Allan, and Michael Watts. 1992. *Reworking Modernity: Capitalisms and Symbolic Discontent*. New Brunswick, NJ: Rutgers University Press.

Pringle, Rosemary. 1997. Feminist Theory and the World of the Social. In *Feminism in the 1990s*, edited by G. Murray and G. Tulloch. London: Sage.

Rajan, Ravi. 2006. *Modernizing Nature: Forestry and Imperial Eco-Development 1800–1950*. New Delhi: Orient Longman.

Ramdas, Sagari R. 2009. Women, Forestspaces and the Law: Transgressing the Boundaries. *Economic and Political Weekly* XLIV (44): 65–73.

Ramesh, Jairam. 2009. India's Forest and Tree Cover: Contribution as a Carbon Sink. Ministry of Environment and Forests. New Delhi.

Rayner, Jeremy, Alexander Buck, and Pia Katila. 2010. Embracing Complexity: Meeting the Challenges of International Forest Governance In *IUFRO World Series* IUFRO.

Reason, Peter, ed. 1994. *Participation in Human Inquiry, Research with People*. London: Sage.

Reed, Maureen G. 2000. Taking Stands: A Feminist Perspective on 'Other' Women's Activism in Forestry Communities of Northern Vancouver Island. *Gender, Place and Culture* 7 (4): 363–387.

Reskin, Barbara F., and Debra Branch McBrier. 2000. Why not Ascription? Organizations' Employment of Male and Female Managers. *American Sociological Review* 56 (2): 210–233.

Rocheleau, Dianne. 2007. Neoliberal Environments, Technologies of Governance and Governance of Technologies. In *Neoliberal Environments: False Promises and Unnatural Consequences*, edited by N. Heynen, J. McCarthy, S. Prudham and P. Robbins. London: Routledge.

Rocheleau, Dianne, Barbara Thomas-Slayter, and Esther Wangari. 1996. *Feminist Political Ecology: Global Issues and Local Experiences*. Edited by J. Momsen and J. Monk, *International Studies of Women and Place*. London/New York: Routledge.

Rönnblom, Malin. 1996. Kvinnors Organisering i Glesbygd—Resurs eller Utmaning? In *Med periferin i Centrum: Om Landsbygden Som Motor i En Långsiktigt Hållbar Utveckling*, edited by H. Månsson. Östersund: Glesbygdsverket.

Rönnblom, Malin. 2002. Ett Eget Rum? Kvinnors Organisering Möter Etablerad Politik. Ph.D. dissertation, Statsvetenskapliga institutionen, Umeå Universitet, Umeå.

Roseneil, Sasha. 1995. *Disarming Patriarchy: Feminism and Political Action at Greenham*. Buckingham: Open University Press.

Roseneil, Sasha. 2000. Queer Frameworks and Queer Tendencies: Towards an Understanding of Postmodern Transformations of Sexuality. *Sociological Research Online* 5 (3).

Roseneil, Sasha. 2011. Criticality, Not Paranoia: A Generative Register for Feminist Social Research. *NORA—Nordic Journal of Feminist Gender Research* 19 (2): 124–131.

Sahu, Subrat Kumar. 2010a. India's Forests as Carbon Sinks. *InfoChange News and Features India*, http://infochangeindia.org/environment/community-forests-of-orissa/india-s-forests-as-carbon-sinks.html.

Sahu, Subrat Kumar. 2010b. What difference Has the Forest Rights Act Made? *InfoChange News and Features India*,http://infochangeindia.org/environment/community-forests-of-orissa/what-difference-has-the-forest-rights-act-made.html.

Sarin, Madhu and Lipika Ray. 1998. *Who is Gaining? Who is Losing? Gender and Equity Concerns in Joint Forest Management*. New Delhi: Society for the Promotion of Wasteland Development.

Sarin, Madhu with, Neera M. Singh, Nandini Sundar, and Ranu K. Bhogal. 2003. Devolution as a Threat to Democratic Decision-Making in Forestry? Findings from Three States in India. London: Overseas Development Institute.

Saxena, Naresh Chandra. 1996. I Manage, You Participate. Unpublished Report. Bogor: Cetnre for International Forestry Research (CIFOR).

Schlyter, Peter, and Ingrid Stjernquist. 2010. Regulatory Challenges and Forest Goverance in Sweden. In *Environmental Politics and Deliberative Democracy: Examing the Promise of New Modes of Governance*, edited by K. Bäckstrand, J. Khan, A. Kronsell and E. Lövbrand. Cheltenham: Edward Elgar.

Scocco, Sandro, and Alfredsson, Eva. 2008. Konsten att Nå Både Klimatmål och God Tillväxt: Underlag Till En Klimatstrategi för EU, Hållbara Investeringar, Teknik och Regleringar. Östersund: ITPS, Institut för Tillväxt Politiska Studier.

Scott, James C. 1985. *Weapons of the Weak: Everyday Forms of Peasant Resistance*. New Haven: Yale University Press.

Scott, Joan Wallach. 1988. *Gender and the Politics of History*. New York: Columbia University Press.

Scott, Joan Wallach. 1999. Some Reflections on Gender and Politics. In *Revisioning Gender*, edited by M. Marx Ferree, J. Lorber and B.B. Hess. Thousand Oaks: Sage.

Secretariat, Campaign for Survival and Dignity 2009. Court Cases Against the Forest Rights Act http://www.forestrightsact.com/court-cases.

Shakleton, Sheona, Bruce Campbell, Eva Wollenberg, and David Edmunds. 2002. Devolution and Community-Based Natural Resource Management: Creating Space for Local People to Participate and Benefit? London: Overseas Development Institute.

Shiva, Vandana. 1989. *Staying Alive: Women, Ecology and Development.* London: Zed Books.

Sivaramakrishnan, K. 1995. Colonialism and Forestry in India: Imagining the Past in Present Politics. *Comparative Studies in Society and History* 37 (1): 3–40.

Sjöberg, Maria. 2001. Släkt, Kön och Egendom Kring Det Äldre Samhällets Egendomsrättsliga Villkor. In *Kvinnor och Jord Arbete och Ägande Från Medeltid Till Nutid*, edited by B. Liljewall, K. Niskanen and M. Sjöberg. Stockholm: Nordiska Museet.

Sjöberg, Maria. 2002. Kvinnors Jord, Manlig Rätt: Äktenskap, Egendom och Makt i Äldre Tid. In *Kvinnor Arbetsliv i Dalarna Genom Fem Sekler*, edited by A. Östborn. Uppsala: Uppsala Universitet.

Skrivelse, 2001/2002:173. *En Samlad Naturvårdspolitik, Regeringens Skrivelse.* Stockholm, Regeringskansliet.

Skrivelse, 1999/2000. *Jämställdhetspolitiken Inför 2000-talet.* Stockholm. Integrations och Jämställdhets Departmentet .

Skutsch, Margaret M., and Michael McKall. 2010. Reassessing REDD: Governance, Markets and the Hype Cycle. *Climate Change* 100: 395–402.

Smith, Barbara, and Beverley Smith. 1983. Across the Kitchen Table: A Sister-to-Sister Dialogue. In *This Bridge Called My Back: Writings by Radical Women of Color*, edited by C. Moraga and G. Anzadua. New York: Kitchen Table: Women of Color Press.

Smith, Dorothy E. 1987. *The Everyday World as Problematic: A Feminist Sociology.* Boston: Northeastern University Press.

Sörlin, Sverker. 1988. *Framtidslandet: Debatten om Norrland och Naturresurserna Under Det Industriella Genombrottet.* Vol. 33, *Kungl. Skytteanska Samfundets Handlingar. Norrlands bildningshistoria.* Umeå.

SOU. 2005: 66. *Makt att Forma Samhället och Sitt Eget Liv—Jämställdhetspolitiken Mot Nya Mål.* Stockholm: Regeringskansliet.

Spivak, Gayatri Chakravorty. 1990. Poststructuralism, Marginality, Postcoloniality and Value. In *Literary Theory Today*, edited by P. Collier and H. Geyer-Ryan. Oxford: Polity Press.

Springer, Simon. 2010. Public Space as Emancipation: Meditations on Anarchism, Radical Democracy, Neoliberalism and Violence. *Antipode* 43 (2): 525–562.

Stanley, Liz. 1990. *Feminist Praxis: Research Theory and Epistemology in Feminist Sociology.* London: Routledge.

Stanley, Liz, and Sue Wise. 1990. Method, Methodology and Epistemology in Feminist Research Processes. In *Feminist Praxis: Research, Theory and Epistemology in Feminist Sociology*, edited by L. Stanley. London: Routledge.

Stoetzler, Marcel, and Nira Yuval-Davis. 2002. Standpoint Theory, Situated Knowledge and the Situated Imagination. *Feminist Theory* 3 (3):315–333.

Sundar, Nandini, Roger Jefferey, and Neil Thin. 2001. *Branching Out: Joint Forest Management in India*, edited by R. Guha and M. Gadgil, *Studies in Social Ecology and Environmental History.* Oxford: Oxford University Press.

Sundar Rajan, Rajeswari, ed. 1999. *Signposts: Gender issues in post-independence India.* New Delhi: Kali for Women.

SUS. 2001. *Skogsvårdsorganisationens Utvärdering av Skogspolitikens Effekter.* Jönköping: Skogsstyrelsen.

Taylor, Dianna, and Karen Vintges. 2004. Introduction. In *Feminism and the Final Foucault*, edited by D. Taylor and K. Vintges. Urbana: University of Illinois Press.

Tharu, Susie, and Tejaswani Niranjana. 2001. Problems for a Contemporary Theory of Gender. In *Gender and Politics in India*, edited by N. Menon. New Delhi: Oxford University Press.

Tiwari, Mamata n.d. Progress Report of Women's Group Formation: Initiative of BOJBP (in English, translated from the original in Odia). BOJBP. Nayagarh, Orissa.

Tollin, Katharina. 2000. Det Måste Finnas Män Med För Att Det Skall Bli Jämställt: En Utvärdering Av Mainstreamingprojektet Inom Arbetsmarknadsverket i Västerbotten. Umeå: Statsvetenskapliga institutionen, Umeå universitet.

Traweek, Sharon. 1988. *Beamtimes and Lifetimes: The World of High Energy Physicists.* Cambridge/London: Harvard University Press.

Treleaven, Lesley. 1998. Unsettling Tensions: Gender, Power and a New University. Ph.D. dissertation. Sydney: University of Technology.

Tsing, Anna Lowenhaupt. 1993. *In the Realm of the Diamond Queen.* Princeton, NJ: Princeton University Press.

Tsing, Anna Lowenhaupt. 2003. Consider the Problems of Privatization. In *Feminist Futures: Reimagining Women, Culture and Development*, edited by K. Bhavnani, J. Foran and P. Kurian. London: Zed Books.

Varughese, George, and Elinor Ostrom. 2001. The contested role of heterogeneity in collective action: Some evidence from community forestry in Nepal. *World Development* 29 (5):747–765.

Villagrasa, Delia. 2002. Kyoto Protocol Negotiations: Reflections on the Role of Women. *Gender and Development* 10 (2): 40–44.

Vintges, Karen. 2004. Endorsing Practices of Freedom: Feminism in a Global Perspective. In *Feminism and the Final Foucault: Feminism in a Global Perspective*, edited by D. Taylor and K. Vintges. Urbana: University of Illinois Press.

von Linné, Carl. 1734. Iter Dalekarlicum. In *Carl von Linnés Ungdomskrifter* edited by S. af E. Åhrling. Stockholm: Med Stats Understöd Utgifna av K. Vetenskaps-Akademien. Andra Serien.

Watts, Michael. 2007. What Might Resistance to Neoliberalism Consist Of? In *Neoliberal Environments: False Promises and Unnatural Consequences*, edited by N. Heynen, J. McCarthy, W.S. Prudham and P. Robbins. London: Routledge.

Westholm, Erik. 2009. A Territorial Approach to the Politics of Climate Change. In *What Future for Social Investments?* edited by J. Palme, B. Palier and N. Morell. Stockholm. Institute for Future Studies.

Wollenberg, Eva, Jon Anderson, and David Edmunds. 2001. Pluralism and The Less Powerful: Accomodating Multiple Interests in Local Forest Management. *International Journal Agricultural Resources, Governance and Ecology* 1 (3/4):199–222.

World Development Report 2000/2001: Attacking Poverty. New York: World Bank.

Young, Iris Marion. 2010. *Inclusion and Democracy.* Oxford: Oxford University Press.

Index

www.ingramcontent.com/pod-product-compliance
Ingram Content Group UK Ltd.
Pitfield, Milton Keynes, MK11 3LW, UK
UKHW022002180926
475701UK00003B/156
9780415629614